THE HUMAN CREATURE

The Human Creature

EDITED BY GÜNTER ALTNER

WITH PAPERS BY

GERHARD HEBERER
OTTO KOENIG
WOLFGANG WICKLER
BERNHARD RENSCH
GEROLF STEINER
HELMUT BAITSCH

KARL J. NARR
HUBERT WALTER
OTTO KOEHLER
HANS-GÜNTER ZMARZLIK
NIKO TINBERGEN
GÜNTER ALTNER

ANCHOR BOOKS
ANCHOR PRESS / DOUBLEDAY
GARDEN CITY, NEW YORK

KREATUR MENSCH
Edited by Günter Altner
Heinz Moos Verlag   Munich
Copyright © 1969 by Heinz Moos Verlag   Munich

Anchor Books Edition 1974
ISBN: 0-385-04947-1
Library of Congress Catalog Card Number 73–11640
English Translation Copyright © 1974 by George Allen & Unwin Ltd. and Doubleday & Company, Inc.

Chapter 1 Figures 1-1, 1-2, 1-3, 1-4A, 1-4B, 1-5, 1-6, 1-7, 1-8, 1-9a, 1-9b—by Gerhard Heberer, Göttingen. *Chapter 2* Figures 2-1, 2-2, 2-3, 2-4, 2-5, 2-6, 2-7, 2-9, 2-10, 2-11, 2-12, 2-13, 2-14, 2-15, 2-16, 2-17, 2-18, 2-19 by Hubert Walter, Mainz. Figure 2-8: L. v. Bertalanffy and F. Gessner, eds. (1968). *Handbuch der Biologie* III/2. Akademische Verlagsgesellschaft, Frankfurt. *Chapter 3* Fig. 3-1 and 3-3 by H. Mohr (1967). *Wissenschaft und menschliche Existenz.* Rombach, Freiburg. Fig. 3-2 by: W. Fuhrmann and F. Vogel (1968). *Genetische Familienberatung.* Springer, Heidelberg/Berlin/New York. Fig. 3-4: W. v. Knoeringen, ed. (1968). *Geplante Zukunft.* Verlag für Literatur und Zeitgeschehen, Hannover. *Chapter 4* Fig. 4-1 through 4-16 by Karl J. Narr, Münster. *Chapter 5* Fig. 5-1 through 5-7: Otto Koenig, Vienna; Figures 5-1 through 5-6, courtesy of the magazine *Naturwissenschaft und Medizin* (n+m), Mannheim. *Chapter 6* Fig. 6-1: by Irenäus v. Eibl-Eibesfeldt, Seewiesen. *Chapter 7* Fig. 7-1 through 7-7 by Hermann Kacher and Wolfgang Wickler, Seewiesen. Fig. 7-8 through 7-11 by Hermann Kacher and Wolfgang Wickler, Seewiesen. *Chapter 8* Fig. 8-1: Otto Koehler, Freiburg. Fig. 8-2 through 8-7: Otto Koehler, Freiburg. *Plates:* Plates 1, 2, 3, 4, 5, 6, 7, 8, 9: Gerhard Heberer, Göttingen. Plate 10: Verlagsarchiv. Plates 11, 12, 13, 14, 15, 16: Otto Koenig, Vienna. Plates 17, 18, 19, 20, 21, 22, 23, 24, 25: Otto Koenig, Vienna. Plate 26: Bernhard Rensch, Münster. Plates 27 and 28: Niko Tinbergen, Oxford. Plates 29, 30, 31, 32, 33, 34, 35: Wolfgang Wickler, Seewiesen. Plate 36: National Geographic Society, Washington, D.C. Plate 37; Irenäus v. Eibl-Eibesfeldt, Seewiesen. Plate 38, 39, 40, 41, 42, 43, 44, 45, 46, 47: Bernhard Rensch, Münster. Plate 48: Hermann Kacher, Seewiesen.

Contents

Preface

The quest for the true essence of man, his essential humanity, is something that is engaging the minds of people as never before. It is no longer a matter of mere academic discussion. Instead, man's urge to find out about himself—impelled by the tremendous progress that is being achieved in the biomedical sciences and by the increasingly powerful environmental influences exercised by science and technology—has acquired an unmistakably practical urgency. It is most essential to ensure proper and responsible utilisation of the general advance in knowledge in a manner beneficial to mankind today and in the future.

The ethical ambivalence of scientific progress compels us to proceed with extreme caution in planning the future of the human species. The fragility of the traditional ethical standards, the classic separation of the humanities and social sciences from the natural sciences, and the traditional isolation of research from the general social process have furthermore contributed to making mankind very helpless when confronted with itself, despite its vastly increased fund of knowledge. It requires considerable effort to reactivate the dialogue between the sciences, particularly the social sciences, and direct it into the orbit of socio-political relationships.

The Human Creature is an attempt at setting the dialogue in motion. In this book scientists belonging to widely varying disciplines are united in inquiring into the "creatural" components of man. The order in which the individual contributions appear is not of major importance. Indeed, some of the chapters could quite justifiably have been included in any of the three sections of this book. Besides, some of the authors, basing themselves on their respective specialised subjects, have attempted a more comprehensive interpretation of man and humanity, so that the main theme is approached and contemplated from the directions of these several special disciplines. In this way alone is it possible to avoid undue overemphasis on narrowly specialised knowledge and to preserve the open-mindedness that man requires in thinking about himself and in striving to ensure that progress will be to the benefit of future generations. In the light of these considerations the present volume obviously cannot lay claim to completeness or finality. Its aim is to stimulate readers to continue the dialogue about man, each from his own position as regards knowledge and function.

THE HUMAN CREATURE

GERHARD HEBERER

The Evolution of Man

When Charles Darwin wrote his great fundamental scientific treatise, *On the Origin of Species,* published in 1859, he fought shy of dealing more specifically with man in this context. Yet even at that time—having in the course of his worldwide travels in the eighteen-thirties come to recognise that evolution was a provable and indeed a proven theory—he was convinced that man, too, must have an evolutionary history, i.e., that he must have descended from pre-human remote ancestors. He did, it is true, express himself only in cautious and tentative terms, but he did write the well-known words: "Light will be shed on the origin of man and his history."

What light has since been shed on that history is something which can now, after more than a century of research, to some extent be assessed. We know that our nearest relations in the animal kingdom to whom we are genetically linked are the anthropoid apes, but that we are not descended from any of the now living species of ape. Our ancestral species must have been more primitive forms of creatures, now long extinct.

Here we will mention merely two facts which—

man

chimpanzee

pygmy chimpanzee

gorilla

orang-utan

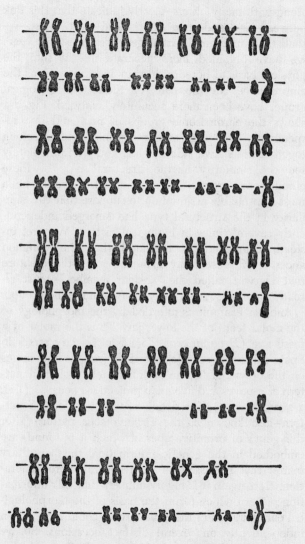

FIG. 1-1: *Comparison of chromosome patterns in man and in apes (according to Klinger).*

along with many others—clearly indicate that this link between ape and man did indeed exist. First, we shall take an example from genetics. In recent years we have obtained more accurate insight into the physical basis of heredity in man and the apes, as the chromosomes in the cells of these two biological groups have been more accurately analysed. Fig. 1-1 shows the chromosome groups of man and ape respectively. The pairs of chromosomes which belong together are shown side by side, and we immediately see the similarity in the structural type of these chromosome groups. To a geneticist it would be a most improbable assumption to suppose that this similarity in the structural type had emerged independently several times in biological history. We are, instead, compelled to conclude that the common ancestor of present-day man and apes—the creature that Darwin called the "ancient member"—must already have possessed this type of chromosome group.

Another example is afforded by the morphology of the molar teeth of the lower jaw. Thus the molar of a fossil ape (*Dryopithecus*) found in Tertiary strata in Spain exhibits a complex set of projections and ridges on the crown. It has an approximately Y-shaped pattern of grooves and five main projections (cusps) (Fig. 1-2 and Plate 1). The details of this so-called 5-Y pattern—also known as the *Dryopithecus* pattern after this genus of primitive apes in which it is found—are embodied in the genetic information, the hereditary matter that is passed on from generation to generation. Here again it is highly unlikely that this information pattern which forms the basis of the morphological configuration of the molar crown could have arisen independently on several distinct occasions. So we must once again draw the same conclusion as in the case of the chromosome groups. The "ancient mem-

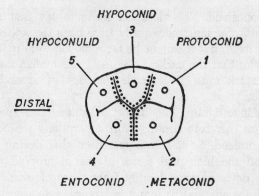

FIG. 1-2: 5-Y pattern on the crown of a lower molar of Dryopithecus showing the main cusps (1-5) and Y-groove (dotted) (according to Robinson).

ber" must essentially have already possessed this typical pattern. It is found also in the molars in the lower jaw which was discovered as far back as 1908 in the oasis of El Fayum—which has since proved to be a rich source of fossil finds—and whose owner was characteristically named Propliopithecus by M. Schlosser. As a result of subsequent excavations two more lower jaws of this creature have come to light (Fig. 1-3).

FIG. 1-3: Lower jaw teeth of Propliopithecus haeckeli from the eyetooth to the third molar (according to Kälin).

This is more or less how the dentition (layout of the teeth) of the lower jaw of the "ancient member" must be conceived. This does not mean to say that *Propliopithecus* must necessarily have been the ancestral form itself, but it cannot be far removed from it. This signifies that the earliest origins of the human ancestral stock must be accorded an age of around 30 million years.

In investigating the history of the human species we are therefore dealing with a very long period of time indeed. So it stands to reason that during this period the biological forms of the anthropoid apes have deviated considerably from those of man. The apes are adapted to living in tropical rain forests of the interior and have evolved a method of arboreal locomotion which is called brachiation, i.e., they swing from branch to branch by their arms. Some ape populations (chimpanzees, in particular) do indeed spend much of their time moving about on the ground instead of climbing about in trees. Also, there are groups of apes (gorillas) which on account of their large size usually walk on the ground even in the depths of the forests. But they have not specifically developed this form of locomotion nor specifically adapted themselves to it; that was something which was achieved only by the early hominids who emerged as a genetically independent group probably not later than the Miocene period and then gradually evolved the typically human adaptational forms.

EVOLUTION OF MAN'S PRECURSORS

Let us take a look at a diagram which presents an over-all picture of man's evolutionary history (Fig. 1-4A). We start from a group designated as Protohominoidea, the precursors of the Hominoidea, which is a category comprising the Pongidae (anthropoid

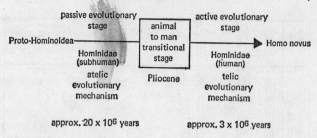

FIG. 1-4A: *Diagram of the evolution of the hominids.*

apes) and Hominidae (humans, contemporary and fossil). The evolutionary history of the Hominidae (hominids) begins with the genetic segregation of a hominoid group which henceforth ceased to have genetic connections with its protohominoid initial forms. Evolutionary research refers to this as a process of isolation or speciation (origin of species). It is thought to have taken place something like 25–30 million years ago. The mechanism underlying the causality of evolution in this early "subhuman" stage of man's history can be conceived as a state of evolutionary passivity in which random mutations occurred and were then subjected to the action of the natural selective mechanism. As yet the early hominids themselves contributed nothing to the causality of their evolution. In this respect they behaved like other animals and vegetable organisms; their evolutionary mechanism was atelic, i.e., without predetermined aim or purpose.

This passive stage was followed by what may be termed the "animal-to-man transitional stage," which was situated in the Pliocene period, probably 3 million years ago or rather earlier. In this stage the subhuman hominids acquired a number of characteristics which enabled them to play an increasingly active

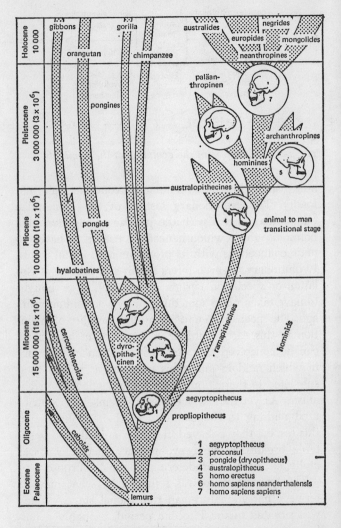

FIG. 1-4B: *Family tree illustrating evolutionary descent of Pongidae (anthropoid apes) and Hominidae (humans and subhumans).*

part in shaping their own evolution by initiating the action of mechanisms which can properly be described as purposive. The evolutionary process thus became telic, i.e., having definite aims; the condition of passivity was transformed into one of activity. The question as to what distinctive characteristics were acquired in the animal-to-man transitional stage constitutes a complex problem. It can, however, be defined in principle: the subhuman hominids acquired the ability not merely to use tools but moreover to improve their tools with a definite future purpose in mind, i.e., to transform elementary tools into purpose-made devices with which consciously planned actions could now more efficiently be performed than had previously been possible. In animals, e.g., in chimpanzees, such improvements have been observed in rudimentary form. A hominid which makes tools and equips itself with purpose-made implements, i.e., a toolmaking creature in the true sense, ranks as a "human" hominid. It should incidentally be noted that in the present context "human" must not be taken to mean that the creature possessed "humanity" in the more exalted sense of the term, as we would expect Homo novus of the future to possess it (cf. Fig. 1-4B).

What did the earliest Hominoidea (hominoids) look like? In the line of descent of the Pongidae (anthropoid apes) we have some fossil remains which appear to be genuinely of very great age. Plate 2 shows an example from the upper Oligocene at the El Fayum oasis, i.e., dating back about 30 million years. This find was made by a team from Yale University under the leadership of Simons, an expert on the Primates. It is the oldest hominoid skull that has hitherto come to light and occupies a fundamental position in the evolution of the Pongidae. As appears from the illustration, this skull is still very animal-like in character. The creature to which it belonged, named *Aegyptopithecus zeuxis,* belongs to a group which comprises the root forms of those fossil apes of the Tertiary period which are represented by numerous remains of jaws and teeth and bear the family is the much-discussed creature which used to be called Proconsul (now often simply referred to as *Dryopithecus*). These "proconsuline" apes were not such accomplished brachiators as some of the modern anthropoid apes. They were, at that remote stage, still in the process of establishing themselves as forest dwellers and acquiring the arboreal way of life. The present-day gorillas and chimpanzees have been derived from them. The gibbons have a somewhat earlier root form, probably derivable from the *Propliopithecus* group. These extremely long-armed arboreal apes, as we now know them, had not yet achieved such a degree of morphological differentiation in the Miocene period as to be directly recognisable as long-armed brachiators. So we see that brachiation in conjunction with long arms constitutes an adaptation which was a relatively late development, and the older theory that the ancestral group of the hominids once lived in the primeval forests, swinging from tree to tree with long arms, was abandoned quite some time ago. Even the orangutan, of which some fossil tooth finds dating from the Pleistocene period are available, is likely to have acquired its ability to swing from tree to tree at a relatively late stage in its evolutionary history. We see therefore that the evolution of the apes has to a great extent proceeded side by side with that of the hominids.

What did the subhuman early forms of the hominids look like? Until fairly recently there were no fossil remains at our disposal to fill in the picture. Anal-

yses of older finds from the Siwalik mountains, foothills
of the Himalayas in India, have since shown, however, that such early hominids are present in the fossil
genus *Ramapithecus* from the upper Miocene period.
Formerly this genus had been classed with the dryo-
pithecine apes and was indeed by no means readily
distinguishable from them. Fig. 1-5 shows a mirror-

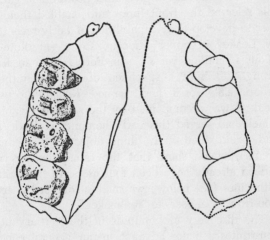

FIG. 1-5: *Upper jaw of* Ramapithecus punjabicus, *with
tentative reconstruction on the left* (according to Simons).

image reconstruction of the upper jaw (one of several
such finds), the two parts of which are here shown
side by side as they once must have been in the living
creature. In this way it was possible to reconstruct the
entire upper jaw dentition and ascertain its form,
which is seen to agree with the pattern found in the
human jaw. The same conclusion can be drawn from
other fossil remains, so that we can say that in the
Miocene period, possibly already in the lower Miocene, the fossil finds contain remains of hominids in

the subhuman stage of development. In these early hominids the front parts of the dental equipment show a reduction, from which it can be inferred that the inadequate functioning of the teeth associated with this reduction must have been compensated for by the increased use of tools. From this it can in turn be concluded that, for example, progress was being made towards achieving an erect posture and gait, for this released the front limbs and enabled them further to develop their capabilities. A fairly recent find by Leakey in upper Miocene strata (absolute age about 14 million years) near Fort Ternan in Kenya brought to light a specimen of the ramapithecine group. This fossil find, named *Kenyapithecus* by Leakey, was accompanied by the remains of animals which had served this early hominid as food. They had been killed with blunt objects (stone implements), which show that the ramapithecines must indeed already have been tool users. In the australopithecines (see below) we shall encounter the transition from "tool user" to "toolmaker."

The discovery of hominids in the Tertiary period constitutes a major advance in our general concepts concerning the evolutionary history of our species. On the evidence of our present knowledge of the subhuman stage of that history we may regard the ramapithecines as forming a group of creatures which walked erect. When standing upright they were better able to see their natural enemies, which gave them a significant advantage in this respect over their precursors, who moved about on all fours and had to locate their enemies from that position. It cannot be ruled out that these early hominids climbed trees to seek protection from attackers. Descended as they were from tree-dwelling ancestors, the ramapithecines were well equipped for three-dimensional visual perception. The eyes had become larger and directed forward so as to make stereoscopic vision possible. Creatures endowed in this way must be regarded as particularly favoured in terms of natural selection, and the increased availability of the hands for the manipulation of objects was likewise a major advantage in this respect. Thus we have hypothetically some factors to account for the resulting emergence of the human from the subhuman. It seems likely that further exploration of the sites of such finds in northern India and in East Africa will in the near future make our knowledge of the Tertiary hominids more complete.

THE EMERGENCE OF EARLY MAN

Evidence for the existence of "primitive man" is provided by upwards of three hundred fossil fragments from two sites: the Transvaal and East Africa (East Serengeti and farther north: Peninj and Omo). The circumstances in which the discoveries were made in these regions vary considerably, however, and nothing is as yet reliably known about their interrelationship in time. Research on early man received an impetus when, in 1924, near Taung in the border area between the Transvaal and Bechuanaland, a child's skull (the teeth indicate that this individual must have been about six years old) was discovered in a cave or cleft in the palaeozoic dolomite plateau which covers the Transvaal. The anatomist R. A. Dart of Witwatersrand University, Johannesburg, described this skull and subsequently also other remains of these so-called australopithecines (*Australopithecus* is a generic name meaning "southern ape"). That relatively plentiful remains of these creatures have survived is attributable to the fact that the palaeozoic

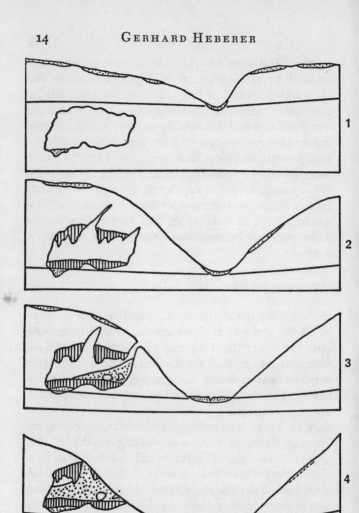

FIG. 1-6: *Profile diagrams illustrating changes affecting a cave in the Transvaal Dolomites (according to Brain).*

dolomite deposits in which they were found contained numerous clefts and caves which, as a result of progressive erosion of the dolomite rock, eventually established open communication with the outer world. Wind carried sand into these caves, animal and human remains found their way—actively or passively—into them and the constant action of lime-bearing water turned the contents of the caves into a solid mass (Fig. 1-6). Excavation of such cave fillings revealed fossil monkeys (baboons) and what at first were thought to be apelike creatures and which in fact turned out to be australopithecines, i.e., hominids. (To the well-known expert on mammal-like Karroo reptiles, R. Broom, belongs the credit of also having saved and collected the remains of adult australopithecines at sites in the region of Johannesburg [Sterkfontein].) From the shape of the child's skull found at Taung and the configuration of its teeth it was already suspected that we were here dealing with an anthropomorphous creature, i.e., a very humanlike form—at any rate, more so than any previously known fossil creature of comparable age. From the evidence of subsequent plentiful finds we now know that this form must indeed be regarded as already truly human, not subhuman in the sense applicable to the ramapithecine group of man's precursors.

In 1959 it was discovered that these human australopithecines had also lived in East Africa. Leakey found their fossil remains in the basal strata of the Olduvai Gorge in the Serengeti steppes (Plate 3). The australopithecines of the Transvaal as well as those of the Serengeti region belong to the lower Pleistocene (Villafranchium) period, and according to currently held views their absolute age must be put at about 2 million years.

What did these early human beings look like? Plate 4 shows the best-preserved skull of an adult australopithecine (*Australopithecus africanus*) found at Sterkfontein near Johannesburg (Krugersdorp). It is a remarkable skull in that its proportions are still similar to those generally found in anthropoid ape skulls. This is evident from Fig. 1-7, where the outline of the

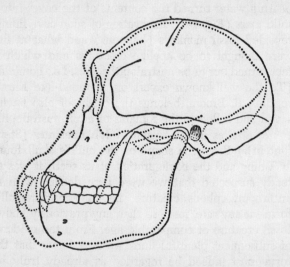

FIG. 1-7: *Comparison of skull outlines of an australopithecine (solid line) and a chimpanzee (dotted).*

skull of an adult individual of *Australopithecus africanus* (solid line) is compared with that of an adult chimpanzee's skull (dotted). It is directly evident that the general skull proportions of these two creatures are approximately similar: small brain case, prominent facial and jaw development. But as soon as we analyse the *Australopithecus* skull in detail with regard to its morphology, we come to the conclusion that it is essentially human, not apelike. This is more particularly evident from a comparison of the teeth in a modern human skull and those of an australopithecine (Plate 5). The two sets of teeth are almost identical, and the teeth are set close up against one another, except that the australopithecine teeth differ from those of modern man in the relative sizes of the individual teeth: the front teeth (incisors and canine teeth) are relatively very small, while the grinders (molars and premolars) are relatively very large. Both sets of teeth differ considerably from the dentition of anthropoid apes (Plate 6). The australopithecines—and this applies equally to both of the groups mentioned below—are thus seen to have a decidedly human type of dentition.

At the present time a fairly clear subdivision can be made into two australopithecine groups, though it is not known whether these groups were genetically separate. One group, which is to be regarded as comprising the australopithecines in the more specific sense (A group), has somewhat smaller teeth than the other group, which is the so-called *Paranthropus* group (P group). The representatives of the P group had a vertical bony ridge on the skull, which served to increase the attachment surface for the masticatory muscles. Here, at the centre of the cranium, the muscles from the left-hand and the right-hand side converge to form a sort of crest rather similar to that found on the breastbones of flying birds. Although this median ridge is reminiscent of the ridges found on ape skulls, its morphology is in fact different, and there is no ridge extending transversely across the occipital region, such as occurs in apes. It is therefore a specifically human feature, a kind of response of the small cranium to the powerful masticatory musculature needed for the proper functioning of the large set of teeth. Without this ridge the skull in the *Paran-*

thropus group would not provide a sufficiently large attachment surface for these muscles (Plate 7).

We also know something about the skeletal features of the trunk and the limbs of the australopithecines. It has been conclusively established that both types walked upright on their hind limbs. At five sites remains of pelvic bones and the skeleton of a foot have been found. The lower-limb bones found in East Africa (Olduvai Gorge), as well as the skeletal remains of a foot, clearly indicate that the australopithecines walked erect. The structure of the skeleton as a whole is also fundamentally hominid in character. We may try to visualise and reconstruct the head and facial features of such small-brained erect bipeds from the lower Pleistocene period—a "primitive man" in fact. Attempts of this kind have been made, independently of each other, by the Natural History Museum in London and by the Anthropological Research Centre at Göttingen, in Germany, and it is of interest to note that the results of these two attempts at reconstruction are substantially in agreement with each other. As in all such cases, we do not of course really know whether this long-extinct creature accurately conformed to our reconstruction, but it cannot reasonably be disputed that an australopithecine may well have looked like this and that the reconstruction is conceivably a close likeness to the original form that once existed (Plate 8). Can these small-brained erect bipedal creatures really be regarded as human (as distinct from subhuman) hominids? Their brain size was no greater than that of anthropoid apes; indeed, they had smaller brains than some modern apes. Yet the brain size must not be judged in absolute terms, without reference to body size. Thus a gorilla weighing 5 hundredweights and with a cranial capacity of 750 cm.[3] has a relatively smaller brain than an australopithecine whose cranial capacity is 600 cm.³ but whose weight is only 1 hundredweight. In assessing the potentialities of the australopithecine mind we therefore cannot base ourselves on brain size alone; in addition, we must seek pointers which will enable us to form a conception of the mental abilities of these creatures. For this purpose we can make use of clues provided by vital manifestations which are acknowledged to have been derived from the australopithecines.

The question we must ask ourselves in the first place is: did those early men already possess greater brain power than the anthropoid apes of our present time? They certainly used tools, as indeed the more primitive ramapithecines can be assumed to have done. That the australopithecines of the A group were tool users has been established beyond doubt; besides, we now know that they not only used but also made tools, that is to say, they deliberately fashioned implements to serve a particular purpose. The materials from which they made their tools were pebbles which were suitably chipped to obtain cutting edges. The finds from the Olduvai Gorge must be similarly judged. At Makapansgat (central Transvaal) Dart furthermore discovered a varied bone tool culture and evidence of purpose-made stone implements. We must therefore regard the australopithecines as having been the first known toolmakers. They had greater capabilities than any animal; in particular, they excelled the anthropoid apes, which, according to recent research, are on the threshold of toolmaking, but have not yet actually acquired this ability. To make tools for a definite purpose is something first encountered in the australopithecines, not before. These, then, must be regarded as the first true "primitive men." With

them we have definitely entered the human stage of
man's evolutionary development.

THE EVOLUTION OF MODERN MAN

We have thus briefly outlined the process of evolution
from prehominid to primitively human. The latter in
turn provided the substratum for the development of
"modern man," which has in fact run a very varied
and complex course. How we may conceive this is indicated in Fig. 1-8. The group of forms which consti-

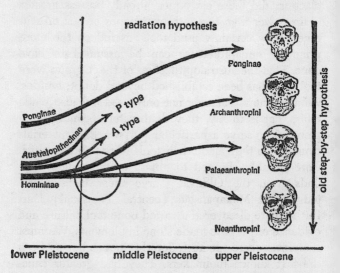

FIG. 1-8: *Diagram illustrating the splitting up of the hominidae during the Pleistocene period. Comparison of the
step-by-step and the radiation hypotheses.*

tuted the ancestral stock from which the hominids of
the genus *Homo* were evolved still appears somewhat
problematical at the present time. Finds in the Oldu-

vai Gorge provide clues that perhaps already among the australopithecines there existed types which could be regarded as belonging to the genus *Homo;* they were the earliest representatives of the genus, which may then have further evolved into primitive men, the archanthropines, with the species *Homo erectus.* This initial group is named *Homo habilis* by some anthropologists. There is, however, considerable divergence of opinion on the subject. From *Homo erectus,* of which there are several subspecies, was split off the *Homo sapiens* group. The most important prehistoric subspecies in this latter group was Neanderthal man (*Homo sapiens neanderthalensis:* Plate 9). At the same time the precursor of modern man, *Homo sapiens,* was split off from the common ancestral stock. The many races of man (polytypism) now in existence all belong to this species. It used to be supposed that there had been progressive step-by-step evolutionary divergence of the archanthropines ("early men"), the palaeoanthropines (to which Neanderthal man belonged) and the neoanthropines (*Homo sapiens*). More recently, however, a rather different view of man's evolutionary history during the last million years has emerged. It is known as the radiation hypothesis (Fig. 1-8). According to that hypothesis, the true hominines ("human" hominids) developed from an australopithecine root located in the lower Pleistocene period (Villafranchium) and then, at the transition from lower to middle Pleistocene, they manifested the "radiation" into the now known fossil and living archanthropines, palaeoanthropines and neoanthropines. Of course, this is merely a provisional picture, based on our present palaeoanthropological knowledge. But there is a fair probability of its being correct in essentials.

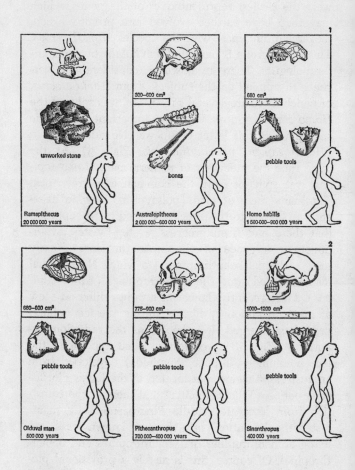

Ramapithecus
20 000 000 years
unworked stone

Australopithecus
2 000 000–600 000 years
bones
300–600 cm³

Homo habilis
1 500 000–900 000 years
pebble tools
680 cm³

Olduvai man
500 000 years
pebble tools
680–800 cm³

Pithecanthropus
700 000–400 000 years
pebble tools
775–900 cm³

Sinanthropus
400 000 years
pebble tools
1000–1200 cm³

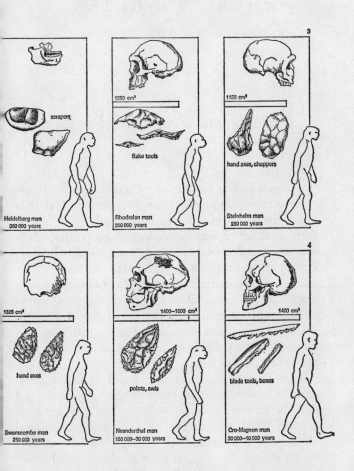

FIG. 1-9: *The diagrams on these pages illustrate the evolution of the hominids from Ramapithecus to Homo sapiens. In each diagram the skull and cranial capacity, the type of implements used and the probable over-all appearance of the creature are shown (according to Heberer, with modifications).*

HUBERT WALTER

Heredity and Environment in Man

It is a well-known fact that people differ from one an-other—not only in physical characteristics such as stat-ure or the colour of the eyes, hair and skin, but also in their intellectual and psychological properties, abili-ties, and modes of behaviour, such as intelligence, temperament or character. To establish these differ-ences between individuals and also between groups of people (races, social strata, urban and rural popu-lation) with precision, to describe them and to in-vestigate them with regard to their possible causes, all come within the scope of research conducted by scientific anthropology.

There can be no reasonable doubt as to the exist-ence of intellectual and psychological differences not only between human individuals, but also between groups. With the now available, largely standardised anthropological methods of research we can, at least in the domain of physical characteristics, reliably de-tect and map out individual as well as group-specific differences; and, what is very important, the results thus obtained are reproducible, i.e., scientifically veri-fiable, which is an essential prerequisite to answering the question regarding their possible causes. That these research methods have not yet been developed and, especially, standardised with the same degree of success for intellectual and psychological properties is due not least to the complexity of man's mental being. It is therefore often very difficult to isolate or pinpoint the separate properties and abilities from the over-all intellectual/psychological complex. An additional complicating feature is that in a psychological investigation the person subjected to it is liable to undergo an unverifiable change in consequence of the investigation procedure itself. However, substantial efforts are being made to overcome these difficulties, so that it will, in the foreseeable future, certainly be possible to determine also the psychological differences between people reliably and reproducibly. But the elaboration of these methods is not so much the task of science. Unfortunately, this has not always been, and is still not always, the approach actually adopted. Even long before adequate methods for the objective treatment of this problem were available it was the subject of lively discussion, which gradually gave rise to two extreme theories, both laying claim to exclusive rightness: the environmental theory and the theory of heredity. In our present century the environmental theory has been stoutly defended more particularly by J. B. Watson: (1878–1958), one of the originators of the theory of behaviourism in America. This theory regarded the human environment as the sole cause for the emergence of differences between people. It asserts that a human being arrives in this world more or less as a blank sheet, and his physical and more particularly also his intellectual/psychological characteristics and properties are produced by the action of his specific environment, education and training. According to this theory, differences between people

are due entirely to environmental differences; if the
latter could be wiped out, people would all become
very similar to one another. The theory of heredity,
on the contrary, states that all our physical and our
intellectual and psychological properties are inborn
and unchangeable, i.e., the human being is, as it were,
programmed from birth. Although both sides, environ-
mentalists and hereditarians, exerted a great deal of
effort to prove their respective doctrines, neither was
by itself able fully and satistfactorily to explain the
diversity of human beings and its causes. Besides,
both schools of thought eventually sank into scientific
dogmatism which tolerated no objective discussion of
the phenomena. E. von Eickstedt (1937) and Mühlmann (1968) have described in detail the history of
these two theories in their intellectual and cultural-
historical context and consequences.

It was only with the advent of modern biology that
these two rigid extreme positions at last became more
flexible, so that it now became possible to make an
objective and unbiased approach to the "problem of
heredity versus environment," not least as a result of
the progress achieved in the science of genetics (the
study of heredity and variation). Although it has not
yet proved possible fully to elucidate this problem in
every detail so far as man is concerned, this much at
least is certain: no living creature—and this is true of
man, too—is solely the product of its environment, nor
is it solely the product of heredity; in reality, the two
sets of influences, heredity and environment, together
bring about what manifests itself to us as an individual or group of individuals with their specific physical and mental equipment. To analyse the interaction
of heredity and environment in developing and
moulding individuals and groups of individuals, and
to estimate the respective effects of these two sets of

influences, is one of the most important tasks of present-day biology and thus also of anthropology.

THE BASIS OF HEREDITY

The development of a human being begins with fertilisation, i.e., the fusion of two special cells (gametes), more specifically the ovum (female gamete) and the spermatozoon (male gamete). The resulting cell, called the zygote, develops by continued division and differentiation in the process of prenatal ontogeny which occurs during the period of gestation, which normally lasts 280 days. Not all zygotes result in births, however; about 30 per cent die during this phase of development and are discharged from the mother's body; this percentage is somewhat higher for male than for female zygotes (Fig. 2-1). At birth the development of the human individual is by no means complete, however. It continues intensively until adulthood, i.e., until the individual is about twenty-one years old.

This process of development is based primarily upon endogenic factors which are contributed by spermatozoon and ovum respectively and which become active from the instant of fertilisation onward. These hereditary factors, known as genes, are located in the chromosomes, which are present in the nucleus of each cell. Whether factors located in the cytoplasm (the protoplasm of the cell excluding the nucleus) also transmit hereditary characteristics and intervene in the development process is as yet unproved in man.

The number of chromosomes in each cell of the human body is normally 46 (23 pairs, this being known as the diploid set of chromosomes), comprising 22 pairs of autosomes and one pair of sex chromosomes.

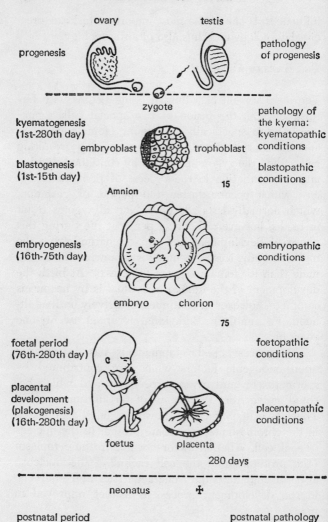

FIG. 2-1: *Stages in prenatal development of the human being (according to Görttler).*

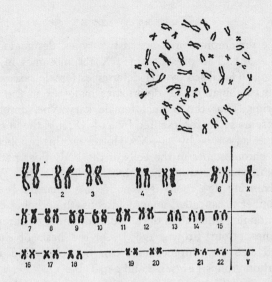

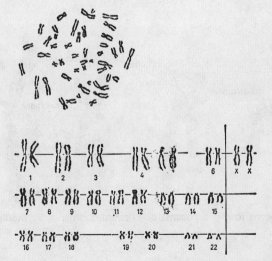

FIG. 2-2: *The human chromosomes; right: male; left: female.*

The sex chromosomes are of two types, designated as
X and Y. The presence of 2 X chromosomes in the
zygote (fertilised ovum) determines female sex, while
the combination XY determines male sex in the offspring. Thus the normal female karyotype, or chromosome set, is represented by 44+XX, and the normal
male karyotype by 44+XY. However, this number of
46 chromosomes in the cells of the body does not remain constant throughout the individual's life. With
advancing age there is a noticeable increase in the
number of so-called aneuploid cells, these being cells
containing other than the standard number of chromosomes (Court-Brown, 1967). On the basis of shape
and size the chromosomes can be subdivided into
certain groups (Figs. 2-2 and 2-3; Table 1).

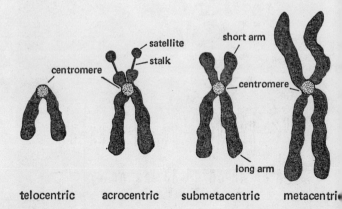

FIG. 2-3: *Chromosome types. Telocentric chromosomes
are not normally present in human cells (redrawn from V.
A. McKusick).*

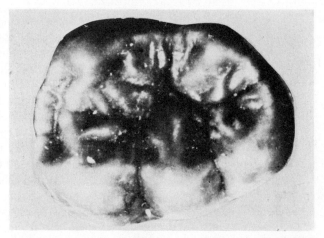

PLATE 1: *Pattern of ridges and projections on the crown of a lower molar of a fossil ape* (Dryopithecus) *from Spain (according to Frisch).*

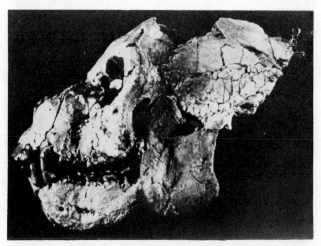

PLATE 2: *Skull of* Aegyptopithecus zeuxis, *the oldest-known hominoid skull, from the upper Oligocene (about 30 million years old), found at the El Fayum oasis (according to Simons).*

PLATE 3: *View of the Olduvai Gorge at its deepest point. In the distant background is the Lemagrut volcano. Leakey is seen standing on the left edge of the gorge which intersects the relatively flat Serengeti country. The concordantly deposited strata are clearly visible. The red rock corresponds to a group of strata designated as III, which at this point is interrupted by a fault. The australopithecine remains occur in the strata I and II which underlie the red rock.*

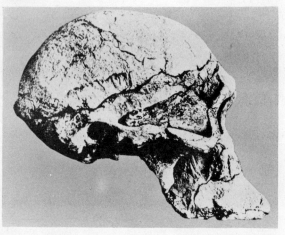

PLATE 4: *Side view of the best-preserved skull of a Transvaal australopithecine (according to Le Gros Clark).*

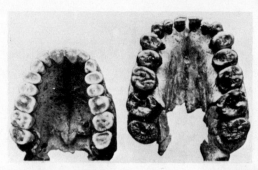

PLATE 5: *Comparison of the teeth in a modern human skull (left) and those of an australopithecine (Paranthropus bosei) from the Olduvai Gorge (right). The australopithecine teeth are disposed in a decidedly human parabolic arc (according to Leakey).*

PLATE 6: *Comparison between milk teeth and permanent teeth of anthropoid apes and hominids. Left-hand row: human canine tooth and molar (A); the corresponding teeth in an australopithecine (B) are essentially human in character; comparison with the corresponding teeth of apes (C, D, E) clearly shows the difference: here the two teeth of this group are separated from each other, and the first molar has a single point instead of four cusps as in the hominids. The foregoing are all examples of milk teeth. Permanent teeth are illustrated in the right-hand row: hominid molars (A and B) with large internal cusps; in the apes (C, D, E) the molars generally have a single point (according to Le Gros Clark).*

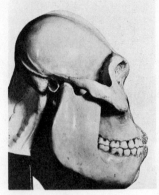
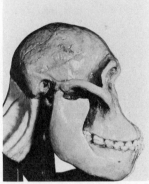

PLATE 7: *Reconstructions of skulls of australopithecines of the A group (right) and P group (left) (Transvaal Museum).*

PLATE 8: *Tentative reconstruction of an australopithecine of the A group (Anthropological Research Centre, University of Göttingen).*

PLATE 9: *Front view of a "Neanderthal man's" skullcap.*

Table 1: SUBDIVISION OF HUMAN CHROMOSOMES INTO GROUPS

Group	Size of chromosomes and position of centromere	Idiogram number	Number in a diploid cell
A	Large; median/submedian	1-3	6
B	Large; submedian		
C	Medium; submedian	6-12 and X	15 (man) or 16 (woman)
D	Medium; subterminal		
E	Small; median/submedian		
F	Very small; median		
G	Very small; subterminal	21, 22 and Y	5 (man) or 4 (woman)

As the normal number of chromosomes is the same in all human cells, there must exist a mechanism which ensures that with each successive cell division (mitosis) in the course of the individual's development this number remains constant. This is achieved by longitudinal division of each chromosome in the mother cell (this occurs in the so-called metaphase), followed by separation of the resulting duplicates, so that two complete sets of chromosomes are obtained. One such set goes into each of the two daughter cells, so that these receive an identical complement of chromosomes (this occurs in the anaphase) (Fig. 2-

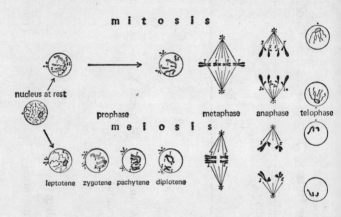

FIG. 2-4: *Schematic representation of an ordinary cell division (mitosis) and a reduction division (meiosis).*

Mitosis: The four chromosomes (two pairs I and II) appear double at the beginning of the prophase. The nucleolus disappears during the prophase and reappears in the telophase. Division of the centromeres begins in the anaphase (centromere of each chromosome marked by circle) and is, in meiosis, accomplished only in the second anaphase of the second division (not shown).

Meiosis: In the first stage of the prophase, the leptotene, the undivided chromosomes appear (thinner than in mitosis), become paired and shortened in the zygotene, are doubled and further shortened in the pachytene, and begin to separate in the diplotene. The chromosomes, which may have interchanged pieces with their partner chromosomes in the pachytene, now are equally divided between the two new nuclei (according to H. Fritz-Niggli).

4). Each daughter cell thus normally contains the same number of chromosomes and the same genetic material as the mother cell.

In the process of sexual reproduction, involving fertilisation, the fusion of the female gamete (ovum) with a male gamete (spermatozoon) would result in a doubling of the number of chromosomes in the zygote unless the number present in each gamete were half the number normally contained in each cell of the human body. In the maturing of the gametes there does indeed occur a halving of the number of chromosomes. This is achieved by a special cell-division process called meiosis (reduction division) to distinguish it from the usual process of mitosis already described. Thus the two gametes are haploid, meaning that they each contain only half the number of chromosomes normally found in the other cells of the body, so that when these two cells undergo fusion, the resulting zygote is a diploid cell, i.e., containing the normal number of paired chromosomes (those in the gametes are unpaired). The female gamete always has a chromosome complement of 22 autosomes and one X chromosome, whereas the male gamete contains either one X chromosome or one Y chromosome in addition to the 22 autosomes. This differentiation of the male gametes into two types, present in equal numbers, means that 50 per cent of the zygotes will have the sex chromosome pattern XX (female) and 50 per cent will have the pattern XY (male) (see Fig. 2-5). In actual fact, however, somewhat more boys than girls are born (the ratio is about 106 to 100), which indicates that more Y-chromosome than X-chromosome sperms achieve fertilisation. Why this should be so has not yet been fully clarified.

The chromosome pattern is what determines normal sexual development with all its physical and in-

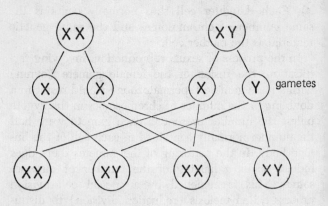

50% female individuals
50% male·individuals

FIG. 2-5: *Schematic illustration of sex inheritance.*

tellectual/psychological characteristics: the XX pattern is the prerequisite for normal female, and the XY pattern for normal male development. In recent years, however, a number of cases have been observed in which there were deviations from the normal number of chromosomes. The cause of these chromosome aberrations is believed to lie in disturbances during the process of meiosis which prevent equal distribution of the chromosomes among the daughter cells, so that some of the gametes contain two homologous chromosomes (i.e., a pair of similar chromosomes), while others are a chromosome short. Such errors in distribution are denoted by the term non-disjunction; they are also encountered in the autosomes (Fig. 2-6). All these chromosome aberrations are associated with irregularities in the individual's intellectual development; in most cases, too, there is disturbed development of the sexual organs and reduced fertility or

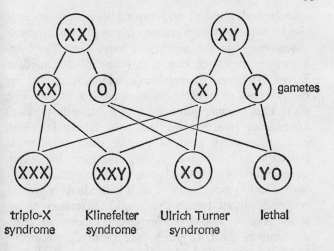

FIG. 2-6: *Schematic illustration of non-disjunction.*

indeed infertility. The presence of more than two X chromosomes therefore adversely affects physical and mental development, and the resulting defects not infrequently cause difficulties in social adjustment and thus give rise to conflict situations. This is more particularly true of the XYY syndrome, which reportedly causes a very high degree of social maladjustment; men with this chromosome pattern are usually characterised by increased aggressiveness, which, according to Mergen (1968), manifests itself already at an early age in crimes of violence such as robbery and murder. Evidently, the Y chromosome contains genetic information for the development of specifically male patterns of behaviour; if this genetic material is present in "double strength" (in the XYY syndrome), the individual in question will be predisposed to anti-social behaviour.

Disturbed physical and mental development may also be caused by an increase (trisomy) or a decrease (monosomy) in the number of autosomes. The best-known example of this is the so-called Langdon-Down syndrome (mongolism), which is caused by the presence of an extra chromosome No. 21 (see Fig. 2-2). This trisomy produces a characteristic physical appearance (small round head with flattened occiput, epicanthus, thick grooved tongue, short thick neck, short stubby hands and fingers) and, more important, a considerably disturbed mental development (idiocy); the life expectancy of such individuals is greatly reduced (about twenty-five years). Instances of trisomy have been observed for several other small chromosomes in the D-G group (see Table 1). According to Fuhrmann (1965), mort than 1 per cent of all live-born children are affected by chromosome anomalies, i.e., quite a high proportion. They are especially frequent in children born to older mothers (over forty years old), which signifies that in their ova non-disjunctive effects occur more frequently than in those of younger women.

All 46 chromosomes in the human cell contain genetic information which is responsible for the development of the physical and intellectual/psychological characteristics and properties and which is transmitted from generation to generation in accordance with particular rules. This information has its material basis in the genes, which are arranged linearly in the chromosomes. The number of genes in the human cell has been estimated at between 6 and 7 million. It is now generally accepted that the carrier substance for the genetic information is the compound named deoxyribonucleic acid(DNA), whose composition and construction have been determined more especially by

James Watson and Francis Crick, who were awarded the Nobel Prize. That this compound is indeed the carrier of inherited information has been established by a number of experiments. Further support is provided by the observed fact that the diploid cells of the body contain about twice as much DNA as the haploid gametes. For human beings the following data are, for example, available: the DNA content of liver and kidney cells is 5.6×10^{-12}g, while that of sperms is 2.5×10^{-12}g. The principal constituents of DNA are: the purine bases adenine and guanine, the pyrimidine bases cytosine and thymine, phosphoric acid, and the sugar deoxyribose (Fig. 2-7). The DNA

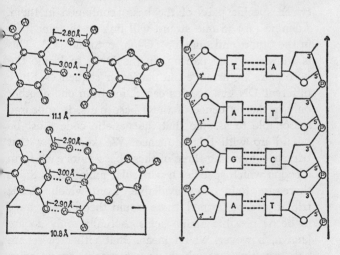

FIG. 2-7: *Model of DNA according to Watson and Crick. Left: thymine-adenine base pairing with two hydrogen bonds (top), cytosine-guanine base pairing with three hydrogen bonds (bottom). Right: sequence of base pairs in the DNA molecule; the base pairs are linked by deoxyribose and phosphoric acid (P) (redrawn after E. A. Carlson).*

molecule consists of two strands which are coiled
round a common axis and thus form a double helix.
The bases are interconnected by hydrogen bonds.
When the chromosomes divide in the ordinary cell division process (mitosis), the DNA molecule repro-
duces itself in the sense that the two parent strands
become separated from each other, somewhat in the
manner of the two parts of a zipper, and then each
strand forms a new matching strand. This process continues until two identical double helixes have been
formed, each of which contains one parent strand and
one newly synthesised strand.

Two strands of DNA can associate by bonds between specific pairs of the bases contained in them.
Adenine (A) in one strand will link to thymine (T)
in the other; and guanine (G) to cytosine (C). This
is known as base pairing. In the DNA molecule the
base pairs are arranged in particular sequences. Since
different DNA molecules can differ from one another
only in the sequence of these base pairs, it appeared
reasonable to assume that the genetic code must be
bound up with this sequence. We know now that
triplets comprising three of these base pairs each form
a codon which specifies a particular amino acid. Since
there are four bases available, from which $4^3=64$
triplets can be formed, there would theoretically have
to be 64 possible amino acids. Actually, only 20 are
known, however, which means that either there are
base combinations which do not specify amino acids
or, more probably, several triplets are able to specify
the same amino acids (degenerated code). These
triplets (codons) do not overlap one another; each begins where the preceding one stops. It is also known
that the genetic code can be "read" only in one direction and only from particular starting points onward.

Schematically this can be represented as follows:
———→ direction of reading

GAA	CTG	GCA	TCA	ACT	CTT
CTT	GAC	CGT	AGT	TGA	CAA
V	V	V	V	V	V	=product X

animo acids

If a change takes place in one of these codons, e.g., in consequence of the loss of one base pair or the addition of another, the information content of this codon, and therefore the whole code, will be changed: instead of the product X, a product X^1 will be formed. Such changes in the structure of DNA, which may take place spontaneously or be caused by chemicals or X rays, are referred to as mutations.

This genetic code possesses a high degree of universality: it is equally applicable to the synthesis of amino acids in the mose diverse organisms, ranging from bacteria to human beings. Nirenberg estimates its age at 500 million years. Since we now know which amino acids are built up by which codons, it has become possible to compile a kind of "dictionary" of amino acids and codons. This dictionary is also of importance to human biology, for with its aid it has for the first time become possible to draw inferences as to the fundamental genetic code for particular characteristics in man also (haemoglobin).

Now how is the genetic information embodied in the DNA code translated into reality? It has in recent years become possible to obtain clear ideas about this, too. Although this research has been concerned mainly with microorganisms, the results thus obtained are perfectly applicable to higher organisms, including man. The process of translating genetic information into phenotypically recognisable genetic effects, e.g., the formation of proteins, apparently proceeds in two stages. First the DNA code is translated into a ribonucleic acid (RNA) code, which forms a complementary copy of the DNA code. RNA differs from DNA in that it contains ribose in lieu of deoxyribose, and uracil in lieu of thymine. This RNA has a relatively short-lived existence; its function consists in transmitting the genetic information to the ribosomes, which exist as granules in the cytoplasm of the cells and are the site of protein synthesis, i.e., it is here that the formation of proteins takes place. So-called messenger RNA (mRNA), the ribonucleic acid molecule that conveys from the DNA the information that is to be translated into amino acids, attaches itself to the ribosomes. At the latter the actual formation of the amino acids is now accomplished with the aid of transfer RNA (tRNA). There is a different kind of tRNA for each of the twenty fundamental amino acids, which are joined together (with the co-operation of guanine-triphosphate) to form polypeptides (compounds formed of three or more amino acids) which become detached from the ribosomes and thus make room for the formation of further polypeptides (see Fig. 2-8). Whereas the mRNA can in each instance initiate the formation only of specific amino-acid sequences which are coded within it, the ribosomes are non-specific and can be made to produce different polypeptides by different mRNAs.

The analysis of the realisation of genetic information has moreover yielded further insight into the way in which the genes work and has shown that the genes can, on the basis of their various functions, be classified into structural genes and regulator genes. The genetic information for producing the various

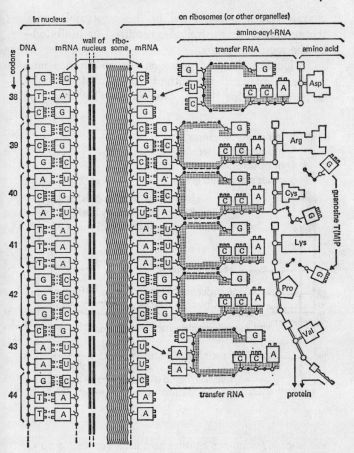

FIG. 2-8: *Diagram illustrating the transfer of information in the formation of a protein. Left: translation of the base sequence of DNA into the complementary sequence of mRNA. Center: arrangement of various kind of amino-acyl-DNA along the mRNA with the aid of the specific base triplets. Right: linking of the amino acids with the aid of guanosine triphosphate to form a polypeptide, and the detachment thereof (according to Barthelmess).*

characteristics is contained in the structural genes, whose activity is controlled—permitted or inhibited—by the regulator genes.

To locate individual genes on the 46 chromosomes in the human cell has hitherto been achieved with certainty only for the X chromosome (Fig. 2-9), on

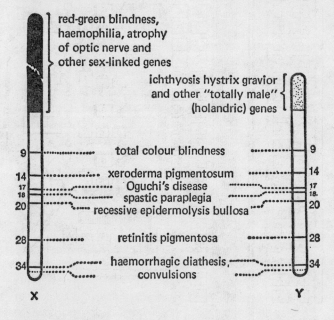

FIG. 2-9: *Human sex chromosome map (according to O. V. Verschuer).*

which 119 gene positions (loci) have been localised by McKusick (1968). Localisation of the genes in the Y chromosome has not yet been accomplished with sufficient certainty, nor has it yet been done for the autosomes (i.e., the chromosomes other than sex chromosomes).

How is the genetic information transmitted from generation to generation? Before any such heredity analyses by means of family investigations can be undertaken, it is necessary to examine the fundamental question whether a particular normal or pathological characteristic, be it a psychological property or a behaviour pattern, is in fact genetically determined. This question can be answered by research on twins.

This research bases itself on the hypothesis that, in consequence of particular circumstances, identical (monozygotic) twins or fraternal (dizygotic) twins may be born. Whereas identical twins are always of the same sex, fraternal twins may be of the same or different sexes (Fig. 2-10). Since identical twins have developed from the same zygote, they have fundamentally identical material of inheritance, though it is now believed that somatic mutations in early stages of development may give rise to certain genetic differentiations even in identical twins. Ignoring this possibility, it can therefore be assumed that differences in characteristics between identical twins are due to environmental factors. On the basis of this assumption is determined the concordance (degree of agreement) or the discordance (degree of disagreement) between identical twins; from comparisons with fraternal twins it is thus possible to draw conclusions with regard to the hereditability of a charactertistic. According to Verschuer (1959), the inference that a characteristic is "predominantly hereditary" can be drawn when the concordance in identical twins is significantly greater than in fraternal twins. On the other hand, a characteristic is to be rated as "predominantly environmental" when the same degree of concordance is found both in identical and in fraternal twins.

Research on twins provides the first step in establishing the genetic determination of particular char-

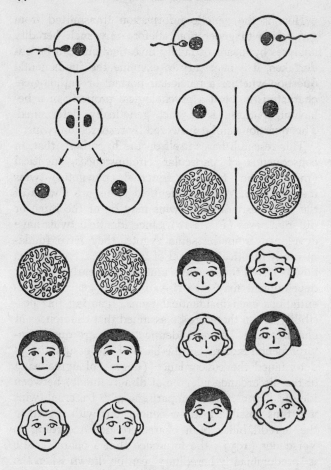

FIG. 2-10: *Mechanisms involved in twinning. Left: how identical twins develop from zygote. Right: twins develop from separate zygotes and have different hereditary characteristics (redrawn from A. Scheinfeld).*

acteristics. Further analysis concerning possible regularities in the transmission of genetic information from one generation to the next has to rely on methods such as are available in family research. In this connection the analysis of family trees plays a major part. The following forms of inheritance are observable in man:

Dominant inheritance patterns (Fig. 2-11) are

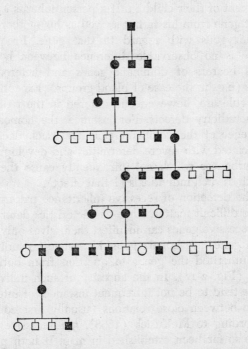

FIG. 2-11: *Dominant inheritance* (*night blindness*) (*redrawn from H. Fritz-Niggli*).

characterised in that genes on which they are based (e.g., for night blindness) generally become manifest

in each generation. Both sexes are affected with equal
frequency. According to McKusick (1968), 837 genes
exhibiting dominant behaviour are now known. When
one parent is homozygous (i.e., having identical genes
in two corresponding loci of a pair of chromosomes)
and the other is heterozygous (i.e., having different
genes in corresponding loci), the particular characteristic under consideration will manifest itself in 50
per cent of their children. If a person inherits a dominant gene from his father as well as his mother, he is
homozygous with regard to that gene. Frequently
there is no observable difference between homozygous bearers of dominant genes and heterozygous
ones (e.g., in the case of blood groups). Exceptions to
this rule are, however, encountered in the pathology
of hereditary defects. For instance, the homozygous
presence of the dominant gene for brachydactyly is
associated with severe deformities and developmental
disturbances which not infrequently cause the early
death of such individuals (lethal effect).

The detection of recessive inheritance patterns is a
more difficult matter, since characteristics determined
by recessive genes can manifest themselves only when
such genes are homozygous, i.e., when an individual
has inherited the genes in question from both parents (Fig. 2-12). In the ancestry of such individuals
there tend to be not infrequent instances of intermar-
riage between close relations (usually first cousins).
According to McKusick (1968), 531 recessive genes
have so far been established in man. If both parents
are homozygous in respect of a recessive gene, then
all their children will be homozygous and manifest
the same characteristic. On the other hand, if both
parents are heterozygous, then 25 per cent of their
children will be homozygous for the gene in question
and will therefore manifest the characteristic. Both

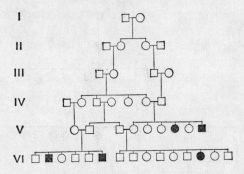

FIG. 2-12: *Recessive inheritance* (*myoclonic epilepsy*) (*redrawn from V. A. McKusick*).

sexes will be equally affected. In external appearance heterozygous carriers of recessive genes are generally no different from individuals who are homozygously free from that hereditary characteristic. With the aid of modern biochemical methods it is nevertheless possible also to detect such heterozygous carriers of the gene, especially in cases where anomalies in metabolism are concerned. Special tests for heterozygotes have been developed for the purpose (Linneweh 1962, Schreier 1963).

So far, we have considered inheritance patterns associated with autosomal genes, i.e., located in one of the 44 autosomes. If the genes are, on the other hand, located in either of the two sex chromosomes, then we obtain so-called sex-linked inheritance. A feature of the X-chromosomal dominant inheritance pattern (Fig. 2-13) is that all daughters of fathers bearing the characteristic and mothers free from it will possess the dominant gene, since they have inherited one of their two X chromosomes from the father. When a woman who manifests the characteristic marries a man free from it, 50 per cent of their sons and

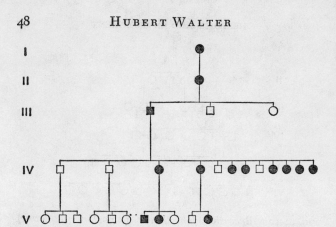

FIG. 2-13: *Sex-linked dominant inheritance (absence of dental enamel) (redrawn from H. Fritz-Niggli).*

50 per cent of their daughters will likewise possess the dominant gene and therefore manifest the characteristic. In the case of rare sex-linked dominant genes the frequency of the gene manifestation is about twice as high in the female as it is in the male sex.

With X-chromosomal recessive inheritance (Fig. 2-14), which occurs, inter alia, in haemophilia (disease in which blood clotting is defective) and red-green colour blindness, the recessive gene can in general manifest itself only in the male sex. The rule is that the father's X chromosome is transmitted only to his daughter, never to his sons. The sons receive their X chromosome always from the mother, whereas the daughters receive theirs from each parent. A sex-linked recessive gene is therefore transmitted from the man bearing the characteristic through the daughter (who does not manifest the characteristic) to the grandsons or though the daughter and granddaughter (neither of whom manifest the characteristic) to the great-grandsons, and so on.

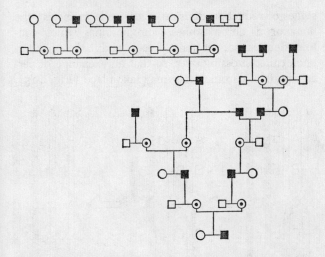

FIG. 2-14: *Sex-linked dominant inheritance (red-green colour blindness). The defect manifests itself only in the male members of the family (black squares); the females transmit the genes (dotted circles) (redrawn from H. Fritz-Niggli).*

With the aid of family research it is therefore possible to draw inferences as to the inheritance patterns of particular characteristics. But we can go further and analyse the family data to ascertain whether or not the genes are inherited independently of one another. If it is observed that certain characteristics occur together with above-average frequency, it can be suspected that the genes on which they are based are located close together in the same chromosome and are somehow associated with each other and tend to pass from generation to generation as an inseparable unit (this is known as linkage). Besides, the relative distances between such genes can be determined, this being based on the fact that in certain stages of reduction division of the cells (meiosis) the homologous chromosomes (chromosomes which contain identical sets of genes) may exhibit the phenomenon called crossing over, so that an exchange of certain parts of chromosomes may take place (Fig. 2-15).

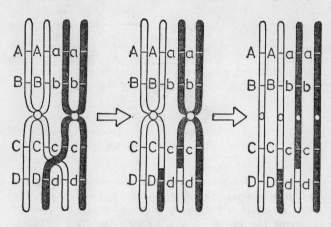

FIG. 2-15: *Schematic representation of crossing over (redrawn from H. E. Sutton). Table 2: Inheritance of intelligence (according to F. Reinöhl).*

The farther apart the loci (gene positions) in a particular chromosome are situated, the greater is the probability of crossing over, so that, conversely, it is possible to draw from the crossing-over frequency an inference as to the relative spacing of the loci in the chromosome. The distances determined in this way are expressed in Morgan units. For man a number of gene linkages have already been discovered, e.g., for the red-green colour blindness gene and that of haemophilia. From researches into linkage and crossing-over values it has proved possible to prepare so-called chromosome maps (Fig. 2-9), which show the positions of the genes in a chromosome.

Such inheritance pattern and linkage investigations are possible only for characteristics of the simple hereditary type, i.e., produced by the action of a single pair of genes (monomerism). For a great many characteristics this is not the case, however. In particular, characteristics such as a person's stature or his facial shape and dimensions are determined by the combined action of a number of gene pairs (polymerism). In such circumstances the patterns of inheritance become very complex and almost impossible to analyse accurately. Since the action of genes may moreover be modified by environmental influences, it is often so obscured that a satisfactory separation of hereditary from environmental contributions in bringing about polygenously produced characteristics is not possible.

INHERITANCE OF PHYSICAL AND MENTAL CHARACTERISTICS

Heredity, or biological inheritance, can be defined as the transmission of genetic information from generation to generation, which transmission conforms to certain definite rules which are now understood to a greater or less extent. In the zygote (fertilised ovum) the information transmitted by the father and mother, respectively, is combined, so that every human individual starts his development with an information program which—except in identical twins—is in a greater or less degree different from that of any other individual. The question now arises: to what extent is this program carried out with rigorous precision or, if not, to what extent can its realisation be influenced by non-genetic factors?

Research on twins and families has shown that there are categories of characteristics which are strictly he-

reditary and which are therefore reproduced in exact
accordance with the genetic information programme
which the bearers of these characteristics have inherited from their parents. These categories comprise the
blood group systems, the serum group systems, the
enzyme systems and the haemoglobin variants. The
conditions of inheritance in these systems are furthermore relatively simple and easy to comprehend.
Hence it is not only possible in individual cases to
draw conclusions as to the specific genetic principles
from the characteristic patterns detectable with various serological and biochemical methods, but it is
also, from the frequency with which the various characteristics occur in populations, possible to make estimates of the frequencies with which the genes that
produce these characteristics are present. Rigorous
and analysable genetic factors also control the development of many pathological characteristics of the
skeletal system, various growth disturbances producing dwarfism, as well as a number of metabolic abnormalities. This means that genetic programs—even
when they deviate from the normal patterns, as in
these cases—are carried out by the organism independently of prevailing external conditions.

These rigorously hereditary categories of characteristics, which are therefore stable in the sense of being
unaffected by environmental circumstances, include
the characteristics of the papillary system (projections on the skin) or the iris structure, though here the
genetic principles are so complex that they are not
yet amenable to detailed analysis. Other characteristics which are largely independent of environment
comprise stature, shape of the head and facial features, physiognomical characteristics and the colour
of the eyes and hair. The genetic basis of these cate-

gories of characteristics is also extremely complex and not yet analysable in detail. This means that, for one thing, it is not possible from observed characteristics and patterns of characteristics to draw reliable inferences as to the underlying genetic principles and that, furthermore, reliable predictions as to the characteristics that will emerge in the offspring of a certain man and woman are not possible either. A complicating feature affecting genetic analyses both in individual cases and in the study of populations is that stature, as well as the shape of the head and facial features, may in part be determined to an unpredictable extent also by non-genetic factors, i.e., environmental influences. On the other hand, a person's weight is largely governed by environmental factors, as investigations have revealed; it is (apart from pathological exceptions) apparently only to a very limited extent genetically determined.

With regard to physical characteristics we may therefore sum up the situation by stating that, as a rule, they are genetically determined, although the genetic information program is not always strictly carried out (as, for example, in the case of blood groups) but may be modified to some extent by factors still to be discovered (in the case of stature, for instance).

What about the genetic basis with regard to psychological properties and modes of behaviour? Considering abnormal psychological behaviour patterns, such as manifest themselves in the insane, it can be asserted that, on the basis of elaborate investigations of twins and members of whole families, it has been possible to demonstrate fundamental genetic causes. Admittedly, this causal relationship is so complex that it has not yet yielded to precise genetic analysis. Yet fundamental participation of genetic factors has been proved, for example, in mental disorders such as schizophrenia and manic-depressive psychosis. According to Elsässer (1952), the probability that children born to schizophrenic parents will also be schizophrenic is 39.2 per cent, while the corresponding figure for manic-depressives is 44.4 per cent. Against this, the average frequencies with which these mental disorders occur in the population at large are 1 per cent and 0.4 per cent respectively. Apparently it is only the predisposition to these disorders that is inherited, not the particular course that they will run in the individuals affected. Detailed genetic investigations have also been carried out with regard to imbecility. It would seem that the genetic information program which, whatever its particular details may be, manifests itself as imbecility is rigorously carried out and can only to a very slight degree be modified by environmental conditions.

Of greater interest in the present context, however, are those psychological properties and modes of behaviour which come within the definition of "normal." Comprehensive research on twins and families has also been conducted with a view to finding out to what extent intelligence or differences in intelligence measured with the aid of specific test methods have a genetic basis. It has been found that the intelligence quotients of identical twins are significantly closer together than those of fraternal twins, and furthermore that in scholastic achievement, which is correlated with intelligence, there are close relationships between parents and children (Table 2). These observations undoubtedly point to participation of genetic factors in the moulding of intelligence.

What is more particularly important in this connection, however, is the observation that identical twins who have grown up separately may differ greatly

TABLE 2: INHERITANCE OF INTELLIGENCE
(ACCORDING TO F. REINÖHL)

Parents	% of children		
	good	medium	low
good×good	71.5	25.4	3.0
good×low	33.4	42.8	23.7
medium×low	18.6	66.9	14.5
low×low	5.4	34.4	60.1

from each other in their individual achievements.
From this it is to be inferred that although differences
in the genetic equipment have a share in determining the differences in intelligence between individuals, they are certainly not alone responsible for the
observed differences. Particularly the research on
identical twins brought up and educated separately,
which has been carried out also for other psychological properties such as temperament or character, reveals how great is the share that non-genetic factors—
i.e., the environment in the widest sense of the term—
have in producing individual psychological differences
(Shields 1962, Koch 1966). This is also true of psychological differences between human groups, e.g., between races or social classes.

Extensive investigations have also been carried out
in connection with special talents or aptitudes, e.g.,
musical or mathematical talent, for which it has been
possible, on the basis of investigations on twins and
families, to establish the existence of genetic components. Such components have also been detected

for less complex properties such as attentiveness, memory, powers of observation, imagination, and receptiveness to shape and colour, as well as for basic conditions (drive, sensitivity, irritability), expressive movements associated with mimicry and gestures, and psychomotor rate (Vogel 1961). Certain behaviour patterns which are also present in babies are also known to have a genetic basis: crying, laughing, sucking, exploratory automatisms, seizing and clasping reflexes (Eibl-Eibesfeldt 1970).

A very difficult problem to solve is that concerning the genetic causes of criminal behaviour. It appears to have been established with certainty that there are no specific genes or combinations of genes that necessarily give rise to such behaviour. To what extent individual misbehaviour that is liable to result in conflict with the social environment is genetically determined is still an entirely open question which it has not yet been possible to decide satisfactorily, despite numerous investigations on the subject. That we nevertheless have to reckon with endogenic conditions which predestine the individual to criminal behaviour is revealed by observations on men with the XYY chromosome pattern. According to Mergen (1968), however, a human being who has criminal tendencies caused by his "congenital constitution" will actually turn into a criminal only if nothing is done *for* him in time.

The available information relating to the problem of inheritance of psychological properties and modes of behaviour can be summed up by stating that these too are fundamentally governed by genetic information programs. In respect of their nature and realisation these programs appear to be exceedingly complex, so that they have hitherto eluded accurate analysis. Also, it would appear that they run a less rigid course than the genetic programs for physical characteristics. Psychological properties and modes of behaviour can therefore be influenced and moulded to a far higher degree by non-genetic factors and are therefore more highly dependent upon the environmental conditions in which the intellectual and psychological development takes place.

THE CONCEPT OF ENVIRONMENT

According to Just, the term "environmental" must be taken to mean the "totality of the external conditions that act upon a living process"—i.e., all those factors which, from the moment of fertilisation onwards, intervene in the realisation of the genetic information programme, promote it, inhibit it or perhaps even upset it. These factors may exist in man's natural environment, e.g., in the specific nutritional or climatic conditions under which a human being grows up; on the other hand, they may exist in his cultural environment, i.e., in the specific circumstances of the social class, level of civilisation and period of history into which he has been born. Of course, the natural and the cultural environmental factors cannot be sharply separated from one another; on the contrary, being complex, they often act in co-operation. Yet it would seem that the natural environment generally is of greater importance to physical development, whereas the cultural environment most strongly affects intellectual and psychological development.

MODIFICATION OF THE INDIVIDUAL'S ENVIRONMENT

Modification of individual development patterns by non-genetic factors, i.e., by environmental influences, already is possible in the prenatal stage. This is revealed by observations on identical twins which may, at birth, sometimes differ considerably from each other in the shape of the head and facial features, stature and weight. According to Verschuer (1959), such differences are due to mutual obstruction of the embryos in the uterus. When this environmental influence—for this is what it indeed is—ceases to act, these differences generally disappear.

More serious are modifications which occur in the developing embryo as the effects of drugs and medicines. In the so-called "phenocritical phases," in which the formation of the organs begins, these may give rise to serious developmental disturbances and sometimes even to the premature death of the embryo (abortion). In recent years a number of such "teratogenic agents," i.e., causing malformations of the structure of organisms, have achieved notoriety, including thalidomide, aminopterin and quinine. Virus infections such as German measles may also seriously endanger the developing embryo. Deformities due to these causes are not hereditary. Misuse of medical drugs or exposure to infectious diseases during certain phases of prenatal development may therefore drastically affect the genetic information program in its process of realisation.

The modifiability of physical development and form after birth has been established more particularly by research on identical twins which have been brought up under different environmental conditions. Thus Verschuer (1954) studied the life histories of a hundred pairs of identical twins, who were investigated first in 1924–25 and finally in 1950, so that observations extended over a period of twenty-five years. From these investigations it emerged that the shape of the body had remained surprisingly constant. Only the fat and the water content of the tissues were subject to major variations, and the physical measurements dependent on these (such as weight and girth) showed a definite relationship with the environmental conditions. Skeletal measurements, such as shoulder width, length of the head, circumference of the head, cheekbone width, lower jaw angle and stature, on the other hand, revealed hardly any differences between twins (Fig. 2-16). Similar re-

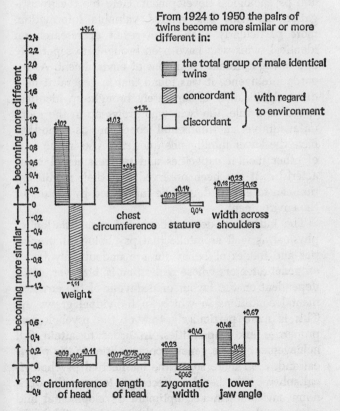

FIG. 2-16: *Environmental modification in identical twins (redrawn from O. V. Verschuer).*

sults were obtained by Shields (1962), who does,
however, emphasise that environmental differences in
early childhood significantly affect physical development and may give rise to distinct differences between identical twins. Differences in nutrition more
particularly play an important part in this respect.

Of especial interest in this connection is the question as to the effect of environment on intellectual
and psychological development. Here too the investigation of twins has yielded valuable information,
more particularly again as a result of research on
identical twins who have been brought up separately
and under different conditions of environment. As regards intelligence it was found that in general it may
differ significantly in separately brought-up identical
twins: as a rule, the twin who grows up in the more
unfavourable environmental conditions is found to
have the lower intelligence quotient. Also in the case
of other mental capacities and temperamental characteristics it has been observed that their manifestation can to a high degree be influenced by factors of
the environment.

The individual development and manifestation of
physical as well as intellectual/psychological properties and modes of behaviour are undoubtedly based
on genetic factors whose realisation is, however, often
dependent on the favour or disfavour of the environmental conditions in which an individual grows up.
This is more particularly true of the psychological
properties and capabilities. In order to attain full
achievement of the genetic potentialities in the physical and, even more so, in the intellectual/psychologi-
cal sphere, it is therefore necessary to have the optimum environment, i.e., optimum developmental and
educational opportunities for the growing child. Mohr
(1967) has accordingly called for the establishment

of a system of education that will ensure the greatest possible development of the individual's genetic potential.

MODIFICATION OF THE ENVIRONMENT OF POPULATIONS

Just as between individuals so there are physical and intellectual/psychological differences to be observed between populations or population groups (social strata, urban and rural population, etc.), and here too arises the question: to what extent are these differences genetically determined or to be regarded as the result of modifying environmental factors? Insofar as we are confronted with differences in frequency and intensity of manifestation of characteristics that are strictly genetically determined and develop quite independently of environment (for example, the characteristics of the various blood groups, serum protein groups, enzyme systems, or papillary systems of the skin) a definite answer can be given to the question as to the causes of the observed differences: the differences between groups of people are due to differences in genetic composition and therefore to differences in the frequency of particular genes. These can (for the serological characteristics systems) now be determined so reliably that exact inferences concerning the genetic structure of a population are possible.

More difficult is the analysis of differences between populations or groups in the case of many other physical characteristics, such as stature or the measurements and shape of the head and facial features, for here it is not possible to make a sufficiently clear-cut assessment of the respective proportions of genetic and non-genetic causal factors associated with the manifestation of differences. This applies, for example, to the differences in stature according to social class—something that has long been known in Europe, but has latterly also been observed in Africa (Jügens 1968). The members of higher classes, or strata, of society are as a rule taller than those of lower classes; the observed differences in average stature range up to 10 cm. Social differences have also definitely been established for other characteristics. Ascertainable differences also exist between urban and rural populations: the former are generally taller, with longer heads, and have narrower and longer faces. Finally, there are differences in physical and sexual maturing patterns between different social classes and also between urban and rural populations: on an average, upper-class children and town-dwelling children grow faster and attain sexual maturity more quickly than those of lower classes and those living in rural environments respectively.

The causes of these differences, the existence of which has been confirmed by many investigations, are very complex. Schwidetzky (1950, 1965) attributes them in part to the action of sifting processes in consequence of which, in the advance up the social ladder or in the migration from country to town, certain variants preferentially participate. This sifting hypothesis is not, however, adequate as the sole explanation, since it has been shown that modification due to changed environmental conditions (town as against country, upper as against lower social classes) can claim a significant share in producing the above-mentioned differences. This is more particularly evident from the process of change in the shape of the head and facial features of Europeans—which has been observed to be in progress already for a long time—and indeed in the physical growth and maturing phenomena in general. Changes in the fundamental genetic constitution of the population cannot be held responsible for these physical changes. Thus, in Europe, there has occurred in historic times a large-scale process of brachycephalisation (relative shortening or broadening of the skull, i.e., a trend towards increased roundheadedness). As a result, in the last eight hundred or a thousand years the proportion of dolichocephalic (long-skulled) individuals in the population has been substantially reduced, while the proportion of brachycephalic (broad-skulled) individuals has correspondingly increased. The assumption that the shape of the head (as expressed more particularly by the cephalic index: the ratio of the maximum breadth to the maximum length of the skull) and also the facial features and shape of the body are subject to environmental modification is supported by numerous investigations on emigrant groups.

The importance of environmental conditions, especially nutrition, manifests itself even more markedly for physical growth and sexual maturing. This has been ascertained from investigations on Scottish, English and Swiss children; in these tests one group of children received extra milk rations for a year, whereas another group of the same age did not. In the first group the annual growth was 6.0–6.7 cm., in the second it was only 4.7–4.9 cm. Better and more nourishing food manifests itself not only in faster increase in stature and weight, but also in the rate of ossification of the bones and the rate of sexual maturing. In times of war and in immediate postwar periods, as indeed in any period of economic crisis with nutritional difficulties, these processes of growth and maturing are greatly inhibited, as is attested by numerous examples from every country in Europe.

Changes in the nutritional conditions, more particularly the increase in the consumption of fat and meat, are evidently also the most important cause of the increase in average stature which has been observed in all European countries over the past hundred years (Fig. 2-17). In some countries, notably

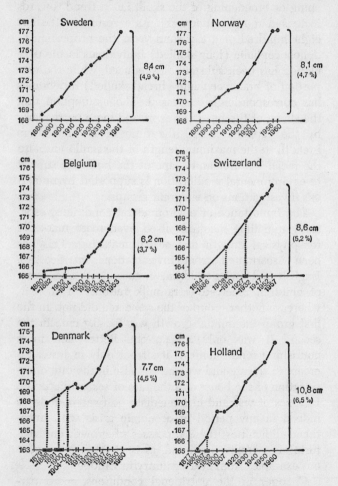

FIG. 2-17: *Increase in stature in some European countries (according to R. Knussmann).*

Sweden, this increase has been as much as 10 cm. Increase in stature is, however, merely a symptom of the changed conditions of growth and maturing. More rapid development is ascertainable already at the pre-natal stage, inasmuch as lengths and weights of babies at birth have shown a distinct increase in comparison with former generations. Thus the average weight at birth has increased from 3100 g. to 3300 g. (6.8 to 7.3 lbs.) in the first half of the present century, while the increase in length over the same period has been from 50 cm. to 53 cm. Also, faster growth is observable in infants and school children. The differences between present-day children and children of the same age in earlier generations are particularly great in puberty, revealing a marked shift towards a more youthful age. Associated with this is the earlier formation of the milk teeth and of the permanent teeth in children (about 6–9 months earlier), and earlier occurrence of disorders such as rheumatism, gastric ulcers and chorea (a nervous disorder characterised by spasmodic jerky movements)—at least three years earlier. More particularly the sexual maturing phenomena now commence at a significantly more youthful age, this being strikingly manifested by menstruation, which has shifted forward some 2–3 years (Fig. 2-18). In boys, too, sexual maturity is reached more speedily. The social effects of these biological phenomena will not be discussed, though clearly they are notable. Whether this acceleration in physical development has been attended with an acceleration in mental development has hitherto not been clearly established.

With a view to explaining the acceleration phenomena which have been outlined above various hypotheses have been put forward in addition to Lenz's nutrition hypothesis (1959). To go into them here

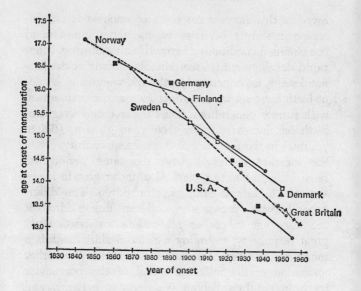

FIG. 2-18: *Shift in age at which menstruation first occurs in some European countries and in the U.S.A. (according to R. Knussmann).*

would be outside the scope of this article. A more recent critical assessment has been given by Knussmann (1968). It can in any case be asserted that this developmental acceleration is primarily due to factors of the environment, including more particularly changes in the pattern of nutrition. Evidently these changes have resulted in better utilisation of the genetic potential for physical development. In other words: the increasing optimisation of the environment has to an increasing extent made possible the maximum realisation of the genetic information programs. At the present time there appears to be some levelling-off of the acceleration rate, since, despite continuing undiminished increase in fat and meat consumption, the average stature is showing little further increase in all age groups. This could signify that the limits of the genetic development potential have now almost been reached.

Reverting once more to the differences in stature correlated to social distinctions, it can, from what has been said above, be surmised that such differences are due not so much to genetic causes as to some significant cause in the very different environmental conditions, especially with regard to nutrition, in which—at least in former generations—children of different social strata grew up. It has indeed been demonstrated by Lenz (1959) that the increase in stature during the past hundred years has been greater in the lower than in the upper classes of society. Since the living conditions more particularly of the lower classes have improved considerably during this same period, which has been not least to the benefit of the growing children, the social differences in average stature must be regarded as being largely environmental modifications, in which genetic factors have little or no share.

While physical differences between social groups or between urban and rural populations must thus, in view of what has been said above, to a great extent be conceived as modifications due to environmental causes, this is at least to the same extent equally true of the differences in intellectual ability found to exist between these various groups. According to social-anthropological researches conducted in many European countries, the members of the social upper classes are, on an average, of greater intelligence than those of the lower classes, a fact which in the majority of investigations has been established on the basis of the learning achievements of school children (Müller 1956). These phenomena are explained as the result of sifting processes which are supposed to have caused a greater accumulation of genes for intellectual capacity in the upper classes of society. There is no doubt that intelligence is based on genetic components, but equally there is no doubt that both the degree and the nature of intellectual ability are determined also by non-genetic factors, i.e., by the multiple complex of the social environment in which a human individual grows up. In this connection we need only be reminded of what has been revealed by research on identical twins who have been brought up separately and in different environments. It is true that at present we are still unable to decide with certainty what proportion of the differences in intelligence between social groups is attributable to environment. The same can be said of the differences in intelligence often observed to exist between one race of people and another, e.g., between Negroes and whites in the United States. As there is as yet no conclusive evidence to support the assumption that social or racial differences in average intellectual capacity are due entirely to genetic factors, it can be supposed that they at least in part reflect differences in environmental conditions of development. In any case it must be endeavoured to provide all social groups and races with optimum and equal possibilities for realising their intellectual and psychological capacities and thus fully utilising their genetic potential.

In conclusion, it can be said that genetic as well as non-genetic factors have their respective shares in producing the typical differences between population groups in intellectual/psychological and to some extent also in physical characteristics. As yet, however, it is not possible to make sharp distinctions between these two sets of factors as regards their effects and relative importance. More particularly in the sphere of intellectual and psychological prospects, abilities and modes of behaviour it is, however, becoming increasingly clear how much the inherited genetic information programs need optimum environmental conditions in order to achieve full realisation. To create such conditions in the form of up-to-date and many-sided education institutions which are open to all sections of the population is therefore an extremely important socio-political duty.

MAN's ADAPTATION TO HIS NATURAL ENVIRONMENT

In the course of its evolution mankind has taken possession of almost the whole world and has therefore adapted itself to the widely varying geographical and climatic conditions of the various continents and latitudes. By adaptation in this sense we understand the development of certain physical (and possibly also intellectual/psychological) characteristics which enable the individual populations to live permanently under the environmental conditions of their respective territories. In these adaptation processes, which certainly have taken long periods of time to accomplish, natural selection must undoubtedly have played an important part, largely resulting in the elimination of the non-adaptable individuals in a population, so that only those survived and were able to propagate who possessed the requisite adaptability, which in turn is based on the genetic constitution of individuals and populations, as we now know and as will be further illustrated by means of examples. Finally, this adaptation to geographical and climatic environmental conditions led also to the differentiation of the human species into the now existing races, namely, the Europoids in Europe, the Near East,

Southern Asia and North Africa, the Negroids in Africa south of the Sahara, the Mongoloids in Central and Eastern Asia and in the Indonesian archipelago, the Indianoids in America, and the Australoids in Australia. To give a detailed discussion of the races of mankind and their development would be outside the scope of this article. Information on the subject is to be found, inter alia, in the writings of Schwidetzky (1962) and Saller (1968).

Of especial interest in this connection are the relationships between geographical distribution of physique and pigmentation, on the one hand, and climate, on the other, the more so as similar relationships have long been known to exist in many animal species (climatic rules in zoology). Thus it has been demonstrated also with regard to the human species that in all racial groups there is, generally speaking, a decrease in stature the closer one gets to the equator. But more particularly for the body weight a distinct negative correlation between the average annual temperature and the average weight of the individuals in a population has been shown to exist. Schreider has calculated the ratio of body weight to body surface area (this ratio is an important criterion with regard to the heat regulation of the human organism) and found it generally to have a lower value for tropical populations than for non-tropical ones. A similar relationship exists for the ratio of body volume and body surface area. According to Roberts, these climatic correlations can only in part be regarded as modifications caused by environmental factors. He, and many other authors on the subject, consider them as most probably being the result of long processes of natural selection, which are conceived as follows: The heat dissipation from the body is proportional to its surface area, whereas the heat generated within the body is proportional to its mass. Now with large bodies the surface-area-to-mass ratio is lower than with small bodies. In a cold climate, or when the climate of a region becomes colder, the larger individuals in the population are at an advantage in that they are better able to withstand the lower temperature on account of the relatively smaller surface area of their bodies. So we may suppose that in regions with different climates (e.g., the Arctic as opposed to the tropics) different respective combinations of genes were advantageous in terms of natural selection, so that these combinations were able to maintain and increasingly consolidate themselves in the course of thousands of years, thus bringing about the now existing climate-correlated geographical differences in the distribution of body weight and height. How this supposed process of selection was precisely accomplished—whether through deposition of fat, basal metabolism, or growth-controlling hormone systems—cannot as yet be determined, however.

The geographical distribution of the colour of the skin is also to be regarded as an adaptation to special climatic conditions (Walter). It has been shown that in all racial groups the most highly pigmented, i.e., the darkest-skinned, populations are those which live in regions exposed to the highest intensity of ultraviolet radiation. A certain amount of this radiation is necessary to the human organism more particularly for producing the growth-stimulating vitamin D from the provitamin ergosterol. On the other hand, excessive exposure to ultraviolet rays may be deleterious to health and sometimes even have fatal consequences. A heavily pigmented skin, such as Negroes or Australian aborigines have, absorbs some of these rays and thus has a protective function. In regions with high radiation intensity a dark skin is therefore biologically advantageous. So it appears probable that human skin colour distribution throughout the world is likewise a result of selective processes which have caused certain genes to occur in specific frequencies.

One group of features associated with man's natural environment is his affliction with certain infectious diseases. In this respect, too, genetic adaptation has taken place, as has been demonstrated in recent years on the basis of the analysis of the geographical distribution of the A, B and O blood groups and of the abnormal haemoglobin designated as HbS (sickle-cell haemoglobin).

The geographical distribution of the blood groups reveals that, for example, the group B—and therefore the gene that produces it—is particularly frequent in Asia, but also in parts of Africa (Nile region, West Africa). Vogel has shown that people with group B blood are much less liable to be infected by, or die from, plague or smallpox than people with blood belonging to group A or O. In those parts of the world where these diseases have been endemic and have taken their toll of human life for thousands of years, the B gene has had a selective advantage and has increased in relation to the other groups. By thus shifting, as a result of natural selection, towards a high percentage of individuals possessing the B gene associated with better resistance to plague and smallpox, the populations of the regions in question have managed to adapt themselves to this environmental hazard and have thus survived.

Similar considerations apply to the distribution of HbS haemoglobin, which is especially frequent in the malaria regions of Africa and Asia (Fig. 2-19). Investigations have shown that individuals with the homozygous genetic constitution for the normal haemoglobin gene, i.e., HbA/HbA individuals, in those

FIG. 2-19: *Geographic distribution of malaria (top) and of HbS haemoglobin (bottom).*

regions are often fatally infected by malaria at a young age, whereas HbS/HbS homozygous individuals show a high mortality rate due to anaemia. On the other hand, heterozygous individuals, i.e., with HbS/HbA genetic constitution, are hardly affected by malaria. From this it is inferred that the malaria-causing microorganism (*Plasmodium falciparum*) is adapted in its way of life, more particularly its metabolic needs, to human blood containing normal haemoglobin, and that it can scarcely develop in blood containing the abnormal haemoglobin HbS. At all events, in the malaria-afflicted regions the HbS gene has a definite selective advantage, which has led to genetic adaptations of the populations of malaria regions to the specific conditions of their environment. Of interest in this connection are Livingstone's observations. He found that the history of the settlement of the Negro populations is closely bound up with the frequency of the HbS gene. Since the larvae of the malaria mosquito (*Anopheles gambiae*) cannot survive in fast-flowing water or shaded water, there are hardly any areas in the tropical rain forests where conditions are favourable to the development of this mosquito. Such areas appear only when clearings are made in the forests, i.e., when the population ceases to be nomadic and establishes itself in fixed settlements. The territories in Africa inhabited by forest dwellers, such as the Pygmies, are indeed relatively free from malaria. Genetic adaptation to malaria as an environmental feature has not been necessary in these circumstances and has not occurred: among these people there is only a very low incidence of HbS haemoglobin. We can therefore draw the conclusion that human populations have adapted themselves to the conditions of the regions in which they live, i.e., to their natural environment, and that natural selection has played and is still playing a major part in this process of adaptation. These selective adaptation phenomena have been associated with the emergence of gene frequencies which are specific to certain populations and indeed to certain biotopes. With the methods of modern population genetics it is becoming increasingly possible to track down and interpret these phenomena.

In the course of their evolution the races and populations of mankind have adapted themselves to their respective environments, but not merely in the manner that has been briefly described here. They have not played simply a passive role, but have had an active share in shaping their evolution by learning better and better to control and utilise their environment, as Heberer has pointed out. As a result of the progress of civilisation and technology, the various races and populations have not only become more or less independent of the circumstances of their natural environment, but there has also been a "slackening" of the natural selection process—as can be observed more particularly in the populations belonging to the Europide racial group (Nachtsheim 1966). This has not been without effect upon the genetic conditions. The danger that threatens mankind from the direction of an ever more comprehensive and all-embracing civilisation is that in consequence of the slackening of the selective processes and furthermore in consequence of increasing pollution of our environment with mutagenic substances the frequency of unfavourable genes will increase, thus adding to the "genetic burden." This potential danger must lead us to consider ways and means of counteracting the increasing degeneration of mankind's biological inheritance.

HELMUT BAITSCH

Future Aspects of Human Genetics

In the first decade after the Second World War scientists seldom concerned themselves with questions about the distant future of mankind; the survivors of the war were not disposed to look beyond the urgent problems of the present day. In retrospect it would seem, however, that despite the pressure of immediate day-to-day needs we ought not, at the time, to have failed to look ahead. Many of the difficulties with which we are faced today may have had their origins in that failure.

With a mixture of dismay and fascination scientists and politicians are now seriously concerning themselves with man's future. Indeed, the problem has become rather a fashionable one. And always the discussion of the subject leads up to the question of the biological future of the human species. Fears and anxieties dominate the arguments; man, it is declared, has so transformed his environment that the response potentialities of the genetically determined "design" of the species have by now already become overstrained by the demands of this environment that we ourselves have changed and are changing. But not only the disparity between the environmental demands and our limited response capacity is a perilous feature; it is also to be feared that man's genetic factors are steadily deteriorating because, while the rate of biological mutation remains unchanged or is perhaps even increasing, modern medical skill in preserving and ensuring the survival of the unfit is steadily adding to the number of diseased and defective genetic factors in the species. In this more and more highly sophisticated welfare society—the pessimists assert—the pressure of natural selection is on the decline: diseased and defective people will propagate themselves more frequently and more numerously than before, thus transmitting their unsound genetic factors to the next generation. All this must, in the long run, result in the genetic extinction of the human species.

And already we hear the call for the "new man," who will be better adapted to this world than the defective species *Homo sapiens*. Already there is talk about the possibilities of modern biology—"genetic engineering"—which will enable us, in the not very distant future, to "repair" defective genetic factors. Thus it will not be long before we can, by our own efforts, rid ourselves of all the shortcomings and faults that mar our biological perfection. Thus an earthly paradise populated by perfect human specimens would emerge. Apparently there are many who have put their faith in the expectation of this sort of scientific progress and are inclined to regard modern biology as a kind of deus ex machina which, in a few giant strides, will lead mankind out of all its misery.

These fears and anxieties, but also these hopes and beliefs, are by no means new. Nearly a century ago the British zoologist Wallace reported a conversation that he had had with Darwin. What he says can be regarded as representative of what many others of his contemporaries were thinking: "In my last conversation with Darwin he expressed himself in very despondent terms about the future of mankind, basing this on the observation that in our modern civilisation no natural selection is taking place and that the fittest do not survive. The successful ones in the struggle for wealth are by no means the best or the most intelligent specimens, and, as you know, in each generation our population is renewed to a greater extent from the lower than from the middle and upper classes."

This pessimistic reasoning by Darwin is characteristic of the mood towards the close of the nineteen century and long continued to influence the thinking of many scientists and politicians. The disastrous link between biological knowledge, the theories derived from it and political actions based on them has been very fully discussed with reference to social Darwinism in H.-G. Zmarzlik's article in this book.

PROGRESS IN RESEARCH ON HUMAN GENETICS

What can the scientist—the geneticist and the anthropologist—say today in reply to the question about man's biological and genetic future?

Since the Second World War a radical change has taken place in human biology. There has been tremendous expansion and development of human genetic studies in the United States and in most Western European countries, and a great many new research institutes have been established.

This interest is manifesting itself also in Germany, though with some time lag. The domination of national socialism had harmed and hindered the development of this scientific field. In this context, too, it is depressing to note that progress in anthropology and human genetics—the two sciences that form the cornerstones of the biology of the human species—has for a

long time been virtually at a standstill in the Soviet
Union and indeed in most other Communist countries.

The knowledge that has been gained about hereditary processes in man in the period since 1950 is many
times more than the sum total of the previously existing knowledge on the subject. Instead of simple theories and hypotheses which had for many years been
dished up in the textbooks as the virtually unvarying
and unchallenged substance of human genetics—and
which, in their oversimplification, invited the attention of politicians desirous of using them as basis and
motivation to serve their particular ends—we now
have an extremely complex texture of new facts and
theories. The expansion of these branches of science
is proceeding at a rapid, almost explosive, rate. And
there is no sign that this will slow down in the foreseeable future: on the contrary, there are more and
more indications that many scientists who previously
had concentrated on genetic research into microorganisms are turning their attention to higher organisms and to man himself.

The progress achieved in anthropology and human
genetics will now be briefly outlined. Of major importance is the fact that the new methods of general
genetics, more particularly the biochemical methods
and the methods of cytogenetics, are quickly coming
to the fore in the genetics of the human species, a field
that has hitherto largely been dominated by formal
genetics. Interest is now no longer focused so much
on finding out the inheritance patterns of particular
diseases or defects. The problems have changed:
what the researchers are now chiefly interested in is
how the genetic information is translated into specific
actions performed by the cell. It is being attempted—
with some success—to reduce complex disease pat-

terns by a process of causal analysis to the level of direct gene actions. These problems can be tackled only by the methods of molecular genetics, which comprises a group of procedures that has become part and parcel of the methodological equipment of modern research institutes. Interest is also concentrated on the problem of what triggers off mutations (sudden changes in genetic characteristics) in human beings: mutation rates can be estimated, the dangers of mutagenic (mutation-causing) agents are recognised and the mechanisms associated with the occurrence of such mutations can be investigated. How man can and should be protected from mutagenic agents is a question that must also be faced.

The unusually important and interesting problem of the origin and control of genetically caused variability of the human species, the phenomenon of polymorphism due to genetic factors, is likewise recognised for what it is. The existence of ambivalence in certain variants is of importance to the theory of natural selection and puts a different complexion on the oversimplified conceptual model previously accepted, namely, that a particular genetically determined characteristic can only be either beneficial or harmful. Enlightening insight into the way in which polymorphism is controlled is provided more particularly by investigations into the relationships between blood groups and infectious diseases. The complex genetic mechanisms that operate in human populations and are responsible for the emergence of the races of mankind are beginning to reveal themselves in intelligible outline, while on the other hand questions concerning the relative value or "superiority" of races are fast receding into the background.

Furthermore, we now realise that the old question "What is hereditary and what is determined by environment?" is—to some extent, at least—fundamentally a spurious problem. To the modern scientific mind it seems only natural and obvious that environment and hereditary character must always be working together, interacting. Besides, they are not independent of each other (Fig. 3-1). Having regard to this

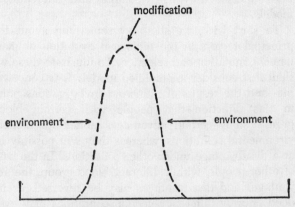

reaction range of a human being
(determined by the genotype of the fertilised ovum)

FIG. 3-1: *The object of this diagram is to show that even in the ontogeny of a human being the modifying environment (or, more precisely: the environmental factors exercising a modifying influence with regard to one particular characteristic) can act effectively only within the scope afforded by the genetically determined reaction range for that characteristic. The concept of "modification" refers to the particular manifestation of a characteristic within this genetically determined range.*

shift in outlook, the concepts of adaptation or adjustment, health, disease are coming more and more to be seen as relative ones.

From this brief outline of the more salient features of present-day genetics and anthropology we shall now pick out for closer consideration a few problems that are important in connection with the question about man's genetic future. At the same time, these examples will show that the oversimplified theories that used to be put forward in illustration of the conceptual model of the "struggle for existence" have now been superseded by highly complex and differentiated models.

To start with, we shall say something about the principal factors in the biological evolution of man, namely, mutation and selection. To illustrate these we shall first consider a simplified model: It is conceivable—and the results of numerous investigations point in this direction—that people with certain blood groups enjoy certain advantages under specific environmental conditions, whereas they will possibly be at a disadvantage under other conditions. In the case of other people, with a different blood group, the advantages and disadvantages may be reversed, or indeed entirely different selection conditions may exist in the same or an altered environment. There are many indications to suggest that in this way a state of balance which maintains variability with regard to blood groups is becoming established.

Now the environmental conditions may change in course of time, with or without human intervention. As factors in the external world in relation to this model we must mention, for example, infectious diseases, which must certainly have played a major part in connection with the emergence and balancing of the variability of human blood groups. It may be that modern medical science with its impressive record of successes, particularly in combatting infectious diseases, has repeatedly readjusted the balance between the blood groups with changed gene frequencies and altered the selection value of the various genes, thus perhaps changing advantages into disadvantages and, conversely, turning disadvantageous variants into advantageous ones.

What has here been outlined with reference to the simplified model of the variability of blood groups will presumably also be valid for many other, if not most, hereditary characteristics and their associated genes in the human organism. In considering these instances of polymorphism and the balancing mechanisms that are responsible for them we must more than ever become accustomed to the idea that the mutation of an item of genetic information, i.e., a sudden change in a hereditary factor, is not necessarily always to be rated simply as positive or negative, "good" or "bad."

Changes in genes and thus in the characteristics determined by them may be beneficial or detrimental to the individual, or they may merely be neutral, always depending on the kind of environment in which the individual in question has to live or in which these characteristics have to manifest themselves. The more variable the environment in which a population lives, the greater will be the chance that certain mutants will, in some particular set of environmental conditions, prove to be "beneficial," whereas in some other set of conditions the same gene may be "detrimental" to its bearer or, at best, neutral. Now if certain variants, on account of their specific genetic constitution, tend to accumulate in specifically favourable environments and if, in addition, a corresponding selective process due to mating occurs in conjunction with a high degree of mobility of such favoured individuals within the population, the resulting effect is referred to as diversifying selection.

With its culture the human species has created a great many environments, subtly differentiated and extending over a wide spectrum. Quite possibly, diversifying selection acting in conjunction with these environments has been, and may still be, a very important mechanism in increasing the genetic variability of the species. This variability has in turn considerably helped to bring about the differentiation of the environment in the course of man's cultural evolution.

This interdependence—the forward-thrusting impulse developed by cultural evolution interacting with the genetic processes that occur within the population—would at first sight appear strikingly obvious and straightforward. However, from all the evidence so far available, sparse though it is, one thing emerges clearly: only a concrete knowledge of such mechanisms would enable us so to assess the present genetic situation of mankind that really reliable forecasts of the genetic future of the species could be made. It may be that here, in the long run, lie the most dazzling prospects for co-operation between geneticists, sociologists, psychologists and political scientists.

HUMAN EVOLUTION AND THE GENETIC BURDEN

Because of the lack of a firmly established body of facts relating to the mechanism of human evolution we cannot as yet take the practical precautions that the geneticist, constantly on his guard against certain types of mutation in the human species, ought to be able to take. There is no doubt that, along with adaptively ambivalent mutations, there also occur mutations which always or usually—under present conditions, anyway—produce abnormalities of a detrimental kind (disease, deformity) in the individuals in which they manifest themselves. Since it is in the nature of genetic information (as transmitted from generation to generation through the genes) that it can mutate, i.e., undergo sudden random changes, there will probably always have been, for as long as there has been life on earth, some mutations that have had a definitely harmful effect on the individual. We now know for certain that our genes are still continually undergoing mutational changes and that very probably the majority of these mutations are of a detrimental kind. There are a vast number of abnormalities that are due to such adverse mutations. They range from the severest developmental disturbances, which are termed lethal factors and kill the individuals in which they occur, to relatively minor defects giving rise to physical, psychological and possibly also social maladjustment just outside the border lines of the current biological and social standards of normality. Evidently we carry along with us a large number of such mutants: the genetic burden of the human species.

How great and how heavy is this burden? The available estimates do not differ very considerably from one another. The mutation rate, i.e., the frequency of the mutations in proportion to the gene frequency, is of the probable order of magnitude of 10^{-5} per gene per generation. This means that one gamete (reproductive germ cell) in 100,000 carries a new mutant of each gene in each generation. If the human zygote (fertilised ovum) is assumed to contain 40,000 genes, then, on a rough estimate, something like 40 per cent of all zygotes would carry a newly developed mutation. Since we have moreover inherited other mutations from our parents and earlier ancestors, these estimates of our genetic burden lead to some rather alarming figures. On the assumption that a major proportion of these mutations are detrimental rather than beneficial, we are forced to the conclusion—both from theoretical considerations and from the results of calculations based on experimental data—that every human being is the carrier of a number of adversely mutated genes.

We now know with a fair degree of certainty that this genetic burden is steadily increasing. In view of this we must ask ourselves whether this burden may not someday become so large as to cause the genetic extinction of mankind. What future developments can we discern here?

The outlines of some trends are emerging: the mutation rate, i.e., the frequency with which the mutations occur in the genes, will probably increase in consequence of the rising level of radiation to which we are exposed (irradiation of cells with X rays, gamma rays, neutrons, etc. speeds up the occurrence of mutation) and, even more so, the rising degree of exposure to the action of chemical mutagenic agents. We are unable to estimate how great the increase is; but we can do something to reduce it, particularly by the more energetic application of protective measures.

We can take it that, as a result of improved medical therapy, people suffering from hereditary diseases will probably procreate offspring with greater frequency than they did in the past. Yet with increasing genetic guidance, and thanks to the simple methods of birth control now available, this process of "anti-selection" need not have dramatically disastrous consequences.

It seems probable that in the immediate future the mentally deficient will, because of their failure to use contraceptives, multiply at a rather above-average frequency rate. But it is not possible to make anything like an accurate prediction of the quantitative extent of the increase in the number of mentally deficient people that may result from this. It is fairly certain, however, that improved medical care for people with hereditary defects and diseases and the above-average procreation rate of the feeble-minded will not give rise to a disastrous increase in defective genes. In any case, there are no indications that such an increase will occur to present a serious threat to the human species in the foreseeable future.

As opposed to these generally unfavourable genetic developments in the near future there are also some favourable ones. There is reason to suppose that certain ambivalent adaptation mechanisms will fade out of the picture, e.g., the genetic adjustment to many infectious diseases such as malaria, as will also the mechanisms for adaptation to undernourishment. We are here concerned with a very significant interaction between biological evolution, on the one hand, and cultural evolution, on the other. The extent of this development, which must be rated as essentially positive in character, i.e., favourable, is something that cannot as yet be accurately gauged. It is probably quite substantial.

We may also take it that certain physical deformations caused by chromosomal aberrations and mutations are becoming rarer as a result of the shortening and bringing-forward of the reproductive period in man, this shift being due to the increase of deliberate family planning in conjunction with earlier marriage and the tendency towards having smaller families (Fig. 3-2). It can be assumed that with increasing participation of women in professional activities and with the changing meaning of marriage, which is coming to be regarded more as a means of shared self-realisation within the man-and-woman partnership, people will, more than they have done in the past, intentionally forgo parenthood by deciding not to have children.

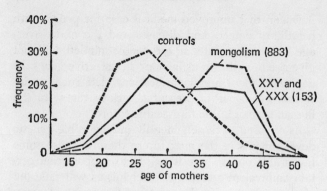

FIG. 3-2: *Age of the mother in cases of mongolism and chromosomal aberrations (XXY and XXX) in offspring, as compared with the population in general (British data, according to Penrose).*

Also of positive significance is the growing effect of diversifying selection in consequence of the progressively greater differentiation of functions and specialisations within the human society, in conjunction with the lowering of social and ethnic barriers, tending towards a society characterised by open classes. The consequences of these processes, which are now in full swing, are at least theoretically clear and also adequately predictable in practical terms: we can expect an increase in genetic variability, and the chances for the emergence of an elite will improve.

Of ambivalent significance to the genetic future of the human species is that, as a result of improvements in the therapy of the phenotype by constantly developing medical skill over a considerable period of time, the concept of disease is becoming more and more a relative one. People will make increasingly extensive use of all sorts of artificial devices to compensate for deficiencies—not just mechanical and optical devices such as false teeth or spectacles, but in future also a variety of dietetic and biochemical aids. We cannot as yet say with certainty whether this trend is to be deplored or welcomed. But we shall in any case have to come to terms with it. We cannot reverse this course of events which is indissolubly linked to our cultural evolution and more particularly to the development of medical science and our attitude towards the sufferings of our fellow men—and indeed we must on no account attempt to.

GENETIC REACTION STANDARDS AND ENVIRONMENTAL CHANGE

Of greater importance to the future of mankind than the trends outlined in the foregoing section would appear to be the problem whether and, if so, to what extent we succeed in keeping control of the environmental conditions created by us ourselves. To highlight the set of problems with which we are here concerned we must consider some further aspects.

Probably the most significant specific characteristic of man is his ability to develop culture. In this process of cultural and civilising evolution, which is ultimately a genetically determined phenomenon, man has created new and continually changing environments. During this process of evolution these environments have not become stabilised or uniform; on the contrary, there is much to suggest that the rate of environmental change in the course of human evolution has become greater and greater and that it will continue to increase. Of decisive importance with regard to our capacity for adjusting ourselves to the new environments that we are constantly creating for ourselves is the question of how much genetic variability is available as the prerequisite for physical and psychological adaptation in human populations (Fig. 3-3).

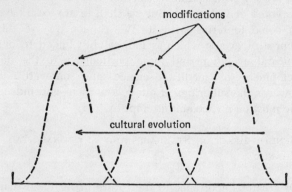

FIG. 3-3: *The object of this diagram is to show that cultural evolution must be conceived as "modificatory evolution." The modification within the reaction range for "cultural capacity," i.e., the cultural state of the population at any particular time, is primarily established by "education."*

What then, in concrete terms, are the difficulties facing us? For example, consider the problem of overnourishment, which has become especially acute in present-day civilised societies, and the crop of physical disorders that follow in its wake: metabolic diseases, high blood pressure, vascular diseases, etc. Or consider the alarming increase in stress situations in certain occupations and certain social patterns, associated with which is the great increase in cardiac and circulatory diseases in the populations of highly civilised countries. Then too, there is the lack of physical exercise that characterises the life pattern of many present-day urban dwellers. This has its adverse consequences in circulatory diseases, overweight, disorders of the ambulatory system and skeletal defects.

One of the most radical and dangerous changes in our environment is that there are more and more people in the world. At present something like 100 million babies are born each year, while the annual death rate runs at only about half that figure. Human beings have not become more fertile than they used to be; in fact, many populations are increasing despite a declining birth rate. The increase in the world's population is because the human genetic constitution has made cultural evolution possible: the kind of culture that has turned out to be an adaptive instrument which has enabled mankind to extend his life span.

It is not just the problem of feeding the vastly increasing population. Even when that problem has been solved, we shall find ourselves up against other problems, arising from the situation where large numbers of people have to live in close proximity to one another. It is being suggested that now already some individuals' capacity for adjustment to the new environmental conditions caused by population growth appears to be overtaxed. In this context must also be viewed the consequences of the drastic increase in the individual life expectation with all its hitherto unsolved problems in the social sphere.

One has to agree with the geneticist Dobzhansky (1965) in stating with regard to this problem: "It does not need a prophet to foresee that, unless mankind destroys itself by nuclear war or some such act of madness, the problem of population increase will in at most a hundred years' time, and probably sooner, overshadow everything else. The urgency of this problem exceeds that of controlling the accumulation of harmful mutating genes and the supposed cessation of natural selection" (Fig. 3-4).

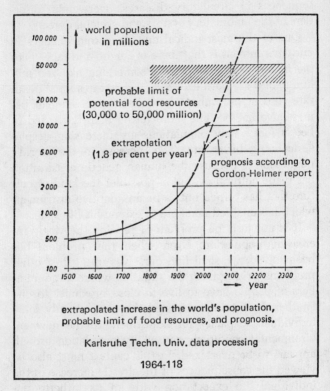

extrapolated increase in the world's population, probable limit of food resources, and prognosis.

Karlsruhe Techn. Univ. data processing

1964-118

FIG. 3-4:   *Increase in the world's population.*

We must ask ourselves what we can do to alter this course of events. Can we be confident that the human species is not already doomed and that we have not irrevocably entered a blind alley in our biological and—connected with this—our cultural evolution? It is the present author's personal opinion that we can, and indeed must, feel confident. Even now we cannot act differently from what we have done throughout the entire evolution of our species: now, exactly as in the past (and presumably also in the foreseeable future), we shall much more often adapt our environment to the genes than our genes to the environment. This was, and still is, mankind's great opportunity: biologically the extraordinary success of this species can be explained only on the assumption that the culture it produced has always been able to change much faster than its genetic constitution.

When we consider what practical steps we can take to influence and control future developments in this sphere, we automatically come up against the question as to what target we are to aim at. Even if we do not as yet discern it and even if we doubt whether such a target can exist at all, there is one thing we can be quite sure of: there is no putting the clock back; we cannot undo our biological and cultural evolution; there is no way back to a past, however golden that may look in retrospect.

Thus it was a fundamental error to believe—as the exponents of German National Socialist doctrine under the Hitler regime did—that the biological and cultural rebirth of a nation could be achieved by building new farms, by proclaiming a mystic "philosophy" of blood and soil or by breeding a race of "Nordic" people. Nowadays we generally take a different view of this trend of development: from the genetic standpoint many of the changes in our modern world, possibly even a large proportion of those which we are inclined to deplore, very probably deserve to be rated as positive. Consider the major changes that have occurred in the social environments of the human species. These changes can be regarded from the angle of their genetic implications: industrialisation and urbanisation are breaking up the rural existence of small population groups, sweeping away isolated genetic groups in the process; large sections of the population which used to have scarcely any contact with one another are now intermingling more and more.

All these processes are almost inevitably leading to increased variability of the human species and thus creating new conditions in which the process of diversifying selection can operate. At the same time we observe, in nearly all contemporary societies, a quite definite tendency to give the individual optimum starting opportunities in life. This equality of opportunity opens up the social groups and classes, and the resulting mobility between the classes is favourable particularly to those things that arise as advantages from the process of diversifying selection: it leads to increased variability, there are better possibilities for the emergence of intellectual elite groups which may well be characterised by the possession of a particularly favourable genetic constitution.

If we are to evolve criteria for our course of action, it is important first and foremost to consider that any extrapolation of our present knowledge into the future will have to allow for an unknown number of as yet unknown factors, not least because social conditions and the functions of people within the social context are now changing so rapidly. We do not know what the social structures of the future will be like and by what ethical standards we shall have to regulate and guide our actions as individuals and as groups. Nor do we know what degrees of freedom we shall preserve with regard to the rapidly increasing numbers of our fellow human beings. But in all our actions it will be of decisive importance to ensure that the freedom needed by the individual for his self-realisation—i.e., for the best possible development of all his inherited potentialities—will remain as great as possible. And in all the proposals that we as doctors and geneticists make in this connection we must always remember and scrupulously make sure not to regard the people entrusted to our care merely as biological specimens or merely as members of a social group or indeed as mere cogs in the technically perfected organisational machinery of the state.

REALISTIC PLANNING FOR THE FUTURE INSTEAD OF UTOPIAN SCHEMES FOR BREEDING SUPERMEN

Having regard to the multitude and diversity of the problems with which we are faced, we cannot expect any one particular measure alone to bring salvation. There is no single panacea. In particular, we must realise that large-scale spectacular interventions in the biological basis of our existence are mere wishful thinking, not only because their technical feasibility must be seriously doubted, but also because they do not individually or collectively hold out any prospect of complete and lasting success. Thus, for example, it will be impossible to eliminate all diseased or defective genes by the traditional method of preventing the procreation of so-called hereditarily tainted individuals. Even if radical coercive measures were applied to attain this end, we could not expect to achieve any decisive success in this way, considering the magnitude of our genetic burden. This does not rule out the fact that, in our capacity as genetic consultants, it does often occur that we advise a couple not to have any children, as the risk of their having a deformed or seriously handicapped child is very high. But any scheme to breed a new type of human being possessing nothing but superior qualities—a superman —will continue to be a mere utopian dream. We not only lack the criteria to know what future generations will rate as "superior" and "desirable," but more particularly we also lack the biological and methodological starting basis for any such scheme. Also, we are unable to intervene directly in the genetic material for the purpose of replacing some defective item of genetic information by an intact one. Despite all the progress that has been achieved in human genetics in recent years, we are still without any possible means of producing controlled and purpose-directed mutations. We do not even know the locations of the genes in the chromosomes, to say nothing of the fact that we are as yet unable definitely to pinpoint particular genes as being responsible for specific characteristics important to us in our existence as human beings. And even if we knew all these things, we should still be—and be likely to remain for a very long time—without any direct means of applying a properly controlled corrective intervention at any one specific point of the genetic information.

What we have to do is not sit back and wait for the realisation of any such utopian schemes but, instead, proceed to take a large number of realistic "small" steps. As a top priority issue it will be necessary to slow down the population explosion; equally urgent is the need to combat pollution of water resources by wastes and effluents. Another important task lies in mutation prophylaxis, i.e., measures aimed at the prevention or reduction of mutations, more particularly by means of better protection from radiation and from mutagenic chemicals. Genetic guidance to people should be increased; in this way it should be possible to avoid much personal distress for individuals and families. We shall, more than has been done in the past, have to engage in environmental research with a view to detecting all those environment-determining factors—mostly of our own making—which in a general or in a partial manner overtax the genetically determined reaction standards in the constructional plan of the human species. Also, it will be of major importance to know how great the variability of these reaction standards is.

We should furthermore support all political efforts aimed at achieving better conditions in which people can live together and at providing equal opportunities for all, especially insofar as education facilities for all members of the species are concerned. Not least important, we must intensify the dialogue with all sciences, and with all political and religious institutions, concerning the ethical standards and the social consequences of our future-directed actions.

Finally, there remains the question of whether all these small steps will be sufficient to ensure the survival of the human species. Certainly, the program outlined here is not a spectacular one. In its aims and scope and in its recommended priorities it reflects the present author's view that the future of mankind is threatened not so much by our admittedly defective genetic equipment but now more than ever by our apparently inadequate ability intelligently and reasonably to regulate interpersonal relationships on a more humane basis and so to control our environmental conditions that they promote optimum development of our genetic potentialities instead of overtaxing them. To take these many small steps will require more than just good intentions. We may appropriately conclude with Albert Einstein's words: "A new kind of thinking is needed if mankind is to go on living."

KARL J. NARR

Cultural Achievements of Early Man

It is man's distinctive function to be not only a creature, a mere product of creation, but also a creator. A science which sets out to investigate this side of human nature in its evolution from its early beginnings finds itself faced with great difficulties, however. It has at its disposal only scanty traces of man's cultural activity, only that little evidence which has managed to survive over long periods of time. Much else has been destroyed and irrevocably lost. On the one hand, this calls for a duly modest approach, in the realisation that it is possible only to build up a skeleton outline, not the complete picture; on the other, the unknown must not be treated simply as non-existent: the reality is bound to have been less one-sided and poor than the picture revealed to us by archaeological finds.

HUMANITY IN EVOLUTION

A serviceable starting point is provided by the earliest known stone implements which can with certainty be regarded as artifacts, i.e., artificially produced. They are more—probably very much more—than a million

years old and belong to the same period as the australopithecines. Whether they were indeed made by
those creatures cannot be established with certainty,
but on the whole it is very likely. These are chopping
tools, which were formed with zigzag sharp edges by
separating smaller pieces from a lump of stone, and
flake tools, which were made by dividing a stone into
thin disc-like pieces also having sharp edges (Fig.
4-1). These types exemplify the two fundamental possibilities of producing sharp working edges on a piece
of stone.

The use of tools, even a crude preparatory treatment of the tools, certain forms of inventiveness,
learning and transmission of knowledge (tradition)
are—though in a simpler and "earlier" form—found
also in apes. But the oldest artificially made stone implements are distinguished by the following characteristics:

1. SHAPE NOT PREDETERMINED: The significant features of the tool—at any rate in the case of flake tools
—are not already pre-established by the natural shape
of the lump of stone from which it is fashioned (as
opposed to, say, a stick, from which it is merely necessary to remove objectionable branches and leaves).

2. FUNCTIONS NOT PREDETERMINED: The tools are
not just (organic) projections, not extensions or en-
hancements of the physical organs (as, for example,
the striking stone is an intensification of the fist, the
stick for reaching out and prodding is an extension of
the arm or the finger), but are used for cutting, i.e.,
for an important new function which does not pre-
exist in physical organs (to be clearly distinguished
from scratching with the nails or tearing with the
teeth). Evidently they are products of real invention
in the sense of establishing a new principle of tech-

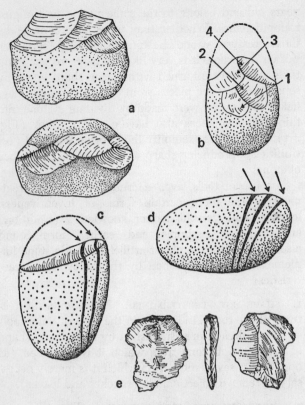

FIG. 4-1: *Making of earliest known forms of unquestion-able artifacts: two views of a "chopping-tool" (a) and pattern of its manufacture by subsequent blows (b); scheme of simple flake chipping from unprepared stone (d) and from truncated lump (c); three views of a crude flake tool (e).*

nique and manipulation based on true insight into conditions and relations.

3. METHOD OF MANUFACTURE NOT PREDETERMINED: The implements are made not merely with the aid of

the available physical organs (hands, teeth), but with
the aid of other implements (hammerstones), though
these in themselves need not necessarily be artifacts.
Thus the use of these latter implements is not the immediate purpose or fulfillment of the toolmaker's activity, but is one step in a systematic—though as yet
simple—sequence of several steps and elements (see
Fig. 4-7).

Even the oldest artificial implements will not have
served only direct purposes (e.g., the chopping up of
animal carcasses), and some of them are so shaped as
to make this unlikely and to suggest, instead, that
they were intended as means for making other implements and weapons from other materials (e.g.,
wood): thus the purpose-directed sequence would be
taken at least one step further. It is not possible to
provide direct proof of this in the form of archaeological finds dating from the very earliest period (see below); but even the manufacture of a simple stone
tool in itself implies the use of tools for making tools.
This represents a characteristic that goes beyond all
known and probably any conceivable animal behaviour: it is based on capabilities and achievements that
we can permissibly regard as specifically human.

ELEMENTS OF A CULTURAL SUBSTRATUM

It can be assumed that tools and weapons made of
organic materials played as great—if not a greater—
part as those made of stone, even though they have
seldom survived on account of their more perishable
character. Sites where remains of australopithecines
have been found in southwest Africa do, it is true,
contain bones and antlers which are sometimes regarded as evidence of the use of tools; but this inference is controversial. What is perhaps more important

is the fact that some of the pieces found in these places appear to have been deliberately fitted together: this would signify that, besides making tools by dividing materials, there were also early attempts at joining parts together. From a later geological horizon,* dating from about 400,000 years ago, trimmed and worked fragments of wood have survived, some of which may have been spears or digging sticks whose points were hardened in the fire. (Definite evidence of the spear with fire-hardened point is not available until about 100,000 years ago, however.) It must be borne in mind, however, that we have to base

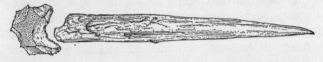

FIG 4-2: *Pointed stick found at Clacton-on-Sea, and stone implement used for shaping such sticks (from K. P. Oakley).*

ourselves on the evidence yielded by oldest-known sites where the conditions for the preservation of such materials through the ages existed at all. The actual earlier existence of such implements in other places therefore cannot be ruled out and is indeed more than likely.

Similar considerations apply to the art of making fire and of sustaining and controlling it. With fire, man had directly subjugated a powerful—and dangerous—force of nature, turning it into a source of heat for warming himself, for cooking his food and for making his implements (such as spears with fire-hardened points)—i.e., using it as a "tool." Definite evidence of the use of fire is available from about the

---

* Synonymous with stratigraphical level, i.e., referring to the systematic position of a stratum on the geological time scale.

same period and, in part, from the same sites which afford the earliest evidence of the use of worked wooden objects. It is not until later in the time scale that we find the remains of campfires and specially constructed hearths with such regularity that we can infer that their users not only knew how to keep a fire going, but were also able to make it artificially as a routine matter. However, it must again be borne in mind that these are only the remains that have survived under special conditions of preservation. For it was only at this period, in the middle Palaeolithic that man began to make more widespread use of caves as dwellings, and in caves much has been preserved which could hardly have survived in the open.

Despite popular belief, early man did not start as "cave man." The earliest archaeological finds relating to man have almost exclusively come from sites out in the open, and the few exceptions to this general pattern are controversial in respect of their character or dating. This must not be taken to mean, however, that early man was a "homeless" creature. One of the oldest sites where stone implements have been found (Olduvai in East Africa) shows an undoubtedly artificial roundish concentration of bones and stones, presumably piled around and forming a boundary to a long-vanished windbreaker screen of branches or some such construction. Clearer evidence is afforded by middle Palaeolithic finds, which reveal similar enclosures around slightly depressed or deepened dwelling places with fireplaces inside them.

At some early sites are found the bones of large numbers of cut-up animal carcasses, including bones which actually show marks made by the cutting tools. Just how the animals were caught and killed in the earliest times is not known; but hunting with spears cannot be ruled out, although definite evidence is again available only for a later period, and then indeed for the hunting of elephants. A notable aspect is the evident disproportion between the size and natural defensive equipment of the wild animals and man's physical inferiority in comparison with them: early man did not possess particular physical organs that specially suited him for hunting, as a carnivorous animal does; instead, he had to compensate for this "inferiority" by artificial means which he created for the purpose. Different species of game were hunted at different times, depending on particularly favourable local opportunities. Evidently, early man sometimes established his camp in the immediate vicinity of good hunting grounds, but there is evidence that he also sometimes carried the desired parts of animals, after cutting them up, long distances to his dwelling place.

Although the remains of early man's meals that have survived are mainly bones, it is very probable that the gathering of plants and small animals (grubs, insects, snails, etc.) for food also played an important part. Again the conditions of preservation of any such remains are such that tangible evidence of these activities is scarce. In any case, this source of food will have been very variable and will have largely depended on the prevailing climatic and vegetation conditions. On cold steppes and tundras the hunting of animals was probably the most important activity, while under different conditions of climate and environment the pattern of food-getting is likely to have been similar to what is today still found among primitive hunters and gatherers of food, whose womenfolk supply something like two thirds of the food requirements by their gathering activities.

The geographical distribution of early man will have largely been determined by environmental circumstances in conjunction with the degree of control that he had achieved over his environment. The oldest known finds of human remains are confined to Africa and the Near East; southern and eastern Asia and southern Europe do not come into the picture until later, and southern central and eastern Europe and the Caucasian region probably even later still. It should be borne in mind that at least during the great ice age (see Fig. 4-3) parts of Indonesia were con-

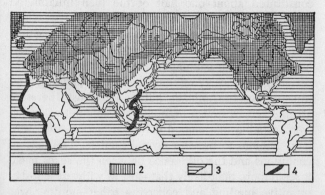

FIG. 4-3: *The inhabited world at the time of the great ice age:* 1=*area covered by ice;* 2=*uninhabited zone with little or no vegetation;* 3=*western and eastern limits of finds of early human remains;* 4=*probable coastlines.*

nected by a land bridge to continental Asia, which readily explains the spread of man into Java. On the other hand, a land bridge—a smaller one—between Europe and Asia Minor played no more than a minor part, so far as we know, and—judging by the formal distinctions in the stone implements—did not promote the migration of man into western Europe. It is more likely that man first entered this latter region from North Africa. These early migrants will therefore have used some kind of vessels (rafts, canoes) for crossing

water obstacles: yet another reason for not judging
their capabilities merely by the simple character of
their stone implements. In forming a conception of
early man's geographical distribution we must rid ourselves of present-day notions and, indeed, take quite
a different view of the relative importance of the
various continents: although there was, at that period,
a considerable land mass off the coasts of Asia, yet
during the main ice age the continent of Africa alone
constituted about one half of the then inhabited
area of the globe (see Fig. 4-3).

Early hunting, especially the hunting of big game,
was largely a communal activity. It called for a certain minimum of communication and organisation for
planning and carrying out the hunt, dividing and
transporting the animals killed. We must therefore
assume the existence of hunting communities which
were capable of planned collective action and were
large enough to provide several hunters. The natural
conditions and the difference between the sexes make
it seem more than likely that—just as with present-day
primitive hunting and collecting tribes—hunting was
mainly the men's task, while the women occupied
themselves with the gathering of food and the care for
the camp. In this sex-determined division of labor
the relationship between men and women, however,
went beyond sexual partnership, to become a bond
between two economic spheres for jointly safeguarding and easing the community's existence. The extension of the period of childhood (as compared with the
apes) must have resulted in a corresponding increase
in the length of time that the parents remained together and lived as a family with their offspring.
(That emotional relationships must also have played
a part is apparent from the fact that the sick and the
crippled, despite their comparative uselessness in eco-

nomic terms, were permitted to go on living under
the protection and care of the community and lived
to what, by the standards of that period, was an old
age.) It would seem therefore that the family as a
unit is something that emerged, as it were, naturally;
for tackling bigger tasks, however, the family has to
ally itself with others: neither the existence of individual family units in isolation from one another nor
the "horde" without family ties can properly cope
with the economic demands and fulfil the natural requirements. Doubtless it was necessary to move camp
at more or less frequent intervals, when one or other
source of food was seasonally or locally exhausted.
Along with the number of members in a community
the space needed to sustain it—estimated at more than
3–4 square kilometres per person in ice-age Europe—
also increased, while there were limits to the distance
that its members could travel each day in search of
food and the absence of appropriate means of transport made it necessary to inhabit a relatively small
area. Hence we must assume that early man existed
in not too numerous local groups which were to some
extent subject to territorial limits.

Whereas there is no actual example or evidence on
which to base the conception of a "primeval horde"
with sexual promiscuity among its members, or the
"group marriage," the community system outlined
above fundamentally resembles what in our present is
still found among primitive hunting and collecting
tribes: evidently these are patterns of social structure
whereby the conflicting demands of the urge for independence and the need to unit into larger groups
in order to meet jointly the challenge of harsh economic conditions are most smoothly and naturally
reconciled.

It is also difficult to conceive how communal life

even of so simple a kind could function without the faculty of communication by real speech. A language is an artificial construct in which meanings are linked to sounds which need not, however, necessarily retain these meanings but which may instead change or lose their original meanings. The powers of abstraction needed for this are something with which we must credit early man, as also the possession of adequate capacity for establishing meaningful sequences and interassociations of actions, in analogy with those manifested in the manufacture of implements (cf. page 110). Also, there were traditions and communal activities involving some degree of planning and organising, which could not have been possible without speech to communicate information about places, times and actions.

From the middle Palaeolithic we have evidence of burials which in part suggest a desire to protect the dead and provide them with food and implements, and in part a desire to confine them in one particular place. Irrespective of which motive—loving care for the dead or fear of them—prompted these burials, they testify to a belief in some form of life after death. Difficult to explain are certain artificial arrangements of animal skulls and bones, but the general situation in which these occur must rule out a profane purpose and would, rather, suggest some kind of religious motive, a sacrifice or something of the sort. These tangible indications of belief in an afterlife and early religious practices are very scarce and of relatively late occurrence. But if we suppose that we are dealing with what is essentially a fully human creature, then there is no reason why we should in advance deny him any emotions or accomplishments compatible with this. To have religion is a general human characteristic, and anyone who insists on having rigorous proof of religion in early man is misconceiving the problem; actually, it is the other way round: it is, instead, the opposite assertion that calls for substantiation.

Although it would appear impossible reliably to say anything specific about the notions and ideas of early man, it is nevertheless possible to establish certain limits, to weigh up what is more and what is less probable. The forms of religion observable in the world today show the religious conceptions, and especially the ideas about God, often to be at least partly determined or coloured by the pattern of the everyday world and the social structure in which any particular religion exists, though of course this should not be taken to mean that these phenomena must necessarily give rise to one or other specific form of religious belief. For simple cultures, initially based on hunting and food-gathering, we can reasonably rule out any religious ideas that are conceivable only in the context of a complex economic and social order, e.g., a hierarchically organised system of gods, the existence of "departmental gods" modelled on a social organisation comprising an advanced division of labour. Furthermore, simple and uncomplicated religious beliefs will as a rule be preoccupied with material and physical rather than with the more highly abstract matters. If only for this reason the conception of a personal creator and ruler is a stronger probability than the conception of some impersonal primeval power or the like. Observations among present-day peoples whose way of life is still very simple and close to nature show at any rate that the situation is not one where a few religious forms commonly regarded as "primitive" (such as "fetishism" or "dynamism") predominate, but that, instead, the conception of a personal creator and sustainer of the world and the world order, i.e., a conception often regarded as evincing a "high moral quality," plays an important part in an "undeveloped" form of culture.

RETROSPECT AND PROSPECT

The oldest makers of stone implements are, by virtue of this achievement, closer to modern man than to modern monkeys, including the anthropoid apes. Besides, they are—according to all available evidence—more closely linked to modern man in the biological evolutionary sense (cf. Fig. 4-4): we may therefore rate them as human beings and consistently seek to understand them as men, in human terms.

If we refuse to do this, i.e., if we insist on regarding the earliest known toolmaking creatures as not human, or not fully human, we shall find ourselves up against the difficulty that at no stage up to the present time can we find any clear and conclusive boundary or transition between such creatures and "true" humans in respect of the phenomena in question. (A true transition, though of a basically different kind, does not occur until about 30,000–25,000 B.C., as explained later.) Certainly there is a sequence in the emergence of various cultural phenomena, but we are not justified in directly regarding them as constituting an evolutionary sequence: the earliest evidence provided by archaeological finds may depend on accidental factors associated with their discovery and especially on the conditions of preservation that have existed in any particular case. This is also true of the scanty clues relating to ritual and religion, burials and sacrificial practices. Such clues as there are have hitherto always been found in caves; out in the open they could not have survived under any but exceptional conditions. Besides, conceptions such as belief in an

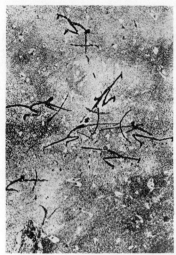

PLATE 10: *These post-ice-age drawings of human figures from eastern Spain differ from the ice-age cave drawings and paintings of southwestern France and northwestern Spain in the content of the scenes and sometimes (as in this example) in the sense of directed movement suggested: here all the movements and the points of the arrows, knees and arms are aimed at the center of the fight.*

PLATE 11: *In Greek mythology the hundred-eyed Argus was placed on guard over Io, with whom Zeus had had an affair and whom the jealous Hera had turned into a cow. But Hermes killed Argus, whereupon Hera took his hundred eyes and put them in the tail of the peacock. The eye markings on the male bird's tail feathers serve to frighten off potential attackers and also play an important part in the mating ritual, more particularly in alluring the hen bird and directing her movements. In southeastern Europe peacock feathers are still often worn to ward off the evil eye.*

PLATE 12: *Odysseus' ship and the sirens (from an ancient Greek vase). A protective eye to preserve the ship and its crew from harm is painted on the bow.*

PLATE 13: *Protective eyes on the bow of an old sailing boat in the harbour of Split (Jugoslavia). The miribota shape is unmistakable. The bows of the vessels of the ancient Egyptians, Etruscans, Greeks, Romans, Chinese and doubtless many other peoples were likewise provided with eyes for warding off evil. The dragon heads carved on Viking ships served a similar purpose.*

PLATE 14: *Embroidered ornaments on a cap, consisting of miribotas, crescent moons, small circular areas and triple-pointed palmettes. All these patterns are eye symbols derived from depictions of eyes. Here, too, we have an example of a highly ritualised system of protection against the evil eye, but used as a decorative pattern whose original meaning is no longer understood or intended.*

PLATE 15: *Emblem on the cap of an officer of the maritime fellowship of Kotor. The* miribota *is clearly recognisable as a protective eye, with pupil, eyelashes and corner of the eye preserved as highly ritualised symbols.*

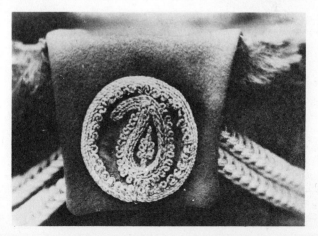

PLATE 16: *Carved foliage pattern on a Neo-Gothic altar. The fact that such patterns are used for the crockets on pinnacles and in various leaf shapes over altars is an indication of their importance. A comparison with derived forms of the miribota reveals that here, too, we have the ancient eye motif. The rounded boss in the middle of the pattern proves its derivation from an eye, despite the plant-like character of the outline.*

PLATE 17: *Bulgarian girdle clasp, comprising two miribotas made of silver. Such clasps, in various sizes and shapes, are still worn by women in Jugoslavian Macedonia. Frequently the position of the pupil—in this instance occupied by three flowers—is marked by a round shiny stone or gem.*

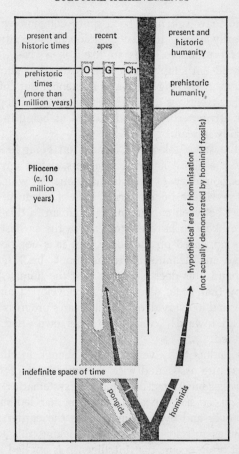

FIG. 4-4: *Diagram of evolutionary place of, and relation between, man and apes: obsolete view (hatched) of immediate relation between modern apes (o=orangoutang, G=gorilla, Ch=chimpanzee) and man (with essentially chimpanzee-like predecessor) in contrast to now undeniable conception of very early separation of the main lines of evolution (black arrows) and separation of men and modern apes by a deep gap (symbolized by black wedge).*

afterlife may well have been quite common without necessarily having found expression in such ritual or sacrificial practices. This in itself is a reason why we should not simply deny the existence of such beliefs in an early stage of man's existence. But this implies that creatures to which such a set of conceptions can be attributed must be regarded as being in principle fully human.

By the same token we cannot, on going back in time to the oldest known toolmakers, detect any conclusive boundary or transitional zone at which we might say: here begins "true" man. (A transition of this sort between subhuman and human in this sense is more likely to have existed *before* the earliest toolmakers appeared on the scene, but it is not possible to make any definite assertions about this.) On the other hand, this does not mean that the human being had, by that time, emerged fully developed and accomplished in every detail or that man's progress along the road towards "coming into his own" had been completed.

The undoubtedly very striking change in the cultural picture associated with the emergence of *Homo sapiens* (as envisaged by zoological systematics) from about 30,000 B.C. onwards, however, has led investigators over and over again to class the earlier forms of man as inferior creatures. In making this assessment it often occurs that intelligence is applied as the sole criterion, and the measure for the development of this faculty is usually taken as being provided by technological evolution. The advance in the level of technology over the period from about 30,000 B.C. to the present time, i.e., within the history of *Homo sapiens* himself, has been incomparably greater than in the entire preceding period. The difficulties associated with judging technological simplicity to be a sign of "primitiveness" or low intelligence become evident when we consider the tremendous technological progress that has been achieved in the last two hundred years. All the preceding centuries put together had nothing comparable to show. Besides, the only surviving evidence that we have for the earliest times is provided by stone implements which can yield only very scanty and fragmentary information. An example may serve to bring home this point more convincingly: A village settlement existed in the third century B.C. at Huaca Prieta, in Peru; the site has yielded archaeological finds which include fishing nets provided with weights and floats (the latter made from cultivated gourds), and remains of cultivated plants, including hybrid cotton. Yet the stone implements found at that site are still very similar to the oldest type known. What would our verdict on this culture have been if under more unfavourable conditions of preservation at this site only the stone implements had survived?

A more important argument is derived from the incredibly long duration of the earliest periods of mankind's history: hundreds of thousands of years, indeed more than a million years. We cannot conceive such lengths of time; and yet hardly any technological progress was achieved during these vast periods (see Fig. 4-5). But it must be considered that the first inventions were certainly the most difficult and must therefore be correspondingly highly rated. It is easier to advance on the basis of progress already achieved. Really new inventions are rare; more often new developments emerge as the result of improving upon known methods. Besides, in early prehistoric times, man lived only in very small groups within large territories. There was less opportunity for exchange of ideas. (To appreciate this point properly, we must

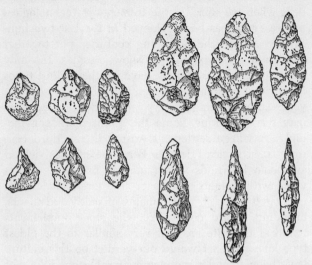

FIG. 4-5: *Technical development of hand axes as found in successive strata in the Olduvai gorge in East Africa: top view (upper) and side view (lower diagram), advancing from the oldest implements on the left to the most "modern" on the right (approx. one third natural size, based on L. S. B. Leakey, redrawn).*

realise how much of our recent technological progress has been due to the numerous possibilities for intellectual contact and communication.) Furthermore, in very small groups based on a very simple economy there was no possibility for social differentiation to develop, nothing conducive to the promotion of special talents. There was little to stimulate technico-economic evolution. But when once the threshold had been crossed, evolution could proceed with almost explosive vigour. This acceleration, the increase in the rate of evolution, is continuing. From the beginning of the specialised hunting cultures of around 30,000 B.C. about 20,000 years elapsed until the start of the agricultural and cattle-breeding cultures; a shorter time elapsed until the emergence of urban cultures, when man had become a town dweller; and so on, at an ever increasing rate, to the breathtaking pace of technological development of our present time. Quite obviously, culture already developed and highly differentiated offers more stimuli, more possibilities for multiple combination of knowledge.

Viewed as a whole, an increase in intelligence is, it is true, a possible cause for the over-all technological progress that has indubitably been achieved; but it is not an essential assumption, i.e., it is a hypothesis which—on the basis of other considerations—is superimposed from outside upon the phenomena in question. These phenomena do not in themselves demand such an explanation, but allow the evolution to be adequately explained in other ways.

SURGING PROGRESS AND NEW EXPRESSION

As compared with the simple cultural picture presented by the earliest periods, a marked evolutionary expansion manifests itself after around 30,000 B.C., at the beginning of the upper Palaeolithic. The new picture that emerges can be characterised by such terms as accumulation, differentiation and specialisation. There is an increase and concentration of cultural goods, a more refined technology with greater variety in the forms of weapons and tools produced and corresponding specialisation of their respective functions (Fig. 4-6), more pronounced economic and

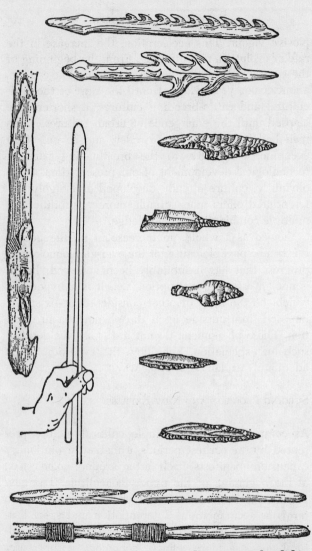

FIG. 4-6: *Tools and weapons of the upper Palaeolithic: stone points and awls (top center), barbed bone and horn points (so-called harpoons, left), composite pointed tool (right), throwing stick and its method of use (bottom).*

general cultural differentiation of individual groups.

At about this same time a whole new dimension of human quality is attained in the earliest works of pictorial art (Plate 10): they mark a new departure whose importance is most closely comparable to the invention of writing and which justifies regarding this as the great watershed in prehistory. Besides—or, rather, above—technico-economic progress and the increasing control over environment there is now a new form of creative representation and expression.

In those parts of the world where proper archaeological investigations have been conducted new cultural forms are found to follow the old with such suddenness that we must assume a well-nigh explosive evolution or an influx of new ideas from other regions. A fact which appears to support the latter hypothesis is that now the earlier forms of man were superseded by the type we call *Homo sapiens*. To attribute the "higher" culture of this type of man to his possession of correspondingly superior mental powers and abilities is not permissible, however, at least so long as this "rapid" succession and the concurrence between cultural and human forms have been properly established only in western and central Europe, i.e., only in a small portion of the then inhabited world.

ADAPTATION TO ENVIRONMENT

The new technological and economic achievements laid the foundation for important advances in man's response to the conditions imposed by his natural environment, for increasing his mastery of unpropitious conditions, especially in cold regions with sparse vegetation, and thus taking possession of hitherto unpopulated parts of the world. By the end of the glacial period, at the latest, man had found ways and

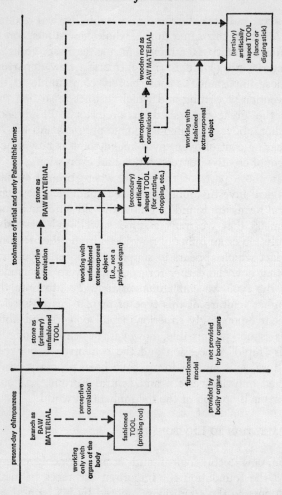

FIG. 4-7: *Scheme of correlation and interaction in simple toolmaking: Different range and degree of sequence and interaction in previous conception (– – →) and actual work (——→). Demonstrated by the "highest" observed achievements of today's wild apes and the earliest-known confirmed artificially-formed tools.*

means which enabled him to live at least for a time under the harsh conditions of cold steppes and bleak tundras. Thus the limits of the inhabited world were pushed farther north (see Fig. 4-8). People even

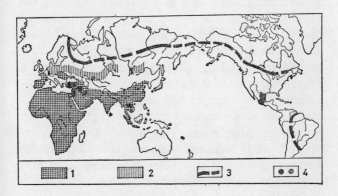

FIG. 4-8:   *Early distribution of man:*
1=until about 300,000 B.C.
2=until about 12,000 B.C. (extending to America, but not adequately traceable for mapping there)
3=until about 5000 B.C.
4=evidence of plant cultivation in the seventh millennium B.C.

migrated into the uninviting northeastern parts of Siberia and spread from there into the American continent, the southernmost tip of which had been reached already before 8000 B.C.

An important new development was the introduction of long-range weapons (see Fig. 4-6), initially the javelin-throwing sling and much later (after 15,000 B.C.) the bow and arrow. Furthermore, cunning new methods of hunting were evolved, such as the stalking of game by hunters wearing animal masks and the use of complex trapping systems, probably also fenced enclosures into which game was driven. Besides big game, which was widely hunted from earliest times, including large creatures such as elephants, the killing or capturing of smaller or more fleet-footed animals such as horses and especially the reindeer became more important. Whereas in the lower and middle Palaeolithic periods the preference for certain species of game was simply due to these early hunters' taking advantage of local favourable conditions, in the later period that we are now considering there emerged real and more advanced specialisation: entire regionally distributed groups, which are distinguishable from one another also by differences in their tools and weapons, specialised in the hunting of particular species of animal and were adapted to living under specific environmental conditions. Some examples will serve to clarify this:

MAMMOTH HUNTERS OF THE COLD STEPPES: The steppes and tundras of eastern Europe in the glacial period, mainly bare and treeless but also comprising regions with tree and scrub vegetation, provided ample grazing for various species of animal, including the mammoth, a form of woolly elephant. Although other animals were also hunted by these steppe dwellers, the mammoth was preferred because it supplied larger quantities of meat and raw materials, including ivory, which was particularly highly prized. Good hunting enabled these people to remain longer in one locality and indeed to settle there. Remains have been found of permanent dwellings, up to 40 metres long and more than 12 metres in width, installed in depressions formed in the ground. The roofs of these dwellings must have been built of large timbers and were probably covered with animal skins or turf. Such permanent structures, with several fire-places inside them, are found chiefly in the river valleys and lowlands, where wood for building and for fuel was more abundantly available. Even under harsh climatic conditions such dwellings provided adequate protection from the weather, and they enabled their inhabitants to survive the rigours of winter even at the northernmost limits of the then inhabited world.

REINDEER AND HORSE HUNTERS: Even during cold periods in the earth's history southwest Germany and Switzerland were covered by tundras with a vegetation of trees and scrub supporting many species of animal. More particularly in caves and under rock shelters we find dwelling places and camps, sometimes provided with a kind of paving and containing fireplaces. Not the mammoth but the reindeer and the horse were chiefly hunted; respectively, they accounted for about 30–40 per cent and 10–20 per cent of the total numbers of animals hunted by these people. Evidently they hunted from bases which were favourably situated in respect of seasonal conditions and concentrated on readily accessible species of game, moving their camps about within relatively small territorial limits.

REINDEER HUNTERS OF THE TREELESS TUNDRA: The treeless tundra region of northern Germany, as it then was, was visited only in summer by large herds of reindeer which moved northwards. There they were pursued by hunting parties who invaded this very inhospitable region only at favourable times of the year and had to travel great distances to do so. On these journeys they lived in pole tents that were easy to set up and dismantle; they were entirely specialised in hunting reindeer, which they were evidently able to kill with bows and arrows. About 80–90 per cent of the animal remains found at these summer camps are those of reindeer. The hunters must have brought at least the poles for building their tents, and probably also the tent coverings (presumably reindeer skins), with them into the treeless tundra. Indeed, this highly unsettled roving life with its continual alternation between wintering in more wooded country farther south and the summer's hunting in the northern region must surely have involved the solving of some transport problems.

Man's newly achieved progress in the control of his environment signified only a minor change in the natural conditions, however. Essentially it went no further than an adaptation by specialisation of the kind described above, i.e., by adjustment to specific conditions (e.g., the intensive hunting of particular species of animal). This could indeed offer substantial advantages, but on the other hand it often made it difficult for such communities to break out of long-established patterns and adapt themselves to subsequent changes in their living conditions. In fact, it would appear that the improvement in the world's climate at the end of the glacial period, so far from making things better for the human communities, gave rise to something like crisis conditions, paradoxical though this may seem: in the ice age it was clearly advantageous for man to compensate for his lack of natural adaptation to his environment and achieve adaptation by artificial means, though evidently at a price, namely, of immobility and dependence on certain patterns, which proved disadvantageous when the conditions changed once again.

The specialised utilisation of natural resources for obtaining food and satisfying other needs will indeed have made it possible for some regions to be more

densely populated than they would otherwise have
been. But we must not overrate the size of the individual communities. The battue, i.e., the driving of
game by beaters, does not require a very great number of men, even when fairly large herds of animals
are hunted in this way; besides, women and youngsters may have taken part as well. The hunting of
particular species of game may, in certain seasons,
have brought together several local communities to
combine their efforts and may very likely have led to
the establishment of ties of kinship between various
communities; but to achieve a permanent increase
and more advanced development of the social and
economic units would have required very favourable
conditions indeed. The finds at the dwelling sites
show that even the rich mammoth hunt in some
eastern European regions was barely sufficient to sustain communities of more than a hundred people, and
usually even fewer, in any one place. To what extent
the social conditions were more highly differentiated
and elaborate than in the preceding period is difficult
to judge. The fact that in burials the men wear
richer ornaments than the women could be an indication of emphasis upon the pre-eminence of the male
hunting element. Certain burials also suggest that the
occupant of the grave may have been a person of
special importance or have been held in special esteem, possibly a great hunter or leader or someone
associated with religious practices or artistic achievements.

In the well-known great paintings and drawings
that have been found on the walls of caves and in
minor artistic expressions (carved or modelled figures,
scratchings) there emerge two polar manifestations
of the artistic urge: naturalistic painting and drawing
in the west; sculpture and geometric ornamentation

in the east. Designations such as "naturalistic" or "realistic" must of course be understood only in an approximate sense and are strictly accurate only for a small proportion of the representations. On the other hand, there are a great many others in which there is undeniable stylising and representational treatment going beyond the physically perceptible. In terms of artistic quality these early paintings can hold their own in a comparison with the art of later periods: details have often been omitted or combined and condensed with a view to producing a striking impression; the artist has confined himself to essentials and has given artistic prominence to the picture's motif. We must accordingly rate these as fully fledged works of art which often radiate a sense of power and depth that has a direct appeal even to the modern viewer.

Against this richness of expression there is a poverty of themes, however. Those prehistoric artists depicted mainly animals, only very rarely human beings and then usually not simply as people, but with animal characteristics or as half human and half animal. This should be taken into account when considering the reasons that prompted them to paint these pictures: always the attention is focussed on the animal or, more rarely, the semi-human, semi-animal hybrid creature. That the pictures were not intended simply as wall decoration—"art for art's sake"—is indeed quite clear from the particular circumstances; but, on the other hand, they cannot be analysed wholly in terms of function and purpose either: there is an "artistic surplus" arising from the sheer joy of painting a picture, the satisfaction of aesthetic needs and a clear desire to fashion something.

The fact that the pictures express the essential nature of the animal, partly in relation to hunting (arrows and javelins are depicted) or to the human figure and sometimes representing a merging of human and animal forms, provides a clue to understanding their purpose. Clearly a special and intimate relationship between man and animal (or other semi-human or semi-animal creatures) going beyond the physically tangible is additionally envisaged: the animal character participates in other spheres of existence: the human and the superhuman and supernatural. The special prominence attaching to hunting in the activities of daily life with its intensification of man's relationship with the animal world is, in these pictures, evidently reflected and enhanced in the spiritual world.

This would correspond, at least in principle, to a basic attitude which at present still governs the religious beliefs current in specialised and advanced hunting cultures. They are centred upon close man-to-animal relationships and an enhanced significance of the animal in the supernatural world. These beliefs include conceptions of animals as guardian spirits and as manifestations of "one's other self"; of the ease with which a being can change from human into animal form and vice versa; of a deity or supernatural power imagined as animal in character, or alternating between animal and human form: lord of animals, hunters and the hunting grounds; of spirits dwelling in the forests and the animals, often associated with traits of ancestors or great legendary heroes; of mediating spirits or personifications of individual characteristics and functions of a supreme deity. In this system of beliefs the animal is no longer merely a creature, nor indeed a being placed on an equal footing with man himself, but may be exalted to the status of a supernatural creator. In what concrete form such beliefs manifested themselves in prehistoric times is of course a question that must largely remain unanswered, but the similarity in fundamental attitudes appears to be clear enough. (The fact that the animals are shown with spears or arrows in their bodies has enhanced the theory that these early cave paintings were intended as a form of magic to ensure success in hunting; but there are far fewer points of similarity to support this view, and as a generalisation it is untenable.)

The interment of whole animal carcasses (e.g., submerging them in a pool) or parts thereof is nowadays still commonly done and was also practised in prehistoric times, as is revealed by the evidence of drawings and finds of bones. Evidently, in some cases these were sacrifices to supernatural beings, but in other cases they partook more of the character of the reanimation of the animals and the preservation of the species. On similar notions is based a "bear ritual" which is nowadays still widely practised with the object of propitiating the animal and mystically sending it back to the lord of animals and of the forest. At least some features of this ritual are attested for the upper Palaeolithic by the evidence of paintings and archaeological finds.

Not so clear are phenomena which subsequently appear as belonging to shamanism, i.e., a highly variable and multi-featured complex of customs and ideas, characterised by states of ecstasy, a belief in guardian spirits, often in animal form, who give help and guidance in the journey to the hereafter, and ideas associated with transformation and transmigration. Evidence at least for ecstatic practices and the belief in birdlike guardian spirits and helpers in the upper Palaeolithic is available in drawings and paintings.

Female fertility as a conceptual characteristic is manifested in the so-called "Venus statuettes," at least insofar as these emphasise the parts of the woman's body more particularly concerned with the reproductive and the infant-feeding functions. Other statuettes are more highly schematised. Comparative studies have shown that the conception of higher female beings, e.g., as the great mother and mistress of animals, as a helper and bringer of success in hunting, as mistress of the underworld and of the forces of nature, must be taken into account in seeking to explain the meaning of these statuettes.

Despite all limitations and uncertainties it emerges that specialisation and differentiation are encountered not only in the economico-technological sphere but also manifest themselves in varied multiplicity in the world of ideas and beliefs.

CHANGING THE ENVIRONMENT

The consequences of the postglacial climatic improvement (after about 8000 B.C.), characterised more particularly by the gradual reafforestation of the northern regions of the world, were mastered apparently by only a few communities which successfully changed their patterns of life and specialisations. In certain parts of the world, outside Europe, it was not until this period that hunting cultures actually evolved. In the steppes and savannahs of Africa it is associated with a wealth of rock drawings which quantitatively far exceed anything to be found in Europe. The American continent was penetrated over its entire width by hunting cultures; not only did these early hunters take possession of the grasslands abounding in game, but they also adapted themselves to living in less hospitable regions, more particularly the dry desert regions in the southwest of the United States and in Mexico.

Such adaptation cannot achieve a decisive break-through to a more advanced way of life, however; this can come about only as a result of achievements involving more profound changes in the natural environment. Mere acquisition and control of the sources of food, in however specialised and subtle a way this might be done, was unable to produce a radical increase and improvement in food supply; this became possible only by active human intervention in the growth of food plants and the breeding of animals, i.e., agriculture and stock-raising.

It seems certain that by the seventh millennium B.C. an important centre of agricultural and stock-raising activities had developed in Asia Minor and the Near East. The plants cultivated in those regions were variants of wheat, barley and leguminous crops (especially peas and lentils). Various other items of food, especially fruits and nuts, were gathered from trees which grew wild or were possibly also tended and protected: pistache nuts, acorns, the fruit of the nettle tree (*Celtis*) and a relative of the American mesquite (*Prosopis*), probably also figs, almonds and walnuts. The wheat and barley varieties cultivated at that period are in some ways very similar to the wild forms of these plants still to be found in these and adjacent regions. Their cultivation must have started in the seventh millennium B.C. in the warm-temperate climatic zone, with mainly dry hot summers and rainy winters, in the coastal regions and peripheral mountains and stepped plateaux of Asia Minor and the Near East from Iran to the Mediterranean or perhaps in regions situated farther to the northeast. (Millet as a cereal crop appeared somewhat later in this region, but was brought into cultivation probably not later than the sixth millennium B.C.; its origin is to be sought in the woodlands and river meadows and also the wooded and dry steppes extending from China to the Sudan.) As the wild forms of peas are distributed from the Mediterranean to India, and the wild lentil extends to regions east of the Himalayas, their potential range of cultivation not only comprises the wheat-growing regions but also a zone farther east, as evidenced by early finds in southern Asia. The often heard assertion that in Asia Minor and the Near East there existed a completely self-contained centre of cultivation of all the food plants which are known to have been in use there at an early period is by no means firmly established.

The first domestic animals—other than the dog— were goats and sheep, which occur concurrently with the cultivation of cereal crops. In the history of animal domestication the dog evidently occupies a special position. Known to have been domesticated in central and western Europe and the Near East not later than the seventh millennium B.C., it appears to have been distributed over an extensive area for a very long time. To what extent the keeping of dogs prompted man to domesticate other animals as well is a question that cannot yet be answered. Since the dog did not achieve any importance as a source of meat or other animal products, but served as a watchdog and helper of man, it did not fundamentally alter the structure of cultures based on the hunting and gathering of food. The same can be said with regard to the origins of the domestication of small ruminants, i.e., so long as these animals continued to be only of secondary importance as a source of food beside hunting. Also, it cannot simply be assumed that in Asia Minor and the Near East the practice of agriculture and of herdsmanship originally occurred as a single combined set of activities. The fact that the taming and utilisation of small ruminants in the mountain-

ous northern regions dates back to the eighth and
possibly the ninth millennium B.C. suggests, instead,
that the domestication of cattle probably originated
in highlands situated farther to the north or the northeast.

It appears likely that in the central parts of the
Near East there occurred an older stage of food-producing economy, prior to the earliest evidence of
cereal crops and domestic animals. Such early agriculture is presumed to have consisted in the cultivation of plants which were entirely perishable and thus
left no archaeologically detectable remains. Its existence can be inferred indirectly from the evidence of
very settled patterns of life, stable settlement in a
region and even early concentrations of relatively
large numbers of people in one place.

In the eighth and ninth millennia B.C. Palestine
consisted of steppes and savannah, interspersed with
small desert areas and with fairly densely wooded
areas in the hill country and in the gullies. On account
of local differences the finds in the desert of Judaea
and in Transjordania are more scanty, while a richer
development manifests itself on the Jordan and Hula
plain and also in the vicinity of the wadies (which
then were probably active watercourses) of Mount
Carmel. Although in some regions the inhabitants
lived in caves and under rock shelters, the characteristic dwelling of this time and place is a round structure
whose foundations and wall bases are constructed in
stone masonry. Many of these dwellings were modified and enlarged a number of times, which testifies
to their constant or repeated use over a considerable
period of time. The basis for such a community might
be localised hunting, fishing and food gathering in a
territory where food was plentiful, but it is more
likely to have been based on an economy which was

already enriched by the cultivation of food crops. This impression is strengthened by the construction of complex and elaborate graves with stone pitching and stacking giving them a rough monumental quality and considerable durability. Such graves were used mainly for collective burials of corpses, but sometimes also for the burial of parts of bodies (skulls and limbs). All the significant and decisive features of this culture are new to the region (as indeed also the type of man who practised this culture) and cannot be traced back to earlier known ones in this region, whereas they do have links with the later agricultural cultures.

This group exhibits well-nigh explosively rapid cultural evolution in the rich archaeological remains found at Jericho. By the end of the eighth millennium B.C. a small but permanent settlement in that locality was enlarged to cover an area of about 4 hectares (10 acres), which was soon enclosed by a massive stone wall up to 1.75 m (5 ft. 9 in.) thick and of considerable height. At one point in the vicinity of the wall is an 8 m (26 ft.) high structure in the shape of a truncated cone, of solid stone construction, whose function and purpose are unknown. Chambers between this "tower" and the wall are considered to have been water storage cisterns by some investigators. The contents of the dwellings in this settlement are very modest and in marked contrast with the quite impressive building achievements of these people. Although there is only scanty evidence that they grew crops or kept domestic animals, it is hardly possible that so large a settlement, which is estimated to have had at least a thousand inhabitants, could have existed in the semi-dry climatic region of the Jordan valley with no food resources other than those provided by hunting and gathering. The most likely con-

jecture is that they had irrigation-based agriculture
whose staple crop need not necessarily have been
cereals, as leguminous plants and fruit growing offered
equally good possibilities.

After an interruption in the habitation of this site
there subsequently appear at Jericho, in the seventh
millennium B.C., sparse remains of domestic animals
(dogs and goats) and some seeds of plants such as
wheat and barley as well as lens, beans, and peas. In
general, new walls follow the alignment of earlier
ones, but some new elements emerge. For instance,
in the undermost level we find arrangements of human
skulls with their lower jaws missing, and burials of
bodies without skulls, but with the lower jaws included. The same burial practice is found also in the
later levels, when the site was reinhabited, but now
the skulls have the facial features modelled in plaster
(Fig. 4-9). On the other hand there is considerable difference in the construction and layout of the houses:
whereas the earlier inhabitants lived in round structures built of mud brick, we now find rectangular
buildings provided with a kind of small porch and
constructed from a new form of brick, in conjunction
with the use of a coloured hard-burned stucco applied
to floors and walls.

The impressive remains at Jericho compellingly
suggest the word "city." Undoubtedly we are here
concerned with a densely populated settlement comprising a substantial number of people, and the well-
planned encircling wall indicates quite a high degree
of organisation. On the other hand, there are no conclusive indications of other urban characteristics. Such
characteristics would comprise: a population largely
dissociated from the basic activities of producing
food, division of labour among different occupations
and crafts, and really significant trade—i.e., a differen-

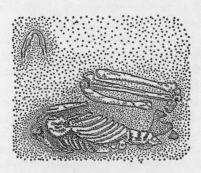

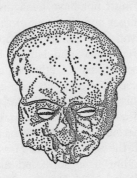

FIG. 4-9: *Skulls with facial features modelled in plaster (no lower jaw; shells for eyes) and burial without skull but including lower jaw: Jericho, seventh millennium* B.C. *(redrawn from K. M. Kenyon).*

tiated, and indeed a stratified, society or a settlement functioning as the centre of a hinterland of simpler socioeconomic structure which contributes substantially to feeding the urban community. On the other hand, a communal centre with some form of division of labour, i.e., the very sort of internal structure that is missing at Jericho, is encountered at the much smaller settlement of Beidha (south of the Dead Sea). There we find, among others, buildings in which very small rooms measuring only about 1 m×1.50 m (3 ft. 3 in.×5 ft.) are arranged in pairs along a narrow corridor and contain materials and tools for a wide variety of activities, such as the cutting up of animals, the working of bone and horn and the production of high-quality stone implements.

In any case it is amazing that at—or at least near— a period of time when agriculture is believed to have first emerged in the Near East we already encounter such phenomena as the above-mentioned early large settlement at Jericho. The question arises as to whether these must not have been preceded, here or elsewhere, by other and simpler forms.

Simple cultivation of plants, without involving the growing of cereal crops and horned cattle breeding, is regarded, on the basis of ethnological and culture-geographical considerations, as the earliest form of agriculture. This is more particularly conceived as having comprised the reproduction of shrubs, root plants and tuberous plants by means of cuttings (as contrasted with the sowing of seed) as is still done in southern Asia; but it is supposed also to have included the cultivation of leguminous plants and the care of fruit-bearing trees. In seeking to apply this theory based on primitive agricultural methods in southern Asia—with which are furthermore associated such practices as cannibalism and the preservation of human skulls for various reasons (head-hunting, ancestor worship)—to the prehistoric material, we find some cultures that present an extremely simple pattern. They comprise burials of complete human skeletons and others in which the skulls are missing; also there are burials of separate skulls together with small collections of other bones. Especially in further India and Indonesia the stone implements belonging to the same culture are extremely simple and crude, often indistinguishable from the rough tools of the early stone age and presumably directly derived from them. At that period, as is now-adays still the case, the use of wood and especially bamboo in those parts of the world was probably so important that stone implements were of relatively minor significance. Whereas the hypothesis that such early communities already practised some form of agriculture has generally remained uncorroborated by actual archaeological evidence, a site in Thailand, where conditions were especially favourable, shows that a community which existed at least as early as the eighth millennium B.C., probably was practising agriculture in the seventh and more likely already by the end of the eighth millennium. The plants which those people are thought to have grown comprise the bottle gourd, the Chinese water nut, the betel nut, beans and probably peas, followed a little later by pumpkins. There may be more surprises in store for us in these as yet little explored parts of the world.

In America we find a different situation. Within a cultural complex which was largely adapted to regions with little rainfall, and in which hunting must have played an important part to judge by the finds of hunting weapons, we encounter, in Mexico, in the sixth and seventh millennia B.C. the bottle gourd and other cultivated species of the pumpkin family, as well as American pepper and avocado pears. Certain species of bean and the amaranth were, at first, probably gathered only from plants growing wild. In the sixth millennium we additionally find a species of millet, and on the threshold of the fifth millennium there appears a form of maize with very small ears, of which it has not yet with certainty been established whether it was in fact a cultivated plant or merely the hitherto unknown wild maize. The cultivation of beans, further cucurbitaceous (pumpkin-type) plants and a variety of maize can definitely be traced to the fifth millennium B.C. Hunting and the gathering of food played an important part besides agriculture. At first the latter may have been a mere adjunct and not significantly have altered the hunting-and-gathering cultural pattern; and although it does gradually increase in importance, it is not until the second millennium B.C. that we can with certainty establish the existence of a really stable and effective village-based agricultural economy and living pattern in central America.

Whether the three centres of early agricultural development (see Fig. 4-8) each evolved independently of the others or whether there were ancient links between them is still undecided and a matter of controversial argument. The social and technological levels differ greatly. There is nothing to suggest that the invention or discovery of agriculture required a highly evolved and differentiated social structure, nor that a high level of technological development was essential to it. In this context it is to be noted that the archaeological remains of the early agricultural cultures of southern Asia and America are in many respects much more primitive than substantially earlier

remains of the hunting communities that existed in
Europe in the old stone age (Fig. 4-10; compare

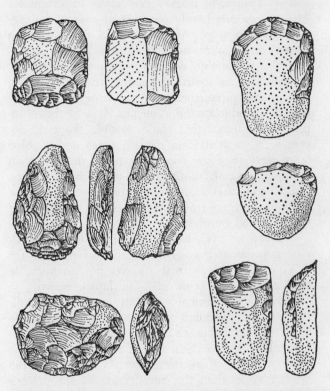

FIG. 4-10: *Hoabinh group, stone implements (about one
third actual size, according to P. I. Boriskovski).*

with Fig. 4-6). Although the question as to the
existence of original intercommunication between the
agricultural regions must remain undecided, the importance of the links established at a much later period must not be underrated. Without the food plants
first grown in America, such as maize and the French

bean (only the broad bean is a native of the Old World), the potato (though not cultivated until later) and the manioc or cassava (especially important for Africa), we can hardly conceive of present-day agriculture in Europe, Africa and Asia. Some of these plants which were introduced into Europe subsequently to Columbus' discovery of America, especially the potato, have contributed not a little to increasing agricultural productivity and to achieving stability and the production of a surplus. It was these improved conditions that made possible the great increases in population in modern times and enabled large sections of the population to be released from agriculture, i.e., from direct food-producing activities. Thus the cultural attainments of prehistoric American Indians constituted an important basic condition for the Industrial Revolution.

The earliest evidence of agriculture and livestock raising precedes the first emergence of pottery. Yet in a period when there was as yet no demonstrable existence of plant cultivation in Japan, namely, in the seventh and probably already in the eighth millennium B.C., ceramic products were being made there, and probably also made their appearance on the mainland of southern Asia at about the same time or very shortly thereafter. Towards the end of the seventh millennium the introduction of the potter's craft marked the beginning of a new period within the agricultural and stock-raising cultures, namely, the New Stone Age in a narrower sense. It occurs also in America since the third millennium B.C. in the Pacific-oriented regions of Ecuador and Colombia and in Panama, where no evidence of agriculture is found even at this period. At first sight one might be inclined to attach little importance to pottery and to rate it as being a mere external aspect of a culture. However, for one thing, as a technological and inventive achievement it must not be underestimated, since its production involves for the first time in human history a true and artificially induced chemical change (by the action of heat) of inorganic material. Furthermore, it is quite an important means of making life easier and more agreeable: with pottery, food can be cooked properly, thus enabling many types of food to be utilised differently and more effectively. Indeed, this may even have been a prerequisite, or at least a contributing factor, to the utilisation of certain plants and their cultivation on a substantial scale. Such an extension of the basic food supply as a result, not of increased production, but of better utilisation of available resources, permitted an increase in the population. It is therefore understandable that in not a few regions the wider expansion and development of village communities based on farming and agriculture were bound up with early pottery.

On the other hand, the use of copper remained initially unimportant, although in some regions it occurred even before the introduction of pottery and was, in the sixth millennium B.C., variously used for making beads and small piercing tools. The smelting and casting of copper, which again constitutes an important technological advance, enabling the advantageous properties of this material to be fully utilised, have been established with certainty not before the fifth millennium.

Roughly concurrent with the introduction of pottery is the emergence of pig breeding in the Near East. It seems a likely assumption that these phenomena both spread from southern Asia, where pig breeding had become an important element of agricultural farming. It is true that the pig is easy to domesticate and that wild pigs were probably available in abundance for the purpose. Yet it is necessary to be cautious with such assumptions. The ancestral form of present-day bovine cattle, the aurochs, also abounded in large areas of the prehistoric world; but this big and dangerous animal cannot have been at all easy to domesticate. Taming it must have made no small demands upon those early people's patience and courage, and it must have been aimed at breeding a smaller variety. So the initial object was not merely to bring a species of animal under control but also to use it for specific breeding purposes. This calls for a substantial amount of experience, which would most likely have been gained with small horned cattle (goats, etc.). Hence the region where the first bovine cattle were tamed can be assumed to be the same region where, according to available evidence, small ruminants had probably already been domesticated before 6000 B.C. The domestication of bovine cattle before that time has not yet been established with certainty; recent claims suggesting greater antiquity still await zoological substantiation.

Prehistoric houses were rectangular or round structures built of daub or bricks, sometimes on stone foundations. Mud floors and mud-plastered walls, occasionally with traces of painting, are variously encountered. Clearly the settlements were, generally speaking, not very large, consisting sometimes of loosely grouped buildings, but often composed of houses joined to one another in the manner of cells, thus forming elaborate complexes in which some parts projected above the level of the others (Fig. 4-11).

The type of settlement was generally the village community, but in some cases it attained a size and concentration suggestive of a city (Çatal Hüyük in

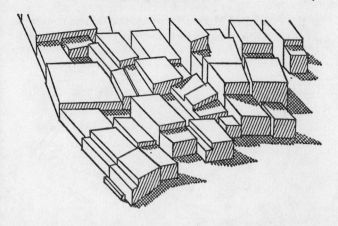

FIG. 4-11: *Çatal Hüyük (Turkey): schematic reconstruction of the settlement, about 6000 B.C. (based on J. Mellaart).*

Turkey is an example), although the internal structural characteristics that would fully justify so calling it were still lacking. These characteristics instead manifest themselves in somewhat later and smaller concentrations, such as a fortress, or citadel, of about 150 m (500 ft.) diameter, dating from the beginning of the fifth millennium, at Hacilar (southwestern Anatolia), which was built on a site prepared by levelling the older settlements that had occupied it. Starting "from scratch," the inhabitants built a wall of imposing thickness—about 4 m (13 ft.)—with small salient features and angular changes of direction. Behind it lie—huddled close together and built against the wall—rectangular chambers, likewise with very thick walls. From details of the finds at this site it appears likely that here already similar conditions existed as

at the citadel of Mersin (also in Asia Minor) around
4000 B.C. (Fig. 4-12). Here, too, the earlier settlement

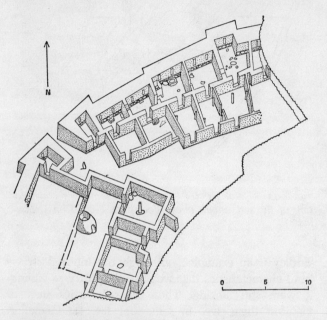

FIG. 4-12: *Citadel of Mersin (Turkey), about* 4000 B.C.,
partial reconstruction (based on G. Garstang).

was completely levelled and a wall of mud bricks on
a stone foundation was constructed, with a gateway
flanked by rectangular towers. The citadel wall also
formed the outer wall of casemate-like pairs of chambers conforming to a standard pattern: directly up
against the wall is a living room with a fireplace, a
fixed built-in millstone and a fair-sized storage re-
ceptacle, together with utensils and vessels of various
kinds and sizes. In the yard behind these rooms lie
heaps of roundish lumps of burned clay to serve as
missiles for slings. There is a larger building contain-

ing a superior type of pottery, suggesting that it was the residence of people in authority or belonging to a higher social stratum.

One interpretation of these archaeological finds, which preserves the concept of a fortified village, assumes that the inhabitants lived in family units in the casemates and served as a kind of city militia in readiness to defend it. A more far-reaching interpretation regards the system as a real fort whose garrison was a kind of standing army of professional fighting men who were relieved of food-producing duties and were therefore fed by other members of the community. The entire nature of these defensive works and their high degree of planning and standardisation suggest stringent organisation, associated with an internal structure which organised towards differentiation of functions and division of labour and which, having regard to the impression of order and discipline, may have belonged to a more authoritarian form of society than existed at, for example, Jericho or Çatal Hüyük.

In general, the village and the village community probably played the most important part, though we cannot say how they were organised in detail. Since indications of social stratification are generally lacking, it seems likely that the members of such communities lived together in co-operative/democratic forms of society. Principles of social order based on the concepts of patriarchy and matriarchy have been shown to exist in historically known and ethnologically investigated agriculture-based cultures. But the archaeological clues are seldom so clear as at Çatal Hüyük, where details of burial practices at least suggest the existence of matriliny (descent and succession through the maternal line) and uxorilocal marriage (the husband lives at the wife's place of residence), presumably on the basis of women's property rights with regard to home and land.

It is also difficult to make definite pronouncements about underlying religious attitudes. Just as in the social sphere, there is likely to have been a multiplicity of forms, so that no general statements are possible. Broadly speaking, however, there can be said to emerge a mainly "female-oriented" religious outlook, which is especially pronounced in simple agriculture-based cultures, with their inescapable interrelation of death and slaying, breeding and procreation, crops and fertility. The male element is, if anything, more particularly linked to the livestock-breeding aspects of religion, and this in turn brings in the ritual use or veneration of animals side by side with, or in lieu of, human sacrifices and the ritual significance of skulls (in connection with ancestor worship and head-hunting) in religious practices. The fertility of the

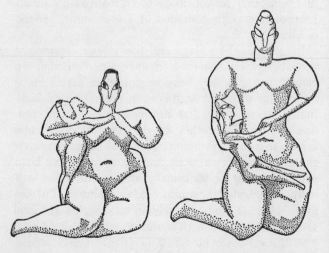

FIG. 4-13: *Hacilar (Turkey): female figurines of clay (actual size 4 in. and 3¼ in.) (redrawn from J. Mellaart).*

soil is linked to female fertility; mother goddesses acquire increased importance, though often in combination with a male principle which displays characteristics of a god of the heavens or represents the heavens. The numerous female statuettes of early occurrence (though seldom with attributes or suggestions of fertility: Fig. 4-13), the lesser frequency of male statuettes, and other indications of this kind can surely be regarded as reflecting such conceptions and religious practices.

Art was evidently to a great extent subservient to religion and concentrated mainly on sculptural and ornamental work. Where wall decorations have been preserved, however—as at Çatal Hüyük—we also encounter polychrome paintings of surprising vitality (Fig. 4-14).

THE THRESHOLD OF CIVILISATION

The new economy and way of life did not, of course, remain confined to the Near East, but spread to other parts of the world. However, this process ranks second to another major development, more particularly in the Near East, namely, the colonisation of the great river valleys. The earlier agriculture-based cultures of this region had been confined to the stepped plateaux and peripheral highlands with adequate rainfall to sustain crop cultivation; sometimes, too, agriculture developed around abundant springs in drier regions (see Fig. 4-15). The early settlers in the valleys of the Euphrates and Tigris had to overcome great difficulties: to make the alluvial deposits of fertile mud useful to agriculture, it was necessary for man to achieve, by his own labour, a "separation of the land from the water" in the true sense of the phrase and to provide artificial irrigation in these re-

FIG. 4-14: *Çatal Hüyük (Turkey): wall painting in brown, red and white (redrawn from J. Mellaart).*

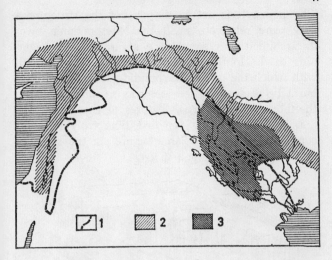

FIG. 4-15: *Early agriculture and rainfall in the Near East:*
1=southern boundary of region with more
than 16 in. rainfall
2=human settlements in this region in sev-
enth and sixth millennia B.C.
3=settlements extended into this region in
fifth millennium B.C.

gions of low rainfall. Thus the origins of human settlement in the alluvial region of southeast Mesopotamia around 5000 B.C. were of a very modest kind. It
should be borne in mind that there was a severe
shortage of important raw materials in this region—
especially stone, but also timber. However, this de-
ficiency was largely compensated by the use of brick,
more particularly unburnt sun-dried brick.

In the circumstances it is surprising how much en-
ergy was devoted to religious architecture. In a typical form of construction a raised central area was
surrounded by a complex of annexes and ancillary
structures whose layout conformed to a definite over-

all scheme. It is not to the size of the structures—
they were relatively small—that Mesopotamia owes
its architectural pre-eminence at around the beginning of the fourth millennium B.C., but to the skill
with which the distinctive building material, the unburnt brick, was utilised and was so integrated into
the internal and external features of these buildings
that we can here for the first time truly call this
constructional activity "architecture" in the sense of
an art of building (Fig. 4-16).

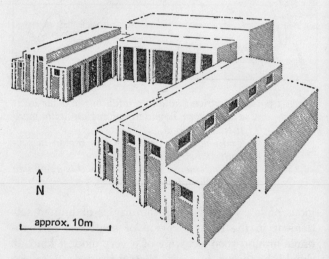

↑
N

approx. 10m

FIG. 4-16: *Temple precinct of Tepe Gawra (Iraq), about
4000 B.C., tentative reconstruction.*

In the fourth millennium the traditions of architecture and craftsmanship were temporarily affected by
major changes: a certain break manifested itself, but
continuity was soon restored. By then the cultural
pattern had meanwhile been enriched with the potter's wheel, the wheel and cart, and the plough. Perhaps the most striking sign of the vigorous new up-

surge is that now limestone was being extensively used for temple construction, the stone being brought from quarries located at distances of about 40–60 km (25–40 miles). Such achievements lead us to infer the existence of well-organised communities living in fair-sized settlements, often large enough to merit being called cities, although only from a small number of sites do we have knowledge of the extent or the internal features of the residential districts.

The compensating for the lack of natural raw materials in the low-lying regions by bringing in materials from distant sources of supply (which obviously required considerable transport achievements), the importation of other desired materials, the improved techniques in the working of metals and in other crafts, the progress in architecture and the lesser arts, in seal cutting and carving—all these activities are hardly conceivable without an advanced division of labour, planning and direction of major enterprises. The relationships were evidently so complex that statistical aids were needed to master them. It is indeed this function that largely governs the character of archaic writings around the transition from the third to the fourth millennium B.C. The progressive release of sections of the population from basic food-producing activities presupposes the production of a surplus of food—i.e., more than required for their own needs —by those engaged in agriculture and farming. This was attainable by having recourse to intensified irrigation. Although the cities each had their own separate irrigation systems and no very extensive networks of canals, the work of enclosing areas of land with dams, opening, closing and maintenance of the watercourses, etc. nevertheless required earth-moving operations on a scale which could hardly be conceivable without well-planned and -directed use of manpower.

Control of the diversified activities connected with these water engineering schemes must in any case have been entrusted to particular individuals. Striking a balance between the available supplies of water and the needs of the crops called for calculation and surveying.

With the accumulation of knowledge and experience came increased harvests, so that larger numbers of people could be fed and larger sections of the population could be released from basic food production, while conversely an increase in the available labour force made it possible to intensify irrigation and step up production. Increase in population and the possibility of closer concentration, instead of migration in search of new sources of food, are both a consequence and a prerequisite of the new economic pattern and organisation. Yet it remains doubtful whether the structural differentiation of the cities and the cultural evolution can be explained solely in terms of such interaction and increase of population and agricultural productivity: side by side with the generally continuous features of this evolution there are some gaps and breaks in the pattern; these may conceal invasions or influxes of other peoples or races who may have imposed themselves as an aristocracy or ruling class and were thus able to exert firm and authoritative control.

In the Nile valley comparable development began at a somewhat later period. Here the first colonisation of the valley, in the fifth millennium, did not—despite the commonly held opinion—take place in a period when the climate was becoming progressively drier, nor was the country in its natural state a region of endless papyrus swamps. The raised banks on each side of the river protected the adjacent land from inundation except at certain high water levels. Systematic cultivation of the land in this region was less difficult than it had been in the Near East, for the construction of regulating embankments in which gaps could be formed to admit water carrying fertile Nile mud onto the fields at times of flood, and the retention of this water by closing those gaps when the water level in the river receded, could surely not have been too difficult. In the fourth millennium B.C. the number of settlements increased. Burial grounds, sometimes of considerable size, indicate a general increase in the population and in the size of the communities. There emerges an element of luxury in the arts and crafts and in toilet requisites. In addition to a wider use of copper there now occur articles made of lapis lazuli, turquoise and glazed earthenware (faience), and by about 3000 B.C. silver and gold appear on the scene. Although all this does not suggest an abrupt drastic change, some details nevertheless point to influences from Mesopotamia. In Egypt, too, conditions were evidently becoming so complex that by the beginning of the third millennium it was no longer possible to manage without mastery of the art of writing.

The details of what actually happened are still very obscure. It is certain, however, that in the river valleys of the Near East and Egypt the threshold to early historic civilisation was crossed towards the end of the fourth and in the early part of the third millennium B.C. The indications pointing to highly differentiated social patterns, organisation based on division of labour, and the concentration of people and power in urban communities become increasingly numerous. A retrospective comparison with other important periods of change shows that the beginning of the late Palaeolithic was the period of specialising adaptation and, above all, brought the breakthrough to artistic expression. The transition to the Neolithic is characterised by the introduction of methods for the production—or rather reproduction—of food instead of having to rely on mere appropriation. On the other hand, the special feature characteristic of the step to civilisation must be seen to consist rather in new forms of social organisation, more particularly the systematic utilisation of human labour in a large way. In the rich expansion of culture, on the one hand, and the advanced social differentiation, on the other, which enabled a minority to skim off an excessive proportion of the goods at the expense of a wide section of the community, lie the glory and the misery of the early civilisations.

OTTO KOENIG

Behaviour Study and Civilisation

New sciences arise in the wake of new knowledge or
in response to problems which cannot be tackled by
any other approach. They are not the products of a
theoretical-philosophical pattern of thought, but are
based on accumulated data requiring scrutiny and
analysis. Hence every emergence of a new science
constitutes a further move in the direction away from
the general and towards the special. Originally it is
part of a matrix, as it were, from which it becomes
detached into something independent by virtue of the
isolation of special material which crystallises and
grows. Thus it acquires properties essentially like
those of an individual or, rather, of a species—which,
after all, is nothing more than a statistical concept of
the totality of individuals recognised to be of the same
kind on the basis of particular criteria.

A science is independent, it has a characteristic
family tree, it can grow and multiply, i.e., can produce
related branches of science, and it can enter into combinations of any conceivable intensity with other systems—up to the point of total absorption. It is subject
to aging processes and is not immortal. Its individual
death as a name or a function does not, however,
mean the extinction of the results it has achieved, for

these are, insofar as they are useful, utilised and traditionally incorporated in the new systems that succeed it.

This entirely biological analogy does, it is true, presuppose establishing a certain analogy between genetic inheritance and the transmission of ideas by tradition. How very much this is possible, and indeed necessary, for a true understanding of human behaviour patterns will be discussed later on. For the present suffice it to point out that an over-all "biology" of the sciences—which has yet to be established—will necessarily have to make use of the phylogenetic analogy, i.e., the concept of the family tree representing the evolutionary descent of a species, in order to arrive at a realistic interpretation. The emergence of a science is just as much an ecologically functional process as the emergence of a new species of animal. In consequence of new environmental conditions, and therefore of changes in the selection pressure, an existing form begins to undergo changes in the parts concerned, until it has adapted itself to the altered situation or is able to exhaust all the possibilities of the new conditions. A new science, a new line of research, should therefore not be regarded as a rival to existing sciences but, instead, as an indication of previously inadequate utilisation of the available possibilities.

The world to which we human beings belong and which we try to understand by our study and research is not in fact subdivided in the manner that our sciences would seem to suggest. The relationship between reality and the behaviour patterns of the various branches of science corresponds approximately to that between a vast unknown territory and the trails blazed by the various explorers who attempt to traverse and chart it. Each contributes precisely that knowledge which it is able to reap by its methods. So anyone who, equipped with different "collecting apparatus," travels a path which has already been travelled before may well succeed in bringing in important additional information that his predecessor missed. A territory to be explored may offer a variety of important data at every point and must not be split up into jealously demarcated areas each reserved for one particular form of research activity. Each tiny shred of information can be of interest to all sciences, for the knowledge possessed by each can promote, correct and supplement that possessed by one or more of the others. It is rather like that tropical tree visited by two species of fruit-eating pigeon. Both eat the fruit of the tree. One species, which has a very soft and delicate stomach wall, can digest only the pulp and excretes the pips intact, whereas the other species has powerful stomach muscles and digests only the pips. Subdivision and demarcation of sciences must never proceed from the object of investigation but solely from the mode of approach and methodology applied. On this is based a part of that much-emphasised freedom of investigation, which applies not merely with regard to other spheres of activity but which must also, and more particularly, exist within the whole field of science. The freedom of research and the natural progressive development of the sciences must not be cramped or restricted by claims of exclusive rights to particular subjects. Espalier trees are out of place in the open country, for it belongs to the nature of a healthy tree that its branches and twigs interlace, overshadow and also support one another.

ETHOLOGY AS A LINKING SCIENCE

Comparative behaviour study (ethology) is often still taken to be equivalent to "animal psychology." This attitude is promoted by the fact that one of the most important German scientific journals in this domain is named *Zeitschrift für Tierpsychologie* (*Journal of Animal Psychology*). But the largest and best-known research centre concerned with this science in Germany is called "Max Planck Institute for Behavior Physiology." Yet, despite the evidently divergent nomenclature, there is really not the slightest difference in content.

For years attempts have been made to establish a true animal psychology. In this context one need only be reminded of the anthropomorphic descriptions in Brehm's famous book on animals, *Tierleben* (*Animal Life*) or the utterly unbiological "psychologisation" of animals by Romanes, a student of Darwin's theories. The experiments which Osten and Krall performed with "calculating" horses and which, though they now appear absurd, used to be taken seriously belong to this category, as does also Pavlov's reflexology and the behaviourism of Small and Watson. On reading the publications on animal psychology which were issued in the interwar years, we can only marvel at the multiplicity of experiments, opinions and fallacies— for example, when Fischel expounds the view that the cell as the physiological-morphological building element has for its psychological counterpart an "effervescing fog" as the element of the soul. Psychologists, zoologists and medical scientists are all striving to construct an animal psychology. The zoologists are doing this in order to extend their knowledge of animals, the psychologists and medical scientists are doing it primarily with the object of improving our understanding of man himself, hoping to find similar possibilities for analogising as are available to anatomists, morphologists and physiologists in experiments with animals.

The most promising step in this direction was actually taken by the psychologist Wolfgang Köhler with his famous experiments with chimpanzees at Teneriffe, which were interrupted by the First World War but were subsequently resumed and further elaborated in the U.S.A. by Yerkes and also in Russia. In this field human psychology made a not inconsiderable contribution to the later behavioural research. The most important preliminary work is, however, due to the two zoologists Oskar Heinroth and Karl von Frisch. The latter discovered the systems whereby bees communicate with one another; Heinroth (1910), thanks to his large-scale comparative breeding experiments with nearly all Central European species of birds, found that relationships and affinities between species can often far better be ascertained on the basis of movements and behaviour patterns than from a comparison of various organs. Thus the efforts to arrive at a correct system of zoological classification, which had hitherto been oriented towards purely morphological and anatomical criteria, now also began to consider the significance of movement sequences and thus led on to the final emergence of an objective animal psychology. The decisive steps were then taken by Konrad Lorenz with his systematic experiments for discovering the laws and thus also the physiological backgrounds of the behaviour phenomena. He was the first investigator who began to formulate theoretically and to classify the practical knowledge yielded by experimental zoology and thus became the actual founder of comparative behaviour study.

The new science dispensed with the name "animal psychology," although it concerned itself with the whole set of problems peculiar to the latter. The well-known work of Otto Koehler on "thinking without words" in animals, as well as his maze experiments

conducted on biologically meaningful principles, established animal psychology as a subdivision of behaviour study. Erich von Holst, for his part, achieved
the direct link-up with psychology. Thus, comparative
behaviour study does in fact occupy a true linking
position and demands from its researchers certain
versatility, for without a proper understanding of
zoological systematics, psychology, physiology and
sociology it is not possible to do serious work in this
field. Very soon, too, close contacts were established
with ecology (the study of the relations of animal
and plant communities to their surroundings), for
without a knowledge of how they fit functionally into
their ecological context it is not possible to arrive at
an understanding of behaviour patterns.

Lorenz originally conceived the word "comparative"
in the phylogenetic sense, but it soon became apparent that phylogeny is a wide-ranging concept
which calls for versatility and therefore provokes
multiple comparisons. Thus the new comparative
behaviour study very rapidly gained a footing in a
great many traditional branches of science, and with
the increasing numbers of students of the new science
corresponding larger numbers of problems could be
tackled. It would be a disastrous mistake to assume
that behaviour study is nothing more than a part of
conventional zoology. It has emerged from zoology,
and it is essential for the researcher to be familiar with
at least some parts of zoology, but these do not in any
sense determine its limits.

Comparative behaviour study arose from problems
associated with zoological systematics, i.e., with matters of phylogenetic descent, and set itself the task of
co-ordinating the classifying of these phenomena
phylogenetically, approximately in the manner of comparative anatomy. Just as anatomy, starting with man,

advances into the animal kingdom, so must behaviour study, coming from the opposite direction, for its part include man in its considerations. But whereas comparative anatomy can concentrate on the so-called "purely biological facts," a science of behaviour must, as soon as it concerns itself with man, necessarily also consider his achievements, i.e., the results of his behaviour. Suppose an ornithologist studies the nest-building motions of a bird, but excludes the building materials as well as the completed nest from his investigations: the result of his efforts must inevitably remain very incomplete. To ignore or indeed to reject the consideration of the whole in the domain of human behaviour patterns would be an analogous and equally unscientific approach. No behaviour researcher would ever think of stopping short at some arbitrary point in the research process merely because to continue would mean advancing into the specifically human domain. In the last resort he, the researcher, is himself a human being and as such the central starting point of his research.

Anyone who observes an animal in action will suddenly, at some point in his observations, find that he cannot help making a comparison with himself. He may do this as a scientist adopting an exact and objectively materialistic approach or he may be succumbing to the emotions of the anthropomorphising animal lover—in any case the flash of supposed "understanding" suddenly comes. This possibility of some form of social contact, however remote, and the recognition of a blurred reflection is indeed not only the great source of the rich multitude of animal fables, the numerous animal stories, the fairy-tale transformations of people into animals and vice versa, as well as other and even older beliefs going right back to the very roots of shamanism, but is also the clearly discernible reason why behaviour study attracts the interest of the public at large. This does not imply a value judgment nor does it mean to suggest that other sciences are of any less interest. It should nevertheless be noted that the comparison with one's own personal attitudes inevitably occurs in nearly every person who is given a description of, for example, the mating behaviour, the search for food, the intimidating postures and the fighting of animals. It is here, too, that we must seek the psychological reason for the comparisons between man and animal which crop up again and again in many different quarters. The procedure adopted by comparative behaviour study in dealing with this set of problems can be described as centripetal, i.e., working inwards towards the centre. Armed with the knowledge of a large number of action systems of many different species of animal, and knowing too the fundamental laws of behaviour and the ecological and sociological relationships, it approaches the objective which it has set itself from the very outset and which is therefore to be regarded as its primary aim: to investigate human behaviour patterns. Lorenz has stated this very clearly (1963): "The road to the knowledge of man goes via an understanding of the animal, just as the evolutionary development of man has undoubtedly proceeded via the animal." And further: "The ultimate goal of our research is not 'animal psychology' but a more profound understanding of man."

ETHOLOGY AND FOLKLORE

Certain social sciences pursue similar aims, more particularly folklore study and ethnology (the study of races, their relations to one another and their characteristics), as these are concerned with human activities as their central feature. One of the most significant and fundamental differences of behaviour study, however, is in the procedure adopted. The methodology of folklore study and ethnology is primarily of a centrifugal character, i.e., it could be described as working from the centre outwards. In these studies, man is not the central objective but the central starting point. Thus the whole operation must lack scientific objectivity and become in the psychological sense a humanly subjective method. Ultimately, the investigator starts from himself, his own zoologically systematic set of forms. This facilitates the collection of information, but it makes it more difficult to establish objective and generally valid classification systems which embody laws of life. In consequence there has emerged a multitude of extremely divergent theories and working hypotheses whose inner logic and intellectual quality are often very tempting but which yield no points of contact with biological reality. The well-known folklorist Peukert once described astrology as one of the most ingeniously and subtly contrived mental systems, absolutely logical within itself and yet entirely unconnected with reality. The social sciences find themselves in a similar situation in cases where they ignore the data that the natural sciences provide. This must not be taken to deny that the disciplines in question have acquired much very valuable knowledge and have revealed important interrelations. It should merely be pointed out that in this domain all sorts of personal attitudes, world views, religious and political dogmas enjoy a large measure of freedom to flourish uninhibitedly, in which a scientific system of scrutiny would be felt to constitute an objectionable constraint. In the sphere of the social sciences it occurs all too easily that discussion is substituted for experiment.

A further difficulty arises from the psychological phenomenon of "shortcutting." If we look down upon the system of roads around a village from high overhead in an aircraft, we see a few major roads leading to it; but if we come closer and closer, we see the roads splitting up and fanning out more and more into branches, each leading to an individual destination. Each individual road user wants to reach his particular destination as quickly as possible by the shortest possible route. Any detour, any deviation from the shortcut is felt to be disagreeable and is therefore avoided.

The researcher is subjected to very similar influences. He finds it subjectively always more difficult to move away from his objective than to move towards it. Anyone who engages in research tends to demarcate his territory in such a manner that he can remain as close as possible to his central objective. The method common to all sciences, namely, to explain complex phenomena in terms of simpler preceding stages, signifies in the realm of ethnology and folklore study that the researcher must delve into the beginnings of human culture. These he finds to be situated far away in space and time, far from his central focus of interest: *Homo sapiens recens*. In his researches he will be disposed to stop at that point, and there draw the boundary of his territory, where from his viewing position he sees the simplest phenomena of his subject to be situated. To go beyond this self-imposed boundary does not appeal to him, as he is liable to lose the thread of his research aims, and every step would lead to the further breakup of the original configuration into separate factors.

The ethologist (behaviour researcher) who adopts a truly scientific approach will proceed quite differently. For him there are no boundaries anywhere along his road of research, but only transitions and connections. We cannot expect him suddenly to stop short on coming to a species of creature which has, since the days of Linnaeus, officially been included in the system of zoological classification and belongs to the order of the Primates—in short: man. For the ethologist it is here, in particular, that the threads of evidence which he has long been following twist themselves into a new cord which evidently and directly leads him to his objective. The practitioner of the above-mentioned social sciences, proceeding centrifugally, stops and turns back under the influence of the shortcutting urge, whereas this same urge causes the ethologist, who is advancing centripetally, to be impelled forward in the direction he is following. In so doing he will be crossing boundaries and making incursions into territory where he has no right to be, or at any rate so it may appear in the eyes of many ethologists and folklorists—who, incidentally, will be evincing a perfectly normal biological reaction in thus resenting an infringement of their territorial rights. Too often the anthropologically oriented investigators fail to understand that particularly the ethologist, having discovered the innate sense of territorial rights and knowing the pertinent ranges of behaviour, really cannot draw the line at the point in question.

Whereas in most countries the study of folklore and ethnology are not clearly separated from each other, but are instead lumped together under the heading of anthropology or ethnology (in a wider sense), in German linguistic usage a sharp distinction is made between these two fields. This separation is merely a reflection of the old traditional way of thinking: "we and the others," which also manifests itself in the ancient Greeks' use of the terms "Hellenes" and "barbarians." One could quite properly distinguish between "national folklore" and "foreign folklore," which would be all the more justified because the modern folklorist, swamped by the avalanche of fresh data, can no longer hope to be an expert on all or even on many of the world's races and peoples; at best he may specialise in one particular continent and thus be classed as an Americanist, an Africanist, etc. The special designation of "folklorist" for someone who should really be called a "Europeanist" is explicable only as a traditional phenomenon or as the manifestation of a tendency to form groups intent upon defending their territory.

These considerations on classification and terminology are presented merely to show how advancing specialisation, and the increasing differentiation of the sciences that goes with it, will break up older entities but will in so doing create new and previously inconceivable possibilities for link-ups. The specialist can justly be called narrow-minded only if he neglects to utilise a newly branched-out or advanced position for communication and discussion with specialists in adjacent scientific fields. The pseudopodium of an amoeba can, from the viewpoint of its owner, be regarded as an "exploratory advance for a special purpose"; from the viewpoint of the creature's environment, however, it is a "feeler put out to seek contact with the world at large." A pseudopodium would be meaningless if it were enclosed within a hard shell which prevented it having contact and interchange with its surroundings. Yet this is precisely what many a specialist does, failing to recognise that he of all people is present at the cradle of a new science for whose growth and vigour it is most essential to have free communication with the world at large. The split-up of the old science complexes, which had become too large and unwieldy, is quite spectacular.

Zoology, too, is now essentially no more than the traditional name for what once used to be a fairly circumscribed field but has now become a vast comprehensive discipline with many subdivisions.

One of the parts that will sooner or later detach itself from zoology is comparative behaviour study, which, already by virtue of the attitude of its founders, is an open-minded and outward-looking science. It could almost be compared to a kind of railway turntable which obtains its material from a wide range of tracks and passes the results onto other tracks leading off in other directions, for every science that is concerned with living creatures of any kind has to deal with behavioural problems. This applies of course also to folklore study and ethnology. To push forward a pseudopodium in this direction is an unavoidable duty of behavioural research. The new direction is called cultural ethology and has arisen solely from the consideration that it is useful and absolutely necessary also to study man's cultural achievements and activities from the viewpoint of behavior study and use its methods to investigate them. So by cultural ethology we simply understand that section of behaviour study (ethology) which is concerned with the social achievements and material production of human beings (culture).

Now these scientific contacts with the social sciences constitute nothing special, for even ethnology itself has in nearly all its theories and doctrines time and again striven to find underlying scientific principles. Let us pass over in silence the fact that zoology, like ethnology, has emerged from the mediaeval collections of curiosities in which all sorts of animal and human specimens from remote parts of the world were exhibited all together, without any specialised classification, in a haphazard manner, such as can still be found in many of the smaller museums today. It was Adolf Bastian, subsequently the director of the Berlin Museum of Ethnology, who in 1859 was the first to introduce a thoroughly "biological" elementary concept into ethnology, namely, that there exists uniform innate basic psychological equipment which is common to all peoples and which made possible a simple basic culture from which the multiplicity of subsequent cultures have developed as a result of contact with various environments. A direct though in effect absolutely incorrect link-up with biology was sought by the evolutionists, who wanted to detect straight lines of development "from the lower to the higher"—for example, from a primitive wild state to civilisation, or from primitive sexual promiscuity to monogamous marriage. It was more particularly the obsolete evolutionist way of thinking, which nowadays has really survived only in traditionally conservative Marxism, that was a contributory factor in causing ethnologists to turn away from the natural sciences. They failed to recognise that biology itself furnishes the most telling evidence against this way of thinking.

Frobenius, too, based his cultural theory on a biological principle by equating the various cultures to independent individuals and introducing concepts such as "cultural morphology, anatomy and physiology." The error lies in the fact that a culture never possesses the self-contained wholeness and unity of an individual in the true sense. As a result of this, the absolutely anti-biological cultural theories of the Vienna school, as developed more particularly by W. Schmidt and W. Koppers, were able to emerge from Frobenius' doctrine. But these also constituted a very dogmatically coloured reaction to the evident errors of the evolutionist school and, like it, had to go into limbo.

A very gratifying approach to biology, and more particularly to behaviour study, was latterly initiated by W. E. Mühlmann with his cultural anthropology and its entirely scientifically empirical procedure. But the functionalist school also bases itself on biological conceptions in that it recognises human life, just like the life of other creatures, to be dependent on natural laws. W. Hirschberg (1965), too, at least with regard to the methodical approach in his ethnohistorical direction, comes close to adopting scientific methods of research in emphasising the so important sequence of sources. Finally, it must be remembered that what to the historian of human affairs is a century or a millennium is to the phylogeneticist merely a second or a minute in his far vaster time scale. With the definition which he gives for "culture" Hirschberg has, with gratifying clarity, though perhaps unwittingly, lent support to the cultural ethology of the Institute for Comparative Behavioural Research of the Austrian Academy of Sciences. He writes: "Culture, the sum total of the intellectual, religious and artistic values produced by a people, as well as its knowledge and skills, behaviour patterns, customs and value judgments, institutions and organisations which, in their structural interassociation, represent the life content of a people in a certain period of time."

As this definition comprises, in principle anyway, everything that a human can possibly accomplish, it must of course also include the innate elements that control and direct his actions. This means, however, that cultural problems cannot be explained without the co-operation of behaviour study. It is therefore in the interests of ethnology that behaviour study examines cultural phenomena, and therefore also cultural products, from its point of view and analyses them by its methods. And indeed it is here that cultural ethology considers its primary tasks to lie.

The distinction between folklore study and ethnology, as reflected more particularly by the terms *Volkskunde* and *Völkerkunde* in the German-speaking countries, is a purely theoretical one, and of no practical significance, from the viewpoint of behavioural research. Where and on what he works is something which, to the ethologist, must depend solely upon the statement of the problem to be tackled. Even Charles Darwin already made an attempt to solve the problem of mimicry in animals by means of a wide-ranging inquiry throughout the British Empire of those days. I. Eibl-Eibesfeldt (1970), who took up these ideas and was more particularly interested in the raising of the eyebrows as an innate gesture of friendliness and greeting, which he studied in a representative cross section of various peoples and races, corrected his material in the course of a world tour. Then again, W. Wickler (1972) investigated the signal function of the penis in baboons and hyenas in the wild state, and in general the significance of penis presentation in primates when sitting on guard. To these observations he linked his very important comparative investigations into representations of the penis in ancient Greek herms (or *hermae:* statues usually surmounted by the head of the god Hermes and provided with a phallus), which were in fact mostly guardian figures. These results found support in Eibl-Eibesfeldt's data collected on expeditions in Indonesia and New Guinea.

Here we clearly see the application of the method employed by the ethologist, who allows himself to be guided only by the subject and its various relations and affinities, but not by geographical regions.

When Konrad Lorenz began his first behaviour

studies on animals, he studied species occurring in his native country: the Danube region of Lower Austria. From the outset it was found to be of fundamental importance to get to know a species in all its activities, since these all fit into a particular biotope. At the start of a project the ethologist does not go about the investigation of a species in the manner of a task-setting interrogator, but as a neutral observer. He must therefore primarily become acquainted with the species in its natural habitat, he must then rear young animals himself, and continue working with tame animals which have become accustomed to him. The interaction between observations under natural conditions and in captivity, repeated rearing, living in the closest possible contact with the animals being studied—these are the methods whereby real knowledge is gained, on the basis of which it becomes possible to carry out systematic experiments which are biologically appropriate to the species of animal under investigation.

On applying this methodology to cultural research, it stands to reason that the researcher will start his work at the point where he can establish contact with his subject most rapidly and is likely to penetrate most deeply. Clearly it is the researcher's own cultural environment that provides these opportunities. It is no exaggeration to assert that the setting-up of a complete system of action as envisaged by behaviour study, even if it were to concern itself with the people in a particular region, would keep a big team of scientists (representing all the several relevant sciences) busy for a good many years. In view of the vast potential scope of the subject, the cultural ethologist is therefore obliged to make a selection, picking out certain sets of problems which he can then subject to the necessary fine analysis. He will find his best start in surroundings where, above all, he possesses an intimate understanding of the language, is able to share a feeling for the customs and practices he encounters and is constitutionally adapted to the climate and to the way of life determined by the nature of the country. Contact with folklore therefore turns out to be essential to research in cultural ethology: just as the investigator of animal behaviour will prefer not to start with some animal from remote parts which is difficult to procure and to breed, so the researcher who studies the behaviour of people will not allow himself to be tempted by the romantic idea of an expedition into the wilds and will therefore not start his investigations with some as yet unknown primitive tribe.

The situation is different with regard to the second step that may be necessary, namely, that of comparison. Lorenz started at Altenberg with grey geese and wild ducks, but now keeps *Anatidae* (the family of aquatic birds comprising ducks, geese and swans) from all parts of the world in lakeside meadows. Wherever that becomes necessary for purposes of comparative study, the cultural ethologist will without hesitation move about within the whole range of ethnological material. The obstacles that are piling up, more particularly in communication, can perhaps be overcome precisely by the ethologist who, in his dealings with animals, is accustomed to establishing contacts with elusive creatures. At any rate, the patience and willingness to try to share the feelings of his fellow creatures which he has acquired in his animal observations are likely to be helpful.

The difficulty of comparison lies more particularly in recognising what actually is comparable. The larger and more complex the whole sets of features are, the more difficult is their comparison. It is therefore necessary to isolate the smallest possible elements, i.e., to split up the whole into its factors in order then to be able to scrutinise their evolution and change. The essential, elementary methodology of behaviour study is based on a comparison, not of wholes, but of factors. Not the total action systems of different species are compared with one another, but always only the phylogenetically related individual phenomena, with additional reference to analogies. This is in principle equally valid for cultural ethology, the only difference being that for phylogeny we must substitute tradition, which performs a similar function in the cultural domain. How important the analysis and the comparison of factors are will be explained with the aid of an example.

BIOLOGY OF COSTUME AND UNIFORM

We are accustomed to regarding the costume worn by the inhabitants of a particular region as a cultural unit. When we visit a region where strict conformity to local costume prevails and where, from childhood onwards, everyone wears the traditional attire which he feels to be right and proper, this view appears to be justified. But if such a region undergoes an economic change in consequence of being opened up and developed for tourism or industrialisation or is otherwise subjected to considerable sociological pressure from outside groups with different habits of dress, then the local costume will begin gradually to disappear. And this takes place in a definite sequence. First it is given up by the male youngsters, then by the adult men and finally by the old men, who may sometimes retain certain less conspicuous items of traditional costume from force of habit. The women's costume almost invariably holds out

longest. But at the same time the women stop making the traditional costume for the little boys and,
instead, dress them in clothes modelled on the new
style of clothing worn by the adult men or on the
fashion of the invading culture. This situation where
the men's clothing undergoes a complete change-
over, while the women continue to wear their original costume, can persist for a very long time, depending on external circumstances. In any case, the
women's costume generally does not begin to disappear until at least some of the traditional male costume features have disappeared. In some instances
the female costume will continue to exist, in a much
simplified form, for a very long time as the respected
attire of elderly matrons.

From this phenomenon, which is not only manifesting itself in our time but has occurred in connection
with every social and cultural shift in consequence of
the intrusion of a foreign group exercising a powerful influence as an example inviting imitation, we
must infer that female costume is always older than
its male counterpart. This has proved indeed to be so
in all the cases hitherto investigated. The woman's
skirt, as the relic of an earlier wrap-round garment,
is older than trousers, a later development. Apart from
what is found among primitive races, wrap-round
garments have survived only among the inhabitants
of certain relatively remote regions, e.g., in Scotland,
where the kilt is still worn. However, an additional
factor is involved here, which will be discussed later.

A comparison between female and male costumes
worn in the Balkans shows the former to be still of a
mediaeval character, whereas the latter almost invariably reflect the influence of the period of Turkish
occupation. In many regions the women still wear
the very ancient double apron, which appears already

on Greek vase paintings, whereas the men's clothing sometimes even comprises elements as "modern" as the nineteenth century. At Dubrovnik the men's costume is purely Turkish, but the women's is so mediaeval-Italian that in its black variety, more particularly in the form worn by widows, it strongly resembles old-fashioned nun's dress. Austrian national costumes of the types known as *Steieranzug* and *Dirndl*, which have received such wide publicity as folklore features in the tourist industry, do not really belong together either. The *Dirndl* female costume, comprising shirt-blouse, skirt and bodice, is already seen in mediaeval pictures and has been worn continuously from those days to the present time. On the other hand, the men's *Steieranzug* in its several varieties comprises variously combined features of Austrian military uniforms of the eighteenth and nineteenth centuries. The peasants wore traditional costume, but in other sections of the population it did not become popular until Archduke Johann and the Emperor Franz Josef set the example. As a result of the example of royalty, nobility and the urban middle classes, the *Steieranzug* gained ground and eventually even supplanted the older Tyrolese costumes from everyday and Sunday wear, leaving them to survive only in the Sharpshooters' Companies, in which they now serve virtually only as uniforms.

It should be furthermore borne in mind that nowadays women's fashions in clothing are nearly all designed by men and that women really always wear what men like to see them in. In this the man's stronger tendency to adopt new things from outside, to imitate examples and to adapt himself to changed situations is clearly manifested.

This evident readiness to adopt new features under certain conditions is bound up with the innate function of the human male to defend his group externally. In the forming of groups he is more sociable than the woman. Women are excellent at nursing and caring for the needs of a family, devoted and willing to make sacrifices; but within the larger extra-familial or super-familial group they tend to be a liability and hardly ever exercise a suitable binding or uniting effect. Whereas the woman is very good at continuous work, the man is far more adjusted to variety and spontaneous effort. This property, in conjunction with the tendency to form male groups, is clearly indicative of men's functions as hunters and as defenders of the community.

He who would defend must be able to stand up to his adversary, however. If he is the weaker of the two or indeed if he is worsted in the contest, he must try to compensate for this disadvantage as quickly as possible. Undoubtedly the first step in that direction is to adopt the tactics, weapons and equipment of one's victorious adversary. Furthermore, from the fighting man's point of view, it is desirable to appear as strong and as formidable as possible, so as to impress and perhaps overawe. The desire to emulate the more successful opponent, or indeed any other person adopted as the model or ideal, coupled with the endeavour somehow to surpass him, is one of the most commonly encountered male characteristics, which manifests itself very strongly and clearly also in the matter of dress. In this context it should be pointed out that in nearly all species of animal the social partnership of the sexes is similar to that in man: the males wear phylogenetically more recent plumage or fur than the more primitively decked-out females. In behavioural research the term "primitive" must be taken to mean "phylogenetically older," just as in ethnology "primitive" signifies "historically older." Immelmann, who bred Australian zebra finches in captivity, found that the males acquired domestication characteristics sooner than the females did.

International military and army history affords many examples where uniforms and other characteristic features of militarily successful countries were copied, which eventually led to a worldwide mix-up of uniforms. A very characteristic example is afforded by the Hungarian hussars, light cavalry whose deeds and skill made them famous and who were copied by nearly all other countries, even Russia, although that country already had its Cossacks. But the Cossacks, too, found their imitators in Austria, Germany and France.

The most famous Prussian general of hussars, von Zielen, used to wear a very conspicuous red uniform with yellow boots, leopard's skin and so-called eagle's wings on his tall busby. Almost identical uniform was worn by the "Hungarian mounted bodyguard," an offshoot of the Hungarian hussars, until the collapse of the monarchy. While von Zielen modelled himself upon the Hungarian hussars, these in turn had copied the uniforms of a famous Turkish guards regiment, the Delis. These bodyguards of the highest Turkish dignitaries took opium before going into battle, where they spearheaded the attack, fighting with blind courage which earned them their name, which in Turkish means something like "madcaps." Such soldiers must of course, in terms of manly courage, have presented an example that particularly invited emulation. This phenomenon of imitating the stronger and therefore aspiring to his rank and his claim to respect can, incidentally, be logically accommodated within the complex of mimicry behaviour that has been very fully treated by W. Wickler (1968).

This marked male human tendency to annex the

winner's attributes is, however, easily liable to turn into resistance to the conqueror if he becomes a hated tyrant. The vanquished may so despise the costume of the oppressor that they begin deliberately to emphasise and cling to their own national costume. Thus the continued existence of the kilt in the highlands of Scotland can be explained in terms of a protest against domination by the English. Similarly the notable preservation of the German male costumes in South Tyrol, particularly in the function of burggrave (governor of a castle), where the pressure of invading Italian influence was particularly great. One might appropriately speak of "costumes of defiance." In such cases it might seem to the casual observer that the men are more conservative than the women, whose traditional costume usually tends to disappear more rapidly in such regions.

Just as male and female dress belong to historical strata of different age, they each for themselves do not form a single whole in unity of time either. Instead, they are composed of numerous parts derived from many different sources. Fundamentally, every costume and every uniform is a complex entity assembled from many parts with a wide variety of origins and can therefore in principle be analysed analogously to a biologically formed entity. No part emerged senselessly or was arbitrarily invented by man but, instead, arose from a specific need or problem which had to be functionally solved. Only when the function becomes lost does the process of ritualisation commence, in which the originally simple feature of the costume or uniform often becomes complicated out of all recognition. When the buttonholes of military tunics were edged with stitching to strengthen them and were trimmed with cloth in the regimental colours, this soon gave rise to ornamental buttonholes

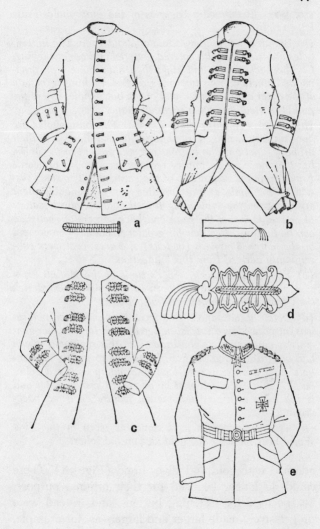

FIG. 5-1: *Evolutionary vagaries of the buttonhole. From left to right:*

(a) *Brandenburg military tunic of about 1700. The button-holes are trimmed with colored material and edge stitching. On the pocket flaps and cuffs they have merely an ornamental function. The two ends of the stitching terminate at the outer end; the inner end of the buttonhole, where the pull is exerted, is given a rounded shape.*

(b) *Prussian infantry tunic (1756). The buttonholes are here already arranged symmetrically and have lost their primary function. The buttons are still present in the holes, but they have for decorative reasons been moved outwards (away from the center line of the garment). The small tassels at the ends of the braiding are an embellishment evolved from the protruding thread ends. A novel feature of this tunic is that the front and back corners of each side can be buttoned together for greater freedom of movement on the march. The flaps (or tails) of a dress coat were subsequently derived from this innovation.*

(c) *Eighteenth-century officer's tunic of the No. 26 Prussian infantry regiment, as worn in the reign of Frederick the Great, with embroidered buttonholes.*

(d) *Detail of buttonhole. In 1900 this embroidered pattern was introduced as a special badge of rank for Prussian generals to commemorate the bravery of this regiment, which had been disbanded in 1806. In its new form this "buttonhole" was worked in gold lace embroidery on a red collar patch. Later it was adopted by all other German states and is still worn as a gold ornamental feature on a red background.*

(e) *Prussian general's field tunic, as worn in the First World War, showing the gold lace on the collar.*

adorned with gold and silver braid (Fig. 5-1). These could no longer be used for their original purpose, i.e., be used for fastening buttons, and instead were progressively made larger and larger—as, for example, in the Austrian Arcières bodyguards' uniform—until they had evolved into large gold areas, the memory of whose nominal buttonhole function was preserved

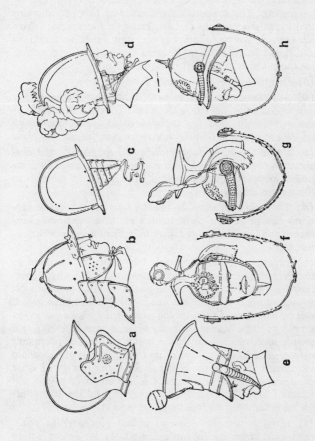

FIG. 5-2: *The evolution of the chin strap—and its eventual transformation into a purely ornamental feature—from helmet parts which originally performed a protective function provides a very good illustration of the subject matter of this article. In the unbroken succession of individual stages in a real and historically recorded evolutionary sequence it demonstrates that laws of biological phylogeny are apparently valid also for certain cultural-historical processes: in*

this case, the gradual loss of functional significance associated with an increase in ornamental character of a particular feature. The irreversible character of this evolutionary trend also emerges. In the last example the original strap has entirely lost its function of securing the helmet, and an additional "secondary" chin strap has had to be provided for the purpose. From left to right:

(a) Helmet of about 1600 with fixed cheek pieces.

(b) Austrian cuirassier's helmet (of the type known as the lobster-tail burgonet) was worn up to about the middle of the eighteenth century, with movable cheek pieces to which are attached leather thongs for tying under the chin.

(c) Helmet worn by foot soldiers and dragoons (mid-seventeenth century) in which the cheek pieces are each composed of four movably jointed iron plates to which the thongs are attached.

(d) This pikeman's helmet (of the type known as the morion) has small iron plates which serve as ornamental attachments for the thongs rather than as real protective features.

(e) Württemberg cavalryman's leather shako, as worn in the Napoleonic period. The ornamental chin strap composed of small scalelike metal plates is now movably attached to the outside of the headdress. When not in use, it can be swung up to rest on the peak of the shako (as in example g). The "scales," usually of brass, are here still of a simple type, reminiscent of the iron plates on the pikeman's helmet, but they are smaller and more numerous to allow movement. At the back of the shako is the vestige of what once was a movable neck guard which could be raised and lowered but which has here become a fixed traditional attachment serving no functional purpose.

(f) Helmet worn by Austrian uhlans (lancers) in 1914, with chin strap which can alternatively be swung up to rest on the peak (as in example g). The main feature is the leather strap with buckle. The actual scales are mere shiny metal embellishments, a fact that is further emphasised by their ornamentally lobed edges.

(h) Austrian gendarme's helmet (1914) with externally mounted ornamental strap formed by two stamped metal parts permanently joined by a rivet instead of a detachable stud. The actual (functional) chin strap is an additional in-

*dependent feature and is attached to the inside of the hel-
met.*

FIG. 5-3: *Evolution of the gorget. From left to right:*
(a, b) Armour of about 1500, front and rear view, show-

ing the gorget forming the transition between helmet and
body armour.

(c) A Brandenburg officer of about 1690 with a large
gorget, from which is still visible the transition between
helmet and body armour.

(d) A Brandenburg infantry officer of about 1710 with the
gorget already smaller and used as an indication of social
rank.

(e) Osceola, a Seminole chief, with a decorative, three-part
gorget that indicates his importance.

FIG. 5-4: *Evolution of the Prussian type of grenadier's
cap.*

(a) Forage cap of the basic baglike type worn by soldiers
around 1700. It consists of four triangular pieces of cloth
sewn together and terminating in a tassel. The edge of the
cap is turned up to make it sit more firmly on the wearer's
head.

(b) Forage cap of about 1750. The seams are trimmed with
tape in colors contrasting with the cap material. The upturned edge is separately sewn and rises to a point in
front, where it bears a lily emblem.

(c) Brandenburg grenadier's cap of about 1700. The front
of the old baglike cap has now been provided with a
pointed vertical metal plate which bears the emblem and
coat of arms and is fastened to the upturned edge.

(d) Brandenburg grenadier guard's cap of about 1700.
The upturned edge here has evolved into a tall, stiff, up-
standing front plate. The bag, however, still survives in its
old form and hangs down at the back.

(e) British grenadier's cap of about 1710. The bag has
been swung upright behind the front plate and attached to
it. The tassel now appears at the topmost point of the
headdress.

(f) Russian grenadier's cap as worn by the Kiev infantry
regiment from about 1700 onwards. This cap clearly shows
its descent from the baglike forage cap, but the upturned
edge and the seams here already show marked decorative
elaboration.

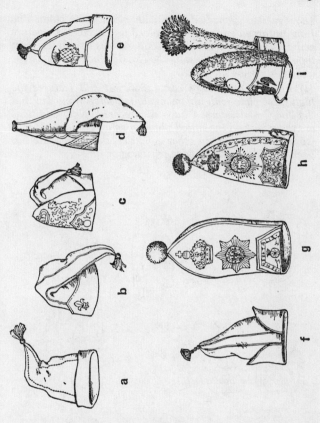

(g) *Cap worn by Prussian soldiers of the Potsdam Red Bodyguards Battalion of Grenadiers No. 6 up to about 1730. The headdress, including the front decoration, is made entirely of cloth, except for the metal badges. The front flap of the upturned edge is still clearly discernible. The tassel of the bag has survived as a woollen pompon on top of the cap.*

(h) Prussian grenadier's cap with metal front plate. The front upturned edge flap is reserved as a decorative feature embossed in the metal. This headdress was developed from type g and was still worn by the No. 6 grenadiers' regiment under Frederick the Great.

(i) Prussian grenadier's cap (1808). It still features the high front plate with ornamentally indicated front flap, but the "bag" and pompon have disappeared. New additions are the peak and the tufted plume. Inspired by the fur caps worn by grenadiers in other countries, the front plate has been provided with an edge trimming of fur.

FIG. 5-5: *The evolution of the bandsman's "wings." From left to right:*

(a, b) *Late mediaeval French costume worn by young men: fur-trimmed jacket with sleeves "slashed" to reveal the sleeves of the undervest. As shown in* (b), *the arms could be passed through the slash apertures.*

(c) *Burgundian duke, fifteenth century. The sleeves of the jacket have now become a purely decorative feature, with the slashes extended to allow the arms to pass through them in the normal way.*

(d) *French nobleman, sixteenth century. The puffed sleeve attachments at the shoulders, as appearing in the earlier garments* (a–c), *have evolved into padded rolls. The sleeves themselves are slit open along their whole length and hang down merely as decorative bands of material.*

(e, f) *French citizens' costumes with vestiges of slashed sleeves retained purely as embellishments. The typical form later adopted for the wings on military uniforms already clearly emerges in* (f). *The pleats may have suggested the vertical ornamental stripes subsequently adopted.*

(g) *Trumpeter of Dutch cavalry, about 1600. As trumpeters had a very important function to perform in transmitting command signals in battle, they wore conspicuous clothing and generally rode grey horses. Their uniforms retained the old style with slashed sleeves as distinctive marks of the trumpeter. The open sleeve fluttered behind the trumpeter as he rode along swiftly and helped to make him more conspicuous. Hence the name "trumpeter's sleeves." The shoulder features from which the bandsman's wings were to evolve are already clearly visible. Also, the sleeves are embellished by the treatment of the seams.*

(h) *Bavarian cavalry trumpeter's coat, about 1720, with "trumpeter's wings" evolved from the vestiges of the slashed sleeves, which were lengthened as bands and moved to the back of the garment. Contrasting in colour with the coat, they fluttered behind the horseman, thus making him very conspicuous.*

(i) *Prussian drummer's coat with epaulettes, about 1760. The fluttering trumpeter's sleeves have now disappeared; instead, their distinctive markings have been transferred to the real sleeves. The trumpeter's tradition was carried on by the military bandsmen.*

(j) *Oboist of the Prussian Fusiliers Bodyguard, 1704.*

(k) German army bandsman, Second World War. The wings are adorned with the traditional decorative strips.

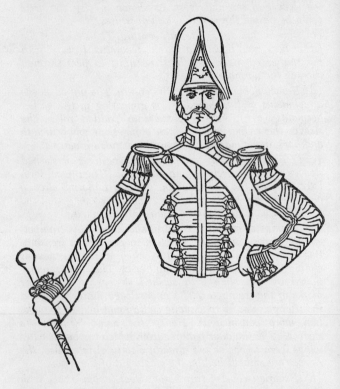

FIG. 5-6: *Russian drum major of the Ismailov regiment, about 1830. The great importance of trumpeters or buglers in battle was reflected in conspicuous features of the uniforms they wore, so as to make them easily recognisable. These decorative features and colours were subsequently adopted for the uniforms of military bandsmen. For reasons of prestige the regimental commanders set much value on splendidly uniformed bands. The drum major marching ahead of the bandsmen was often a splendid figure richly decked out in gold lace. The uniform of this Russian drum major shows every conceivable embellishment. Besides dec-*

orative sleeves with lace at the cuffs and collar embellish-
ments, it has breast facings and embroidered buttonholes
with tassels. Of great interest is the very rarely encountered
combination of epaulettes with wings. This simultaneous
presence of two analogously evolved features is possible be-
cause they derive from different origins. The epaulettes
were developed from shoulder flaps, whereas the wings
originated as sleeve attachments.

in the symbolically indicated slits. In the process of
further development these wide strips evolved into
decorative foliage patterns but with their tendrils still
following the old buttonhole lines. The collar slits encountered in the uniforms of many present-day ar-
mies are a relic of such ornamental buttonholes.

In accordance with the same principle all parts of
costume or uniform can be explained in terms of
evolutionary development—epaulettes, forage caps,
sleeve patches, cuffs, revers, piping or other features
(Figs. 5-2, 5-3, 5-4, 5-5, 5-6). The study of uniforms
offers the behavioural researcher a rich mine of material because, thanks to military thoroughness, every
single modification has been placed on record or has
been the subject of some official order. There are
very few uniforms which have not been preserved at
least in pictures and descriptions, and in Europe in
civilised times there is not a single one of which we
do not know at least the type. The evolution of military uniforms from about 1700 to 1914 constitutes for
the phylogenetically thinking ethologist the "model of
a phylogeny without missing links" and is therefore
eminently suitable for testing the working possibilities for the ethologist in the cultural field.

Only with a knowledge of developments in uniforms as cultural analogues to real (biological) phylogeny did it become possible to extend the investigations to other fields of research. Thus we have in

recent years, by a synoptic assessment of results obtained in behaviour study and in ethnology and folklore study, succeeded in detecting an entirely different and hitherto disregarded phenomenon and in throwing some light on the problems associated with it.

EYE SYMBOLS AS DEFENSIVE DEVICES

In the decorative arts of Europe and Asia there exists a characteristic ornamental pattern which is very widely employed and known under a variety of names. In English it is known as the "Paisley design"; in German it is variously called *Fischblase* (fish bladder), *Palmenblatt* (palm leaf) or *Blumenranke* (flower tendril). In Persia the names *mir, miribota* and *botemiri* are commonly employed. There are doubtless many more names for it. It is in fact a leaf-shaped pattern, without indentation at its wider end and curved back in one direction at its tip (Fig. 5-7). Usually it is outlined with decorative double lines. Its internal detailing does not consist of leaf veins, but at its wider end it often has a small circular area (sometimes formed by a precious stone mounted there) or alternatively a round flower pattern. In Jugoslavian costumes the *miribota* appears in a symmetrical two-sided, often richly ornamented form as a clasp on women's girdles, and is frequently also encountered as a small pendant cut from silver plate and unadorned with any internal pattern.

This ornamental design was a feature of the Persian imperial crown and also appeared as a supporting decorative element on the coronation robe of the Empress of Persia. It is very frequently found on carpets and also regularly appears on oriental shawls, furthermore in a great deal of embroidery on traditional

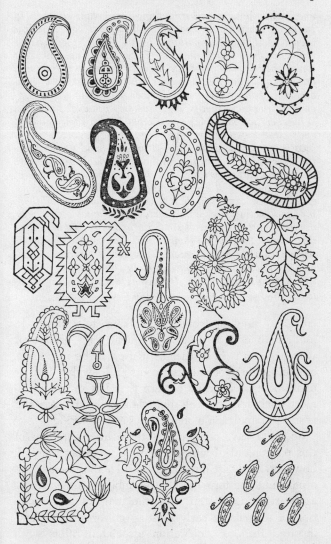

FIG. 5-7: *Various modifications of the* miribota *pattern on carpets and rugs. The word* mir *means "lord" or "illustrious*

one," while bota *means something like "plant cluster." In India the term* budi, *meaning "small plant" or "herb," is used to designate this pattern. Yet the first of these shapes illustrated here shows that the* miribota *does not represent a plant motif, but has been derived from an eye. The pupil and eyelashes are clearly recognisable. The process of ritualisation of the pattern may, however, lead to the emergence of true plant motifs, e.g., clusters of flowers or leaves. Wherever two miribotas are arranged with their rounded ends close together the impression of a pair of eyes in a face is produced, as in the bottom left-hand corner. The frequent occurrence of the* miribota *as a decorative feature on carpets and rugs testifies to its function as a means of warding off the evil eye, inasmuch as nomadic tribes make extensive use of rugs in their tents and sometimes use them for constructing the tents themselves. Camel saddlebags, doorway curtains, etc. all similarly have the magic protective symbol woven into their design. Fear of the evil eye is still widespread among oriental peoples. A European analogy is the age-old traditional practice of applying protective symbols and magic designs as decoration on farmhouses and churches to ward off the powers of evil.*

costumes ranging from the Balkans to Ireland. In modern times it is used as frequently for printed or woven patterns in textiles as it used to be in, for example, Celtic personal ornaments and jewelry. I know of no other decorative pattern that has remained almost unaltered for well-nigh thousands of years and is still so popular in modern times as the *miribota*.

So far, I have come across three interpretations of this pattern, all of which strike me as rather fanciful, however. Some art historians consider the foliage-type ornamental pattern closely resembling the *miribota* as constituting a step from the magical representation of animals in early hunting cultures to a plant-inspired form of decoration associated rather with farming and agriculture. A Dalmatian silver filigree worker explained the *miribota* "a heart driven slightly

PLATE 18: *Greek and Turkish ornaments. The Turkish clasp (right) clearly shows the eye shape with the pupil and has a number of protective amulets suspended from it, all forming a system of safeguarding against the evil eye. In the Greek ornament (left) the process of ritualisation has advanced further, with a tendency to adopt symmetrical shapes; but the basic character still emerges clearly enough to anyone who has studied the significance of eye symbols.*

PLATE 19: *On the backs of garments worn as national or local dress we frequently find conspicuous protective symbols against evil influences, as the wearer is especially vulnerable from the rear. This Croatian coat is adorned with an embroidered pattern in which the miribota has been subdivided into spirals which in themselves are eye symbols. Besides, the pattern comprises a number of "eye stars."*

PLATE 20: *Embroidery on the sleeve of a Serbian jacket. The miribota outline is clearly discernible. Despite the overall symmetry of the pattern, the tip is still slightly curved over to the right. The ancient eye character has almost entirely disappeared, however, as the miribota has here been split up into smaller miribota ornaments.*

PLATE 21: *The Turkish army crossing the river Drau in 1529. All the horsemen and officers, as well as Sultan Soliman (on the right, in the background), are wearing feathers curved in the miribota shape.*

PLATE 22: *Detail of a Persian miniature depicting Mohammed's flight from Mecca to Medina. The warriors are wearing so-called par feathers, whose distinctive feature is their curved shape. The significance of this emerges only when it is considered that Indian warriors often wore the miribota on the headdress. Among the Persians and the Turks this was replaced by similarly curved feathers, especially those of the ostrich and the crane. Both these species of bird were regarded as guardians— a function which was attributed to them probably on account of the supposed resemblance between their display feathers and the miribota.*

PLATE 23: *Head of a Nepalese idol. The eyebrows show the unmistakable miribota shape. On the forehead is a third eye. The ornaments worn on the idol's head are likewise composed of eyes and eye symbols. (From: H. Tichy, 1960, Menschenwege-Götterberge, Vienna.)*

PLATE 24: *(left): Horse harness from the Pinzgau (Austria) with pendant in the shape of a Turkish crescent. Actually, this symbol originally had nothing to do with moon or star, but is a highly ritualised protective eye and performs exactly the same function as the smooth round metal disc seen higher up. The crescent shape was evolved in various ways. Thus, the pupils of two miribota-shaped eyes may become ornamentally merged with each other and finally shift to the centre of the crescent, there to appear as a star. On the other hand, the symbol has also arisen from the amulets worn against the evil eye by the ancient Romans and even by some present-day Italians. In these the whole arch of the eyebrow is represented as a semicircle under which two spots, and subsequently just one spot, were placed. Old keys are sometimes adorned with this double eye pattern. In Italy a key is used as a means of warding off the evil eye. (centre): Harness ornament for draught oxen from Verona. The three stars in circles are protective symbols and represent the triple-eye principle. Cattle which have a light-coloured spot on the forehead as a "third eye" are greatly appreciated by the rural population. In the Austrian Alps it is still common practice to add one such "three-eyed" cow to each herd in the belief that this will ward off evil or misfortune. In the East, starting with the ancient Assyrians, cows' or bulls' heads bearing a rosette on the forehead are encountered in the visual arts. (right): Ancient Cretan bull's head with a whorl marking the "third eye" (Knossos, probably about 1550 B.C.).*

skew by terror," and a Persian carpet dealer was of
the opinion that it represented the imprint of the
underside of a clenched fist with which Persian dignitaries used to sign documents. All these supposed explanations do indeed to some extent account for the
external shape of the pattern, but not for the conspicuous, usually circular internal feature at the wider
end. This leads us to infer that these are merely retrospective hypotheses. We get nearer the truth when
we consider the fact that the *miribota* was used as
an amulet by the ancient Celts (in what is now Ireland), in the Balkans, in Greece and southern Italy,
in the Yemen, in Persia and also in China. In the
Mediterranean region such amulets help to ward off
the evil eye.

On considering other magic signs intended to perform the same function, we find that symbolised representations of eyes are very frequently encountered
in them. Circular mirrors, roundish blue stones and
corresponding tattooed markings are believed to give
protection against the baleful effect of a look from a
blue eye. More realistic representations of eyes are
sometimes used for the purpose. The question thus
arises whether the *miribota* is not also a "ritualised"
representation of an eye. On examining the round
central ornamental feature, often consisting of a
gleaming jewel or pearl or a brightly coloured spot,
we can readily recognise it as the pupil of an eye.
Thus the pattern as a whole must represent an eye.
If we place two miribotas symmetrically side by
side, with the bent-up tips outwards, we find ourselves
looking at the pair of eyes in a face.

On the basis of a great deal of evidence, of which
only a small amount can be adduced here, it can be
assumed with near certainty that the *miribota* is indeed a very ancient representation of an eye which,

though often much embellished and stylised, has recognisably survived as such down to the present time
and which, because of the innate fascination that
any representation of an eye exercises upon human
beings, has retained its appeal and continues to be
used. This assumption is further supported by the
observation that paintings on ancient Greek vases often depict ships which are provided with a pair of
very realistic painted eyes on the bow. Egyptian and
Etruscan ships are known also to have had such eyes,
while at the present time they are painted on the vessels of many primitive tribes. A modified and greatly
ritualised form of these eyes is still to be found on the
old Jugoslavian sailing boats which, now equipped
with engines, still ply between the islands, carrying
cargo. The eyes, bearing a marked resemblance to
the *miribota*, are located in exactly the same position on the vessel's bow as their more realistically depicted predecessors on ancient Greek ships (Plate 12
and Plate 13). That these eyes are indeed intended
to ward off evil is beyond dispute, for frightening
masks and big eyes for scaring off malevolent de-
mons are widespread, occurring in the great majority
of peoples throughout the world. They are to be
found in Gothic cathedrals as well as in old farmhouses in Europe.

Besides warding off evil influences, eyes may also
give aid and protection in a wider context. According
to Greek beliefs they safeguard against perils on voy-
ages and help the ship to find its way. So these eyes
have to perform quite a variety of functions. These
include maintaining a general watchfulness, but it
would seem that on the whole their over-all function
could best be described as defensive in the sense of
warding off.

Anyone who fears invisible dangers and evil spirits

must seek protection against their powers, and since the human being expresses rebuttal largely by facial expressions, he will for this purpose base himself more particularly on the ritualised representation of such expressions. Eyes of course constitute focal points of expression in the human face; they are the only sensory organs of remote perception that can establish reciprocal contact with those of other living creatures. We do not "hear" the ears of another person, but only the words that his mouth speaks; we do not "smell" his nose, but only the odour given off by his body. But we do "see" his "gaze," and we all know from our own experience how important and meaningful the eye-to-eye look can be. Every second that it lasts too long already suggests designs and intentions. Looks can invade a person's private world. The effect of the eye in social intercourse is comparable to that of the sense of touch. Just as we can direct "hand in hand" or "mouth to mouth" contact, so we can have "eye to eye" intercommunication at a distance. Thus the eye has a special significance which makes it appear particularly well suited as a means of protection against the evil eye.

This use of the eye, or the representation of the eye, as a defence against one's enemies is not something new and peculiar to man (Plates 14, 15, 16). The animal kingdom affords many instances of "eye spots" as devices for the intimidation of would-be aggressors. Thus there are butterflies with conspicuous eye spots on the upper surfaces of their wings; when the wings are quickly opened, the spots are suddenly presented to birds or other predators, causing them to back away in alarm. If the eye spots are removed, the butterflies lose their protection from their natural enemies. Birds which were offered food together with eye spots refused to touch it. There are numerous examples from all sections of the animal kingdom which show the importance and success of eye spots as a protective device. Sometimes, as in certain butterfly and fish species, such spots serve as a means of "re-orienting" the animal's body, thus misleading an enemy into attacking in the "wrong" place, where no harm will be done, while the animal's real eyes are relatively small and inconspicuous so as not to distract attention from the "false" eyes. This latter behaviour pattern, i.e., closing the (real) eyes so as not to "catch the enemy's eye," is exemplified by the nightjar as it sits on its eggs or is merely resting. Relying on its protective markings to make it inconspicuous, this bird closes its large eyes—particularly effective for seeing at night—to narrow slits so as not to give itself away.

All animals have their eyes on their heads, and in nearly all vertebrates the head is a part which, being equipped with teeth for biting, performs a very important function in attack or defence. A predator will therefore always try to seize its prey in such a way that the latter's head cannot be brought into action. Being the seat of the brain and the most important sensory organs, it must be eliminated as speedily as possible, and the eyes provide a quick means of recognition for determining the position of the head. When you walk past a timid animal and look the other way, or at least close one eye and half-close the other, you will cause it less alarm than when you look at it with both your eyes wide open. The direct gaze is felt as implying a threat of attack and causes the animal to seek refuge against it.

All this goes to show the importance of the eye as a medium of expression and a signal, thus giving real significance to its use as a means of protection in the culture of human communities. There is of course an important difference between the evolution of defensive eye spots and markings in the animal and in the human world. In animals the effectiveness increases according as the eye spot looks more realistic, so that natural selection towards greater realism takes place; in man, on the other hand, the evil spirits and other malevolent influences which he has imagined for himself do not really react to the artificial defensive eyes. The effectiveness of the amulet is determined entirely by the faith and imagination of its wearer: there is no real, objectively existing enemy to be repelled. Consequently, the door is opened to a wide range of variation, and a vast variety of ritualised forms are derived, often to the point of unrecognisability, sometimes evolving into flower and leaf patterns. This is likely to happen particularly in communities where belief in the evil eye and evil spirits has died out. Alternatively, the innate response to eyes and the pleasure communicated by their shape may well give rise to the adoption of the eye as an ornamental feature, largely independent of any belief in spirits and imaginary dangers. These phenomena are therefore to be regarded as definitely of polyphyletic origin, i.e., having an evolution in which several distinct influences have been at work.

One of the many different starting points for the adoption of the human eye as an ornamental feature must surely have been the eyes painted on the bows of ships in ancient times, particularly in the Mediterranean region. Here the at first realistically represented eye soon began to change, when people realised that the dangers of the unseen world need not be taken too seriously. In an intuitive tendency to conform to physical influences, the front of the eye pattern was rounded so as to give it a teardrop shape, while the rear end was made to end in a point and give an upward curve. This is the shape now still to be found on traditional Jugoslavian sailing boats. Evidently this eye pattern was then in many places adopted as an ornamental feature of costume. The members of the maritime fellowship of Kotor, which was once the organisation to which belonged all the captains and sailors of the Boka Kotorska (great seamen, much sought after for their navigational skill) and whose traditions are hundreds of years old, wear precisely this "defensive eye" as a visible sign on their headgear.

But change and evolution went further (Plates 17–24). The human tendency to arrange things symmetrically caused the one-sided curved "eye" pattern to develop into such varied derivations as the well-known tulip motif of the Persian tree of life, the traditional heart shape, the crescent or the richly embellished crabs on Gothic cathedrals. This does not mean to say that every one of these ornaments must be directly descended from the ships' eyes. The practice of applying make-up around the eyes and, more particularly, often extending the corner of the eye slantingly upwards in the *miribota* shape must also have originated as "defensive magic" and may have been the starting point of subsequent ornamental patterns. In this content it should be noted that stylised representations of eyes are already to be found in Palaeolithic cave paintings and that many shapes, such as the spiral, which very frequently became an eye symbol, may well have survived continuously to the present time. Whatever the actual connections may be, in the final result the central importance of the eye as a means of expression almost invariably emerges. The phenomenon under discussion clearly shows how very much we humans cling to our inborn attitudes of mind and how they affect even those fields of activity which we customarily refer to as art, imagination and intellectuality. In none of his actions and functions is man able to dissociate himself from the biological rules inherent in the basic family tree that all living creatures have in common.

BEHAVIOUR PATTERNS AND CUSTOMS

On the basis of his behavioural equipment man can be designated as a diurnal predatory, i.e., hunting and food-gathering, social creature that lives in small communities, has a preference for broken terrain and dwells under cover. From this combination of attributes emerge his modes of behaviour and his habits. As a diurnal animal, i.e., one that seeks its food by day, he regards darkness as dangerous—a fact which finds expression in the positive value attached to anything that symbolises light (incidentally, such symbols are often used in connection with "putting across" political ideas). Being a hunter in the very essence of his nature, he reacts to moving objects and tries to catch them. All his games are essentially hunting games in which the aim is to outwit or overtake one's adversary or capture something from him. The overtaking urge in motorists is to a great extent a hunting urge. From the vacuum cleaner salesman to the research scientist all men strive to get results, i.e., to get hold of things that elude them. The collecting urge—i.e., the gathering or acquisitive craving—is also so widespread that its inherited character can hardly be doubted. In social intercourse, man tends to prefer the small circle in which all social gradations are duly balanced and only change slowly. In the large social community there is an increased disruptive tendency to split up into factions, so that there is a breakdown into small groups once again.

He is helpful more especially towards people he
knows well, whereas the fate of strangers affects him
only when, as a result of appropriate publicity, it can
become an object of his sympathy. His adjustment
to broken (as distinct from featureless open) country
as his natural environment is apparent from the way
he builds his settlements and his tendency to lay out
parklike scenery in his immediate surroundings. Besides, man is a pronounced "corner seat passenger,"
who likes to seek cover, withdraws into "secret" re-
cesses and is reluctant to sit or sleep alone in the middle of a large hall. His sense of territorial rights
prompts him to lay down frontiers, fix boundaries,
build fences. The tendency to stake out and maintain
his "preserves" arises from an aversion to faeces.
Marmots are territory-conscious animals which, like
certain other animal species in similar ecological circumstances, have their own special "lavatories" and
thus keep their hunting grounds clean. Arboreal
mammals, which normally do not come into contact
with their own faeces, have no aversion to them,
which is something that has objectionable consequences when such animals are kept in cages. Animals that roam far and wide in their search for food
do not display an aversion to their faeces in captivity
either, since such aversion is simply not a biological
necessity to them in their way of life out in the open.

What has here been briefly mentioned could be
proved in detail with reference to the examples already investigated. However, suffice it to say that
comparative behaviour study has already arrived at
a rough over-all evaluation of man, having succeeded
in working out his natural behaviour pattern from the
comparison of a great many action systems in animals. The comparison is of more particular importance in that we are here concerned with phenom-

ena which would escape our attention if we were not able to extricate them from the background of other combinations of activities. Here the comparison between man and animal turns out to be the basic method of research. Sciences such as folklore and ethnology, which are to so great an extent concerned with the behaviour patterns and activities of human beings, cannot afford to ignore this knowledge brought to light by behaviour study. An example derived from the culture-ethological research work of our institute will serve to show how biological laws can play a decisive part also in matters of tradition and customs.

A custom widespread in Europe is the observance of the festival of St. Nicholas (6 December). The essentials can be outlined quite briefly. The saint—known also, and more familiarly, as Sinterklaas in Holland —goes from house to house on the evening of 6 December (in Holland: 5 December, the eve of his birthday) and gives presents to children who deserve them by having been good. In Austria, southern Germany and Holland he appears in the garb of a Catholic bishop, behaving with due decorum and dignity. In other, more northern countries (including Britain), however, he appears as Father Christmas in his red fur-trimmed robe, travelling on foot or in a sleigh drawn by reindeer. In most countries he is accompanied by a servant, who carries the presents and sometimes also administers chastisement to naughty children.

In some regions St. Nicholas' servant is a rather uncouth fellow, whereas in others he is a benevolent, almost angelic character. In Holland he is invariably a blackamoor named Black Peter, who is the saint's servant and groom (for here St. Nicholas travels on horseback); he carries the presents for rewarding the good children and a rod for spanking the naughty ones. In Austria the servant is usually a rather sinister demonlike creature named Krampus. There is a legend which tells us that he really is a devil whom the saintly bishop Nicholas once conquered and forced to act as his servant in bearing gifts to the children. It is not my intention here to discuss the figure of St. Nicholas or that of his servant, except to point out that in folk tradition Krampus is much older than either the bishop or Father Christmas.

In many far-flung parts of Europe—in the Frisian Islands, in the valleys of Switzerland and Austria and in the remote Pyrenees—a great many Krampus-like demon creatures, under a variety of names, go hurrying through the winter nights, ringing their big bells. They are up to all sorts of pranks and mischief, romp tauntingly around passers-by, burst into houses, beat the occupants with rods or drag them out into the street. They also demand gifts, which are handed to them by the women of the house. It is a wild frolic in which the participants, mostly young men all of about the same age, wearing furs and terrifying masks, make their uproarious way through the villages and hamlets. Krampus is a last remaining—one might say: "Christianised"—glimmer of an old custom of undoubtedly heathen origin.

In order to record the precise sequence of activities and the behaviour patterns and to analyse, if possible, the origin and evolution of this custom, working groups of the Vienna Academy Institute began filming it in East Tyrol. For the behavioural researcher, films constitute one of the most important aids with which it is possible to obtain precise and permanent records of movements and which can subsequently be used for accurately analysing the activities in question and breaking them down into their component parts, as well as comparing them with those recorded in other, similar films.

To start with, filming was done in East Tyrolean villages. In those parts Krampus is known by another name, Klaubauf, and is one of the most important traditional characters of all. The young men of a village get together and go on the prowl, wearing masks. They are accompanied by St. Nicholas with his servant, two beggars named Lütterin and Lotte, demanding alms, and a musician. Most important of the participants are, however, the *Kleibeife* (the East Tyrolese plural form of *Klaubauf*) (Plate 25). First, St. Nicholas and his servant enter the room, behaving with proper dignity and distributing confectionery, nuts and figs. Then come the beggars with the musician, who now in their turn receive gifts, and then, to the accompaniment of a deafening ringing of bells, the wild masked Klaubaufs burst into the room, hurl themselves upon the table behind which, on the bench at the household shrine (altar with crucifix and image of the Virgin, this being a Catholic country), are seated the members of the family. The intruders try to seize the table and carry it out of the room. Often there is a wild tug of war, and if there are strong men among the men of the house, the family may win the struggle and keep possession of their table. But usually the Klaubaufs are victorious and carry the table out into the road, where they celebrate their triumph with wild joyous dancing. This illustrates the general character of the Klaubauf frolic. In details there are many differences between one district and another. However, a feature shared by all Klaubaufs is that they are fond of having a scuffle and are boisterous characters who, in the street, try to throw every passer-by to the ground and sometimes even drag all the occupants of a house

outside and roll them in the snow. In many places
this kind of horseplay has been toned down by the
efforts of the village priest or of some organisation
taking an interest in the ancient custom and its preservation as a means of collecting for charitable purposes. At Matrei, however, the rough-and-tumble aspect has been given particular prominence: on three
evenings, in the main square, wild battles are waged
between the Klaubaufs and the "townsmen," who
gather here specially for the purpose. Though quite
rough, these fights are seldom dangerous, because
there is generally a thick blanket of snow on the
ground to break the falls. But the Klaubaufs get most
fun out of chasing and catching girls, who, for their
part, show a keen interest in this side of the proceedings.

Not far from East Tyrol, though separated from it
by the Tauernkamm, a mountain range, lies the Gastein valley in the Salzburg region of Austria. Here, too,
the Klaubauf tradition is firmly rooted and displays in
principle the same elements as are found elsewhere,
but there are marked local differences. Whereas in
East Tyrol the young men of a village all band together into one group of variable size, in the Gastein
valley there has evolved a system of so-called *Passen*,
strictly separate groups, each of which comprises its
own St. Nicholas, a servant, a basket bearer and four
or five Klaubaufs. Each group (*Passe*) forms a
closely knit unit in which St. Nicholas' clothing and
that of his servant are of matching colours, the basket
bearer is always dressed in peasant costume and the
Klaubaufs all wear similar masks. Thus each group
has its own quite separate and distinctive character.
On the other hand, in East Tyrol each participant
wears a different mask, according to his own particular taste, and there are scarcely any Klaubauf

masks with horns on them, whereas the Gastein Klaubaufs wear numerous rams' horns of the greatest possible length on their uniformly black masks.

These differences at once become understandable on examining the two phenotypes from the ecological-social point of view. The East Tyrolese Klaubauf frolics are centred upon their own villages, which they seldom leave. If they nevertheless do so, they are liable to fall foul of neighbouring communities, as any crossing of boundaries is regarded as unfair. In the wide trough-shaped Gastein valley the great majority of the farming population lives in individual farms often situated quite close to one another, and the two townships in the valley—Badgastein and Hofgastein—are tourist centres rather than real local communities. Because of the scattered location of the farms, a Klaubauf group based and operating on East Tyrolese pattern would have to travel for miles along the roads in order to visit a substantial number of them. Under these conditions of population distribution and topography it was not practicable to form one large central group. The many small groups, mostly composed of neighbours and a few close friends, constitute the social form suited to the local situation.

Of course, the patterns of action must also be significantly modified. Fights over territorial infringements are "out," since the various groups have to use the same roads and thus often encounter one another at crossroads and junctions. Also, as regards the houses they visit the groups do, of course, each act independently, as it is not possible to work out a central plan of campaign because there is no central leadership for these activities such as exists in a normal village. Thus many houses, particularly those located at "strategic points" such as bridges over the river, are visited by several groups, so that these are bound sometimes to run into each other on such occasions. From this situation a highly ritualised "encounter ceremony" has been evolved, with solemn signs and words of greeting uttered by the respective St. Nicholases and a kind of completely ceremonial "battle dance" performed by the Klaubaufs.

When a group approaches a house which another group happens to be visiting at that very time, it makes a detour or waits outside, as unobtrusively as possible, until the other group has departed. If the group already "in occupation" happens to become aware of the other's approach, it will speed up the proceedings and leave as quietly as possible through the back door. The system of these strictly observed rules is reminiscent of patterns of behaviour in large animal communities, where, in order to avoid perpetual fights between rivals, there is a great variety of ritualised gestures signifying submission, greeting and menace, which ease matters when two rivals meet and have to pass each other and which indeed make such encounters possible at all without leading to conflict.

The horns are another important factor in relation to this complex social system. In East Tyrol, where sham fights with the "townsmen," i.e., the local inhabitants not wearing masks, romping with the girls and the "invasion" of homes with its attendant horseplay are important features in the proceedings, horns on the masks would be dangerous appendages or indeed a mere nuisance to the contestants. With horned and antlered animals the general rule is that, among related species, those with the biggest and most powerful antlers display the most advanced degree of ritualisation in fights between rivals. In fights within the species dangerous or very large and impressive weapons are normally used only in such a way that no

serious injury is caused to the adversary. Something
very similar applies to the Klaubauf masks of the
Gastein valley. With their huge horns, often in multiple pairs, they would be both dangerous and clumsy
in a fight. Scuffling and romping in the East Tyrolese
manner are not among the activities in this valley.
Instead, they are characterised by some very striking
and peculiar ceremonial dancing in which the dancers
move back and forth, bowing from time to time. These
motions at once become intelligible on observing how
a group enters a house. Because of the big horns on
their heads, they cannot simply walk straight through
the—usually rather low—doorway, but have to stoop.
Even so, the horns often remain sticking, so that the
Klaubauf then has to take one or two steps backwards
in order to try again, stooping lower. This difficult
and clumsy procedure of entering a room has been
formalised, by exaggerating the Klaubaufs' own awk-
wardness, and incorporated into the ceremonial dance.
Inside the house the activities are similar in principle
to those in East Tyrol, but without the rough-and-
tumble and always in a relatively more "decorous"
fashion. The dangerous horned headgear simply
makes it imperative to exercise greater restraint and
caution than is usually found among the East Tyrolese
Klaubaufs. In the Gastein valley each Klaubauf group
is under the control of St. Nicholas; all the Klaubaufs
in the group wear the same sort of mask, so that they
do not create their impression as separate individuals;
instead the group as a whole produces its effect. The
Klaubaufs of East Tyrol, on the other hand, are in-
dividualists each of whom tries to outdo the others
with his mask, bells and behaviour.

Closely associated with the difference in behaviour
between the Klaubaufs in the Matrei and the Gastein
regions, respectively, are also the different values

attached to the anonymity afforded by the masks. At
Matrei, where the scuffles and general rough pranks
are taken more seriously and involve the prestige of
the individual contestants, this anonymity is jealously
guarded. No Klaubauf will remove his mask to a
townsman, and anyone who has the audacity to tear
off a Klaubauf's mask can be sure to receive a sound
thrashing. Even the local police respect this anonymity: if they stop a Klaubauf for questioning and
identification, they conduct him to some quiet side
alley before ordering him to remove his mask. At
Gastein, on the other hand, Klaubaufs may be seen
carrying their masks under their arms in public and
even dancing without them. Also, when served with
drinks on their visits to houses, they immediately remove their masks. Whereas the East Tyrolese Klaubaufs, in order to protect their anonymity, do not use
their voices and, instead, rely on bells to make their
deafening noise, their counterparts in the Gastein valley roar loudly.

The attitude of the Gastein Klaubaufs, which could
in general be described almost as "friendly menace,"
and their small number and correct behaviour, ensure
their admission into every home at which they call.
On the other hand, at Matrei, where the Klaubaufs are
noted for their wild and unpredictable behaviour,
never more than two or at most three will be admitted
into a newly furnished room, and then only on condition that they promise not to indulge in any rough
pranks. In bygone days, when farmers made their own
furniture of a rather primitive kind, a few scratches or
cracks did not matter greatly. But polished or var-
nished factory-made furniture cannot be properly
repaired by do-it-yourself methods, while modern domestic appliances such as washing machines and television sets are far too fragile to permit liberties to be

taken with them. The customary performance of seizing the table, which arose from the desire to get at the womenfolk sitting behind it, is therefore very much on the decline and is practised only in mountain villages where the traditional furnishings survive. More particularly at Matrei itself, where up to forty or so Klaubaufs may be on the prowl, this limitation imposed on their activities has had the result that, instead, they direct their attacks at passers-by and tussle with them.

Anyone who ventures in the streets on the three Klaubauf nights knows exactly what may be in store for him. Therefore the people who are out and about on these nights are mostly high-spirited young men— who may sometimes change sides and themselves act as Klaubaufs—and girls who simply want to be chased and caught. Thus it has become the custom that, when St. Nicholas and his attendants have completed all the prescribed house visits, the whole gang assembles in the main square. St. Nicholas with his servant, the beggars Lütterin and Lotte, and the musician march past, followed by the fur-clad demoniacally masked Klaubaufs, who hurl themselves into the big square, furiously ringing their bells, and immediately start to tussle with the bystanders, who have expectantly been waiting for the fun to begin. The wild frolic continues until midnight. Under the pressure of local conditions there has thus developed a very special form of St. Nicholas-and-Krampus celebration, which could never have been evolved in a small village community. The main impetus came from the change to modern furniture and appliances in the homes, as already mentioned, whereby the Klaubaufs found themselves deprived of a major sphere of activities. In a small community this setback would have caused the whole custom to fall into abeyance, except insofar as it could perhaps be transformed into a peaceable visit by a small group comprising St. Nicholas and a few attendants. At Matrei, a largish and densely populated market centre, with a sufficiently large main square and a sufficient number of interested citizens, on the other hand, the custom evolved into a new form with the character of public entertainment. Such developments are not be expected in the Gastein valley, where in consequence of the low-density population distribution the system is characterised by small groups whose actions are controlled by fairly elaborate ritual. Here the change to modern furniture in the homes has had no effect at all upon the pattern of the custom.

Although only a limited selection of the available factual data has been presented here, it may suffice to show that the method of ethological comparison, as we know it from behaviour study, can also be utilised in the field of folklore and ethnological study, i.e., cultural investigations. But the possible links between ethology and ethnology have not thus been anywhere near fully outlined. The zoological-systematic approach of behaviour study may, at first sight, correspond more to the physical anthropology, but it is precisely this method that forms the exact basis on which it is possible to go purposefully forward. In its most difficult sector, namely, the study of clan and family relationships, it merges imperceptibly into folklore study anyway.

PROBLEMS OF CULTURAL ETHOLOGY

Sociology and psychology, especially the psychology of children, have long overlapped with ethology and indeed merge with it and one another. Thus folklore study and ethnology will have to enter into symbioses and partial fusions with these sciences in order to achieve their central purpose: to obtain a better and fuller understanding of recent man.

If the newly emerged science of cultural ethology, firmly rooted in general comparative behaviour study, is concerned predominantly with the folkloristic sector, this is due to the perfectly realistic consideration that easier, more successful and deeper-penetrating research can be done in one's own national group than in any other, which is liable to adopt a defensive and unco-operative attitude to the intruder. And in any case, the methodology most characteristically peculiar to behaviour study derives from this predilection for working with "tame" and "familiar" creatures. Oskar Heinroth, who was one of Konrad Lorenz's teachers, was the first to apply this procedure. It was he who so successfully compiled the still up-to-date and valid treatise on the birds of Central Europe from information obtained with tame birds bred in captivity. In the metaphorical sense a "tameness effect" of this kind asserts itself as a positive factor also in the study of one's own national folklore.

Besides the greater familiarity that exists between investigator and subject under investigation in one's own folklore, the historical documentary material that is so abundantly available in Western Europe plays a very stimulating part. The assumption that, in studying so-called "primitive races," we are dealing with more primitive and therefore phylogenetically older cultures is not entirely correct. Actually, in many cases they are very pronounced and relatively young cultures specialised to suit particular conditions of climatic and territorial environment. Also, rigid traditions of behaviour and taboos frequently conceal the true relationships and evolutionary patterns. Yet it is specifically the laws of change and development that we have to investigate in order to be able to understand how changes take place and how "fossilised" situations eventually arose. For such investigations the European civilisation, receptive to new influences and in a perpetual state of flux, is far better than, for instance, the tradition-bound population in some out-of-the-way backward tropical region.

This assertion must not be construed as in any sense derogatory to the importance of ethnological studies; it merely seeks to focus attention on the great significance of European folklore to behavioural researchers, the majority of whom do, after all, live in Europe. At all events, in the so essential co-operation of ethology and ethnology, and more particularly in the special manifestation of cultural ethology, we find the evidence of the truth of the assertion that Otto Koehler made at the end of his introduction to Tinbergen's treatise on the theory of instinct (1969): "The farther away the level of behaviour at which one works is from present-day physiology, the more impossible the pure, solely objective representation must appear to him. I am convinced that it is comparative behavioural research which is precisely destined to be the mediator between physiology and psychology, between natural and mental sciences, and should like to keep the door to psychology wide open."

This applies equally to the door to ethology. Essentially, ethology is a science with connections in every direction; for whoever investigates living creatures, whether they be fish, birds, mammals or indeed, within the latter category, man himself, always find himself dealing with behaviour patterns, and the investigation of these constitutes the central set of problems with which ethology is concerned.

NIKO TINBERGEN

On War and Peace in Animals and Man

An ethologist's approach to the biology of aggression.

In 1935 Alexis Carrel published a best seller, *Man— The Unknown.*[1] Today, more than thirty years later, we biologists have once more the duty to remind our fellow men that in many respects we are still, to ourselves, unknown. It is true that we now understand a great deal of the way our bodies function. With this understanding came control: medicine.

The ignorance of ourselves which needs to be stressed today is ignorance about our behaviour—lack of understanding of the causes and effects of the function of our brains. A scientific understanding of our behaviour, leading to its control, may well be the most urgent task that faces mankind today. It is the effects of our behaviour that begin to endanger the very survival of our species and, worse, of all life on earth. By our technological achievements we have attained a mastery of our environment that is without precedent in the history of life. But these achievements are rapidly getting out of hand. The consequences of our "rape of the earth" are now assuming critical proportions. With shortsighted recklessness we deplete the limited natural resources, including even the oxygen and nitrogen of our atmosphere.[2] And Rachel Carson's warning[3] is now being followed by those of scientists, who give us an even gloomier picture of the general pollution of air, soil and water. This pollution is seriously threatening our health and our food supply. Refusal to curb our reproductive behaviour has led to the population explosion. And, as if all this were not enough, we are waging war on each other—men are fighting and killing men on a massive scale. It is because the effects of these behaviour patterns, and of attitudes that determine our behaviour, have now acquired such truly lethal potentialities that I have chosen man's ignorance about his own behaviour as the subject of this paper.

I am an ethologist, a zoologist studying animal behaviour. What gives a student of animal behaviour the temerity to speak about problems of human behaviour? Of course the history of medicine provides the answer. We all know that medical research uses animals on a large scale. This makes sense because animals, particularly vertebrates, are, in spite of all differences, so similar to us; they are our blood relations, however distant.

But this use of zoological research for a better understanding of ourselves is, to most people, acceptable only when we have to do with those bodily functions that we look upon as parts of our physiological machinery—the functions, for instance, of our kidneys, our liver, our hormone-producing glands. The majority of people bridle as soon as it is even suggested that studies of animal behaviour could be useful for an understanding, let alone for the control, of our own behaviour. They do not want to have their own behaviour subjected to scientific scrutiny; they certainly resent being compared with animals, and these rejecting attitudes are both deep-rooted and of complex origin.

But now we are witnessing a turn in this tide of human thought. On the one hand the resistances are weakening, and on the other, a positive awareness is growing of the potentialities of a biology of behaviour. This has become quite clear from the great interest aroused by several recent books that are trying, by comparative studies of animals and man, to trace what we could call "the animal roots of human behaviour." As examples I select Konrad Lorenz's book *On Aggression*[4] and *The Naked Ape* by Desmond Morris.[5] Both books were best sellers from the start. We ethologists are naturally delighted by this sign of rapid growth of interest in our science (even though the growing pains are at times a little hard to endure). But at the same time we are apprehensive, or at least I am.

We are delighted because, from the enormous sales of these and other such books, it is evident that the mental block against self-scrutiny is weakening—that there are masses of people who, so to speak, want to be shaken up.

But I am apprehensive because these books, each admirable in its own way, are being misread. Very few readers give the authors the benefit of the doubt. Far too many either accept uncritically all that the authors say, or (equally uncritically) reject it all. I believe that this is because both Lorenz and Morris emphasise our knowledge rather than our ignorance (and, in addition, present as knowledge a set of statements which are after all no more than likely guesses). In themselves brilliant, these books could stiffen, at a new level, the attitude of certainty, while what we need is a sense of doubt and wonder, and an urge to investigate, to inquire.

POTENTIAL USEFULNESS OF ETHOLOGICAL STUDIES

Now, in a way, I am going to be just as assertative as Lorenz and Morris, but what I am going to stress is how much we do not know. I shall argue that we shall have to make a major research effort. I am of course fully aware of the fact that much research is already being devoted to problems of human, and even of animal, behaviour. I know, for instance, that anthropologists, psychologists, psychiatrists and others are approaching these problems from many angles. But I shall try to show that the research effort has so far made insufficient use of the potential of ethology. Anthropologists, for instance, are beginning to look at animals, but they restrict their work almost entirely to our nearest relatives, the apes and monkeys. Psychologists do study a larger variety of animals, but even they select mainly higher species. They also ignore certain major problems that we biologists think have to be studied. Psychiatrists, at least many of them, show a disturbing tendency to apply the *results* rather than the *methods* of ethology to man.

None of these sciences, not even their combined efforts, are as yet parts of one coherent science of behaviour. Since behaviour is a life process, its study ought to be part of the mainstream of biological research. That is why we zoologists ought to "join the fray." As an ethologist, I am going to try to sketch how my science could assist its sister sciences in their attempts, already well on their way, to make a united, broad-fronted, truly biological attack on the problems of behaviour.

I feel that I can co-operate best by discussing what it is in ethology that could be of use to the other behavioural sciences. What we ethologists do not want, what we consider definitely wrong, is uncritical application of our results to man. Instead, I myself at least feel that it is our method of approach, our rationale, that we can offer,[6] and also a little simple common sense, and discipline.

The potential usefulness of ethology lies in the fact that, unlike other sciences of behaviour, it applies the method or "approach" of biology to the phenomenon behaviour. It has developed a set of concepts and terms that allow us to ask:

(1) In what ways does this phenomenon (behaviour) influence the survival, the success of the animal?

(2) What makes behaviour happen at any given moment? How does its "machinery" work?

(3) How does the behaviour machinery develop as the individual grows up?

(4) How have the behaviour systems of each species evolved until they became what they are now?

The first question, that of survival value, has to do with the effects of behaviour; the other three are, each on a different time scale, concerned with its causes.

These four questions are, as many of my fellow biologists will recognise, the major questions that biology has been pursuing for a long time. What ethology is doing could be simply described by saying that, just as biology investigates the functioning of the organs responsible for digestion, respiration, circulation and so forth, so ethology begins now to do the same with respect to behaviour; it investigates the functioning of organs responsible for movement.

I have to make clear that in my opinion it is the comprehensive, integrated attack on all four problems that characterises ethology. I shall try to show that to ignore the questions of survival value and evolution—as, for instance, most psychologists do—is not only shortsighted but makes it impossible to arrive at an understanding of behavioural problems. Here ethology can make, in fact is already making, positive contributions.

Having stated my case for animal ethology as an essential part of the science of behaviour, I will now have to sketch how this could be done. For this I shall have to consider one concrete example, and I select aggression, the most directly lethal of our behaviours. And, for reasons that will become clear, I shall also make a short excursion into problems of education.

Let me first try to define what I mean by aggression. We all understand the term in a vague, general way, but it is, after all, no more than a catchword. In terms of actual behaviour, aggression involves approaching an opponent, and, when within reach, pushing him away, inflicting damage of some kind, or at least forcing stimuli upon him that subdue him. In this description the effect is already implicit: such behaviour tends to remove the opponent, or at least to make him change his behaviour in such a way that he no longer interferes with the attacker. The methods of attack differ from one species to another, and so do the weapons that are used, the structures that contribute to the effect.

Since I am concentrating on men fighting men, I shall confine myself to intraspecific fighting, and ignore, for instance, fighting between predators and prey. Intraspecific fighting is very common among animals. Many of them fight in two different contexts, which we can call "offensive" and "defensive." Defensive fighting is often shown as a last resort by an animal that, instead of attacking, has been fleeing from an attacker. If it is cornered, it may suddenly turn round upon its enemy and "fight with the courage of despair."

Of the four questions I mentioned before, I shall consider that of the survival value first. Here comparison faces us right at the start with a striking paradox. On the one hand, man is akin to many species of animals in that he fights his own species. But on the other hand he is, among the thousands of species that fight, the only one in which fighting is disruptive.

In animals, intraspecific fighting is usually of distinctive advantage. In addition, all species manage as a rule to settle their disputes without killing one another; in fact, even bloodshed is rare. Man is the only species that is a mass murderer, the only misfit in his own society.

Why should this be so? For an answer, we shall have to turn to the question of causation: What makes animals and man fight their own species? And why is our species "the odd man out"?

CAUSATION OF AGGRESSION

For a fruitful discussion of this question of causation I shall first have to discuss what exactly we mean when we ask it.

I have already indicated that when thinking of causation we have to distinguish between three subquestions, and that these three differ from one another in the stretch of time that is considered. We ask, first: Given an adult animal that fights now and then, what makes each outburst of fighting happen? The time scale in which we consider these recurrent events is usually one of seconds, or minutes. To use an analogy, this subquestion compares with asking what makes a car start or stop each time we use it.

But in asking this same general question of causation ("What makes an animal fight?") we may also be referring to a longer period of time; we may mean "How has the animal, as it grew up, developed this behaviour?" This compares roughly with asking how a car has been constructed in the factory. The distinction between these two subquestions remains useful even though we know that many animals continue their development (much slowed down) even after they have attained adulthood. For instance, they may still continue to learn.

Finally, in biology, as in technology, we can extend this time scale even more, and ask: How have the animal species which we observe today—and which we know have evolved from ancestors that were different—how have they acquired their particular behaviour systems during this evolution? Unfortunately, while we know the evolution of cars because they evolved so quickly and have been so fully recorded, the behaviour of extinct animals cannot be observed, and has to be reconstructed by indirect methods.

I shall try to justify the claim I made earlier, and show how all these four questions—that of behaviour's survival value and the three subquestions of causation —have to enter into the argument if we are to understand the biology of aggression.

Let us first consider the short-term causation; the mechanism of fighting. What makes us fight at any one moment? Lorenz argues in his book that, in animals and in man, there is an internal urge to attack.

An individual does not simply wait to be provoked, but, if actual attack has not been possible for some time, this urge to fight builds up until the individual actively seeks the opportunity to indulge in fighting. Aggression, Lorenz claims, can be spontaneous.

But this view has not gone unchallenged. For instance, R. A. Hinde has written a thorough criticism,[7] based on recent work on aggression in animals, in which he writes that Lorenz's "arguments for the spontaneity of aggression do not bear examination" and that "the contrary view, expressed in nearly every textbook of comparative psychology . . ." is that fighting "derives principally from the situation"; and even more explicitly: "There is no need to postulate causes that are purely internal to the aggressor" (p. 303). At first glance it would seem as if Lorenz and Hinde disagree profoundly. I have read and re-read both authors, and it is to me perfectly clear that loose statements and misunderstandings on both sides have made it appear that there is disagreement where in fact there is something very near to a common opinion. It seems to me that the differences between the two authors lie mainly in the different ways they look at internal and external variables. This in turn seems due to differences of a semantic nature. Lorenz uses the unfortunate term "the spontaneity of aggression." Hinde takes this to mean that external stimuli are in Lorenz's view not necessary at all to make an animal fight. But here he misrepresents Lorenz, for nowhere does Lorenz claim that the internal urge ever makes an animal fight *in vacuo;* somebody or something is attacked. This misunderstanding makes Hinde feel that he has refuted Lorenz's views by saying that "fighting derives principally from the situation." But both authors are fully aware of the fact that fighting is started by a number of variables, of which some are

internal and some external. What both authors know,
and what cannot be doubted, is that fighting behaviour
is not like the simple slot machine that produces one
platform ticket every time one threepenny bit is in-
serted. To mention one animal example: a male stickleback does not always show the full fighting behaviour
in response to an approaching standard opponent; its
response varies from none at all to the optimal stimulus on some occasions, to full attack on even a crude
dummy at other times. This means that its internal
state varies, and in this particular case we know from
the work of Hoar[8] that the level of the male sex
hormone is an important variable.

Another source of misunderstanding seems to have
to do with the stretch of time that the two authors are
taking into account. Lorenz undoubtedly thinks of the
causes of an outburst of fighting in terms of seconds,
or hours—perhaps days. Hinde seems to think of
events which may have happened further back in
time; an event which is at any particular moment
"internal" may well in its turn have been influenced
previously by external agents. In our stickleback example, the level of male sex hormone is influenced by
external agents such as the length of the daily exposure to light over a period of a month or so.[9] Or, less
far back in time, its readiness to attack may have
been influenced by some experience gained, say, half
an hour before the fight.

I admit that I have now been spending a great deal
of time on what would seem to be a perfectly simple
issue: the very first step in the analysis of the short-
term causation, which is to distinguish at any given
moment between variables within the animal and
variables in the environment. It is of course important
for our further understanding to unravel the complex
interactions between these two worlds, and in par-

ticular the physiology of aggressive behaviour. A great deal is being discovered about this, but for my present issue there is no use discussing it as long as even the first step in the analysis has not led to a clearly expressed and generally accepted conclusion. We must remember that we are at the moment concerned with the human problem: "What makes men attack each other?" And for this problem the answer to the first stage of our question is of prime importance: Is our readiness to start an attack constant or not? If it were —if our aggressive behaviour were the outcome of an apparatus with the properties of the slot machine— all we would have to do would be to control the external situation: to stop providing threepenny bits. But since our readiness to start an attack is variable, further studies of both the external and the internal variables are vital to such issues as: Can we reduce fighting by lowering the population density, or by withholding provocative stimuli? Can we do so by changing the hormone balance or other physiological variables? Can we perhaps in addition control our development in such a way as to change the dependence on internal and external factors in adult man? However, before discussing development, I must first return to the fact that I have mentioned before, namely, that man is, among the thousands of other species that fight, the only mass murderer. How do animals in their intraspecific disputes avoid bloodshed?

THE IMPORTANCE OF "FEAR"

The clue to this problem is to recognize the simple fact that aggression in animals rarely occurs in pure form; it is only one of two components of an adaptive system. This is most clearly seen in territorial behaviour, although it is also true of most other types of hostile behaviour. Members of territorial species divide themselves among the available living space and opportunities by each individual defending its home range against competitors. Now in this system of parcelling our living space, avoidance plays as important a part as attack. Put very briefly, animals of territorial species, once they have settled on a territory, attack intruders, but an animal that is still searching for a suitable territory or finds itself outside its home range withdraws when it meets with an already established owner. In terms of function, once you have taken possession of a territory, it pays to drive off competitors; but when you are still looking for a territory (or meet your neighbour at your common boundary), your chances of success are improved by avoiding such established owners. The ruthless fighter who "knows no fear" does not get very far. For an understanding of what follows, this fact, that hostile clashes are controlled by what we could call the "attack-avoidance system," is essential.

When neighbouring territory owners meet near their common boundary, both attack behaviour and withdrawal behaviour are elicited in both animals; each of the two is in a state of motivational conflict. We know a great deal about the variety of movements that appear when these two conflicting, incompatible behaviours are elicited. Many of these expressions of a motivational conflict have, in the course of evolution, acquired signal function; in colloquial language, they signal "Keep out!" We deduce this from the fact that opponents respond to them in an appropriate way: instead of proceeding to intrude, which would require the use of force, trespassers withdraw, and neighbours are contained by each other. This is how such animals have managed to have all the advantges of their hostile behaviour without the disadvantages: they divide their living space in a bloodless way by using as distance-keeping devices these conflict movements ("threat") rather than actual fighting (Plates 26, 27 and 28).

GROUP TERRITORIES

In order to see our wars in their correct biological perspective one more comparison with animals is useful. So far I have discussed animal species that defend individual or at best pair territories. But there are also animals which possess and defend territories belonging to a group, or a clan.[10]

Now it is an essential aspect of group territorialism that the members of a group unite when in hostile confrontation with another group that approaches, or crosses into their feeding territory. The uniting and the aggression are equally important. It is essential to realize that group territorialism does not exclude hostile relations on lower levels when the group is on its own. For instance, within a group there is often a peck order. And within the group there may be individual or pair territories. But frictions due to these relationships fade away during a clash between groups. This temporary elimination is done by means of so-called appeasement and reassurance signals. They indicate "I am a friend," and so diminish the risk that, in the general flare-up of anger, any animal "takes it out" on a fellow member of the same group.[11] Clans meet clans as units, and each individual in an intergroup clash, while united with its fellow members, is (as in inter-individual clashes) torn between attack and withdrawal, and postures and shouts rather than attacks.

We must now examine the hypothesis (which I

consider the most likely one) that man still carries with him the animal heritage of group territoriality. This is a question concerning man's evolutionary origin, and here we are, by the very nature of the subject, forced to speculate. Because I am going to say something about the behaviour of our ancestors of, say, 100,000 years ago, I have to discuss briefly a matter of methodology. It is known to all biologists (but unfortunately unknown to most psychologists) that comparison of present-day species can give us a deep insight, with a probability closely approaching certainty, into the evolutionary history of animal species. Even where fossil evidence is lacking, this comparative method alone can do this. It has to be stressed that this comparison is a highly sophisticated method, and not merely a matter of saying that species A is different from species B.[12] The basic procedure is this. We interpret differences between really allied species as the result of adaptive divergent evolution from common stock, and we interpret similarities between non-allied species as adaptive convergencies to similar ways of life. By studying the adaptive functions of species characteristics we understand how natural selection can have produced both these divergencies and convergencies. To mention one striking example: even if we had no fossil evidence, we could, by this method alone, recognise whales for what they are—mammals that have returned to the water, and, in doing so, have developed some similarities to fish. This special type of comparison, which has been applied so successfully by students of the structure of animals, has now also been used, and with equal success, in several studies of animal behaviour. Two approaches have been applied. One is to see in what respects species of very different origin have convergently adapted to a similar way of life. Von Haartman[13] has applied this to a study of birds of many types that nest in holes—an anti-predator safety device. All such hole-nesters center their territorial fighting on a suitable nest hole. Their courtship consists of luring a female to this hole (often with the use of bright colour patterns). Their young gape when a general darkening signals the arrival of the parent. All but the most recently adapted species lay uniformly coloured, white or light blue eggs that can easily be seen by the parent.

An example of adaptive divergence has been studied by Cullen.[14] Among all the gulls, the kittiwake is unique in that it nests on very narrow ledges on sheer cliffs. Over twenty peculiarities of this species have been recognised by Mrs. Cullen as vital adaptations to this particular habitat.

These and several similar studies[15] demonstrate how comparison reveals, in each species, systems of interrelated and very intricate adaptive features. In this work, speculation is now being followed by careful experimental checking. It would be tempting to elaborate on this, but I must return to our own unfortunate species.

Now, when we include the "Naked Ape" in our comparative studies, it becomes likely (as has been recently worked out in great detail by Morris) that man is a "social Ape who has turned carnivore."[16] On the one hand he is a social primate; on the other, he has developed similarities to wolves, lions and hyenas. In our present context one thing seems to stand out clearly, a conclusion that seems to me of paramount importance to all of us, and yet has not yet been fully accepted as such. As a social, hunting primate, man must originally have been organised on the principle of group territories.

Ethologists tend to believe that we still carry with

us a number of behavioural characteristics of our animal ancestors, which cannot be eliminated by different ways of upbringing, and that our group territorialism is one of those ancestral characters. I shall discuss the problem of the modifiability of our behaviour later, but it is useful to point out here that even if our behaviour were much more modifiable then Lorenz maintains, our cultural evolution, which resulted in the parcelling-out of our living space on lines of tribal, national and now even "bloc" areas, would, if anything, have tended to enhance group territorialism.

GROUP TERRITORIALISM IN MAN?

I put so much emphasis on this issue of group territorialism because most writers who have tried to apply ethology to man have done this in the wrong way. They have made the mistake, to which I objected before, of uncritically extrapolating the results of animal studies to man. They try to explain man's behaviour by using facts that are valid only of some of the animals we studied. And, as ethologists keep stressing, no two species behave alike. Therefore, instead of taking this easy way out, we ought to study man in his own right. And I repeat that the message of the ethologists is that the methods, rather than the results, of ethology should be used for such a study.

Now, the notion of territory was developed by zoologists (to be precise, by ornithologists[17]), and because individual and pair territories are found in so many more species than group territories (which are particularly rare among birds), most animal studies were concerned with such individual and pair territories. Now such low-level territories do occur in man, as does another form of hostile behaviour, the peck order. But the problems created by such low-level frictions are not serious; they can, within a community, be kept in check by the apparatus of law and order; peace within national boundaries can be enforced. In order to understand what makes us go to war, we have to recognise that man behaves very much like a group-territorial species. We too unite in the face of an outside danger to the group; we "forget our differences." We too have threat gestures, for instance, angry facial expressions. And all of us use reassurance and appeasement signals, such as a friendly smile. And (unlike speech) these are universally understood; they are cross-cultural; they are species-specific. And, incidentally, even with a group sharing a common language, they are often more reliable guides to a man's intentions than speech, for speech (as we know now) rarely reflects our true motives, but our facial expressions often "give us away."

If I may digress for a moment: it is humiliating to us ethologists that many non-scientists, particularly novelists and actors, intuitively understand our sign language much better than we scientists ourselves do. Worse, there is a category of human beings who understand intuitively more about the causation of our aggressive behaviour: the great demagogues. They have applied this knowledge in order to control our behaviour in the most clever ways, and often for the most evil purposes. For instance, Hitler (who had modern mass communication at his disposal, which allowed him to inflame a whole nation) played on both fighting tendencies. The "defensive" fighting was whipped up by his passionate statements about "living space," "encirclement," Jewry and Freemasonry as threatening powers which made the Germans feel "cornered." The "attack fighting" was similarly set ablaze by playing the myth of the Herrenvolk. We must make sure that mankind has learned its lesson and will never forget how disastrous the joint effects have been—if only one of the major nations were led now by a man like Hitler, life on earth would be wiped out.

I have argued my case for concentrating on studies of group territoriality rather than on other types of aggression. I must now return, in this context, to the problem of man the mass murderer. Why don't we settle even our international disputes by the relatively harmless, animal method of threat? Why have we become unhinged so that so often our attack erupts without being kept in check by fear? It is not that we have no fear, or that we have no other inhibitions against killing. This problem has to be considered first of all in the general context of the consequences of man having embarked on a new type of evolution.

CULTURAL EVOLUTION

Man has the ability, unparalleled in scale in the animal kingdom, of passing on his experiences from one generation to the next. By this accumulative and exponentially growing process, which we call cultural evolution, he has been able to change his environment progressively out of all recognition. And this includes the social environment. This new type of evolution proceeds at an incomparably faster pace than genetic evolution. Genetically we have not evolved very strikingly since Cro-Magnon man, but culturally we have changed beyond recognition, and are changing at an ever increasing rate. It is of course true that we are highly adjustable individually, and so could hope to keep pace with these changes. But I am not alone in believing that this behavioural adjustability, like all types of modifiability, has its limits. These limits are imposed upon us by our hereditary constitution, a constitution which can only change with the far slower speed of genetic evolution. There are good grounds for the conclusion that man's limited behavioural adjustability has been outpaced by the culturally determined changes in his social environment, and that this is why man is now a misfit in his own society.

We can now, at last, return to the problem of war, of uninhibited mass killing. It seems quite clear that our cultural evolution is at the root of the trouble. It is our cultural evolution that has caused the population explosion. In a nutshell, medical science, aiming at the reduction of suffering, has, in doing so, prolonged life for many individuals as well—prolonged it to well beyond the point at which they produce offspring. Unlike the situation in any wild species, recruitment to the human population consistently surpasses losses through mortality. Agricultural and technical know-how have enabled us to grow food and to exploit other natural resources to such an extent that we can still feed (though only just) the enormous numbers of human beings on our crowded planet. The result is that we now live at a far higher density than that in which genetic evolution has moulded our species. Higher density leads inevitably to more frequent, in fact almost continuous inter-group contact, and so to more frequent external provocation. Improved long-distance communication enables us at the same time to form much larger in-groups than in the past, and it also allows rapid mobilisation of an entire in-group, or nation, for purposes of war.

Yet increased density alone would not necessarily cause more actual intraspecific killing; we still have to understand how it came about that, beyond an increase in inter-group brawls or threatening bouts (as we find in group-territorial animals), we find, in man alone, this frequent wholesale killing of other men. Clearly in man the balance between aggression and factors which keep it in check (such as fear and the responses to appeasement) can readily be upset in favour of aggression. This must be a consequence of our cultural evolution. A few ways in which typically human traits could have produced this unbalance can readily be suggested with reasonable confidence. First of all, the simplest human aggressive act, the fist blow—which stuns and intimidates rather than kills—could easily have become a killing act at the time when man first began to use simple stone implements. Once this happened, another uniquely human attribute would sooner or later come into play: the ability to learn that a dead man does not return, and to act on this knowledge. It is only in the most recent phase of human history that the saying "War does not pay" has actually come true—for many centuries war *did* pay. Although a death does occasionally occur in inter-group or inter-individual fights between animals, there is no evidence that this turns any animal into a killer. The inference that the invention and perfection of long-range weapons have made the act of killing an easier one to commit (by keeping the aggressor away from danger and from the expressions of appeasement and distress of his victims) has been drawn so often that it need hardly be mentioned here. Very few airmen who are willing enough to drop their bombs "on target" could bring themselves to strangle, stab or burn children (or, for that matter, adults) with their own hands.

Once fighting groups have become hierarchically organised (as must have occurred already in the remote past) and once speech had evolved, a social system could develop whereby soldiers could be made to kill with little inhibition. This is achieved by intimidation and brainwashing. The fact that soldiers are often forced to overcome their fear of the enemy by the threat of being executed for cowardice is too well known to require elaboration. Soldiers are also brainwashed into the belief that running away—originally, as we have seen, an adapted type of behaviour—is despicable, "cowardly." It seems that man, accepting that in moral issues death may be preferable to flight, has falsely applied the moral concept of "cowardice" to matters of merely practical significance, such as the division of living space.

Finally, it seems that man stands alone in being able to fuse all his aggressive motivations, i.e., all motivations that "employ" aggressive acts of one kind or another, into one over-all monster motivation. Acts that lead to injury or death of other individuals may, in most animals, be performed in a variety of motivational contexts: they are used not only in intraspecific encounters, but also when dealing with a parasite, with a prey, or when resisting "with the courage of despair" an attack by a predator. While intraspecific fighting is usually kept in check by fear, no or few such inhibitions operate in relation to these other activities.

By systematically being taught to treat their opponent as "vermin," as "monsters"—in short, as nonhuman adversaries—soldiers are made to fight without inhibition. The less human one considers one's opponent, the more ready is one to kill him. But when a predatory animal is engaged in an intraspecific territorial clash, it is, if anything, less likely to kill a prey for food than when it is alone; such different motivational states as intraspecific aggression and hunger are usually mutually exclusive (which ensures that an animal normally does "one thing at a time"). The fusion of a number of normally independent motivations that "employ" the same motor pattern into one super-motivation is somehow more easily achieved in man than in animals.

Finally, as we all know, the most embittered wars were fought over religious issues. Towards an explanation of this, and of the equally fierce inter-racial type of warfare, the animal ethologist can as yet contribute little. But neither have other disciplines succeeded in explaining these aspects of war in scientific terms. The truth is that we still know very little with certainty about either the "animal roots" of our behaviour or our culturally determined transformation to "the killing ape." We should acknowledge this ignorance and intensify the study of both our animal heritage and the cultural evolution of our behaviour. In that study, biological methods such as are being applied in animal ethology may well be of considerable value.

There is a frightening, and ironical paradox in this conclusion: that the human brain, the finest life-preserving device created by evolution, has made our species so successful in mastering the outside world that it suddenly finds itself taken off guard. One could say that our cortex and our brainstem (our "reason" and our "instincts") are at loggerheads. Together they have created a new social environment in which, rather than ensuring our survival, they are about to do the opposite. The brain finds itself seriously threatened by an enemy of its own making. It is its own enemy. We simply have to understand this enemy.

THE DEVELOPMENT OF BEHAVIOUR

I must now leave the question of the moment-to-moment control of fighting, and, looking further back in time, turn to the development of aggressive behaviour in the growing individual. Again we will start from the human problem. This, in the present context, is whether it is within our power to control development in such a way that we reduce or eliminate fighting among adults. Can or cannot education in the widest sense produce non-aggressive men?

The first step in the consideration of this problem is again to distinguish between external and internal influences, but now we must apply this to the growth, the changing, of the behavioural machinery during the individual's development. Here again the way in which we phrase our questions and our conclusions is of the utmost importance.

In order to discuss this issue fruitfully, I have to start once more by considering it in a wider context, which is now that of the "nature-nurture" problem with respect to behaviour in general. This has been discussed more fully by Lorenz in his book *Evolution and Modification of Behaviour;*[18] for a discussion of the environmentalist point of view I refer to the various works of Schneirla.[19]

Lorenz tends to classify behaviour types into innate and acquired or learned behaviour. Schneirla rejects this dichotomy into two classes of behaviour. He stresses that the developmental process, of behaviour as well as of other functions, should be considered, and also that this development forms a highly complicated series of interactions between the growing organism and its environment. I have gradually become convinced that the clue to this difference in approach is to be found in a difference in aims between the two authors. Lorenz claims that "we are justified in leaving, at least for the time being, to the care of the experimental embryologists all those questions which are concerned with the chains of physiological causation leading from the genome to the development of . . . neurosensory structures" (p. 43). In other words, he deliberately refrains from starting his analysis of development prior to the stage at which a fully co-ordinated behaviour is performed for the first time. If one in this way restricts one's studies to the later stages of development, then a classification in "innate" and "learned" behaviour, or behaviour components, can be considered quite justified. And there was a time, some thirty years ago, when the almost grotesquely environmentalist bias of psychology made it imperative for ethologists to stress the extent to which behaviour patterns could appear in perfect or near-perfect form without the aid of anything that could be properly called learning. But I now agree (however belatedly) with Schneirla that we must extend our interest to earlier stages of development and embark on a full program of experimental embryology of behaviour. When we do this, we discover that interactions with the environment can indeed occur at early stages. These interactions may concern small components of the total machinery of a fully functional behaviour pattern, and many of them cannot possibly be called learning. But they are interactions with the environment, and must be taken into account if we follow in the footsteps of the experimental embryologists, and extend our field of interest to the entire sequence of events which lead from the blueprints contained in the zygote to the fully functioning, behaving animal. We simply have to do this if we want an answer to the question to what extent the development of behaviour can be influenced from the outside.

When we follow this procedure the rigid distinction between "innate" or unmodifiable and "acquired" or modifiable behaviour patterns becomes far less sharp. This is owing to the discovery, on the one hand, that "innate" patterns may contain elements that at an early stage developed in interaction with the environment, and, on the other hand, that learning is, from step to step, limited by internally imposed restrictions.

To illustrate the first point, I take the development of the sensory cells in the retina of the eye. Knoll has shown[20] that the rods in the eyes of tadpoles cannot function properly unless they have first been exposed to light. This means that, although any visually guided response of a tadpole may well, in its integrated form, be "innate" in Lorenz's sense, it is so only in the sense of "non-learned," not in that of "having grown without interaction with the environment." Now it has been shown by Cullen[21] that male sticklebacks reared from the egg in complete isolation from other animals will, when adult, show full fighting behaviour to other males and courtship behaviour to females when faced with them for the first time in their lives. This is admittedly an important fact, demonstrating that the various recognised forms of learning do not enter into the programming of these integrated patterns. This is a demonstration of what Lorenz calls an "innate response." But it does not exclude the possibility that parts of the machinery so employed may, at an earlier stage, have been influenced by the environment, as in the case of the tadpoles.

Second, there are also behaviour patterns which do appear in the inexperienced animal, but in an incomplete form, and which require additional development through learning. Thorpe has analysed a clear example of this: when young male chaffinches reared alone begin to produce their song for the first time, they utter a very imperfect warble; this develops into the full song only if, at a certain sensitive stage, the young birds have heard the full song of an adult male.[22]

By far the most interesting aspect of such intermediates between innate and acquired behaviour is the fact that learning is not indiscriminate, but is guided by a certain selectiveness on the part of the animal. This fact has been dimly recognised long ago; the early ethologists have often pointed out that different, even closely related, species learn different things even when developing the same behaviour patterns. This has been emphasised by Lorenz's use of the term "innate teaching mechanism." Other authors use the word "template" in the same context. The best example I know is once more taken from the development of song in certain birds. As I have mentioned, the males of some birds acquire their full song by changing their basic repertoire to resemble the song of adults, which they have to hear during a special sensitive period some months before they sing themselves. It is in this sensitive period that they acquire, without as yet producing the song, the knowledge of "what the song ought to be like." In technical terms, the bird formed a *Sollwert*[23] (literally, "should-value," an ideal) for the feedback they receive when they hear their own first attempts. Experiments have shown[24] that such birds, when they start to sing, do three things: they listen to what they produce; they notice the difference between this feedback and the ideal song; and they correct their next performance.

This example, while demonstrating an internal teaching mechanism, shows, at the same time, that Lorenz made his concept too narrow when he coined the term "innate teaching mechanism." The birds have developed a teaching mechanism, but while it is true that it is internal, it is not innate; the birds have acquired it by listening to their father's song.

These examples show that if behaviour studies are to catch up with experimental embryology our aims, our concepts and our terms must be continually revised.

Before returning to aggression, I should like to elaborate a little further on general aspects of behaviour development, because this will enable me to show the value of animal studies in another context, that of education.

Comparative studies, of different animal species, of different behaviour patterns and of different stages of development, begin to suggest that wherever learning takes a hand in development, it is guided by such *Sollwerte* or templates for the proper feedback, the feedback that reinforces. And it becomes clear that these various *Sollwerte* are of a bewildering variety. In human education one aspect of this has been emphasised in particular, and even applied in the use of teaching machines: the requirement that the reward, in order to have maximum effect, must be immediate. Skinner has stressed this so much because in our own teaching we have imposed an unnatural delay between, say, taking in homework, and giving the pupil his reward in the form of a mark. But we can learn more from animal studies than the need for immediacy of reward. The type of reward is also of great importance, and this may vary from task to task, from stage to stage, from occasion to occasion; the awards may be of almost infinite variety.

Here I have to discuss briefly a behaviour of which I have so far been unable to find the equivalent in the development of structure. This is exploratory behaviour. By this we mean a kind of behaviour in which the animal sets out to acquire as much information about an object or a situation as it can possibly get. The behaviour is intricately adapted to this end, and it terminates when the information has been stored, when the animal has incorporated it in its learned knowledge. This exploration (subjectively we speak of "curiosity") is not confined to the acquisition of information about the external world alone; at least mammals explore their own movements a great deal, and in this way "master new skills." Again, in this exploratory behaviour, *Sollwerte* of expected, "hoped-for" feedbacks play their part.

Without going into more detail, we can characterise the picture we begin to get of the development of behaviour as a series, or rather a web, of events, starting with innate programming instructions contained in the zygote, which straightaway begin to interact with the environment; this interaction may be discontinuous, in that periods of predominantly internal development alternate with periods of interaction, or sensitive periods. The interaction is enhanced by active exploration; it is steered by selective *Sollwerte* of great variety; and stage by stage this process ramifies; level upon level of ever increasing complexity is being incorporated into the programming.

Apply what we have heard for a moment to playing children (I do not, of course, distinguish sharply between "play" and "learning"). At a certain age a child begins to use, say, building blocks. It will at first manipulate them in various ways, one at a time. Each way of manipulating acts as exploratory behaviour: the child learns what a block looks, feels, tastes like and so forth, and so how to put it down so that it stands stably.

Each of these stages "peters out" when the child knows what it wanted to find out. But as the development proceeds, a new level of exploration is added: the child discovers that it can put one block on top of the other; it constructs. The new discovery leads to repetition and variation, for each child develops, at some stage, a desire and a set of *Sollwerte* for such effects of construction, and acts out to the full this new level of exploratory behaviour. In addition, already at this stage the *Sollwert* or ideal does not merely contain what the blocks do, but also what, for instance, the mother does; her approval, her shared enjoyment, is also of great importance. Just as an exploring animal, the child builds a kind of inverted pyramid of experience, built of layers, each set off by a new wave of exploration and each directed by new sets of *Sollwerte*, and so its development "snowballs." All these phases may well have more or less limited sensitive periods, which determine when the fullest effect can be obtained, and when the child is ready for the next step. More important still, if the opportunity for the next stage is offered either too early or too late, development may be damaged, including the development of motivational and emotional attitudes.

Of course gifted teachers of many generations have known all these things[25] or some of them, but the glimpses of insight have not been fully and scientifically systematised. In human education, this would of course involve experimentation. This need not worry us too much, because in our search for better educational procedures we are in effect experimenting on our children all the time. Also, children are fortunately incredibly resilient, and most grow up into pretty viable adults in spite of our fumbling educational efforts. Yet there is, of course, a limit to what we will allow ourselves, and this, I should like to emphasise, is where animal studies may well become even more important than they are already.

CAN EDUCATION END AGGRESSION?

Returning now to the development of animal and human aggression, I hope to have made at least several things clear: that behaviour development is a very complex phenomenon indeed; that we have only begun to analyse it in animals; that with respect to man we are, if anything, behind in comparison with animal studies; and that I cannot do otherwise than repeat what I said in the beginning: we must make a major research effort. In this effort animal studies can help, but we are still very far from drawing very definite conclusions with regard to our question: To what extent shall we be able to render man less aggressive through manipulation of the environment, that is, by educational measures?

In such a situation personal opinions naturally vary a great deal. I do not hesitate to give as my personal opinion that Lorenz's book *On Aggression*, in spite of its assertativeness, in spite of factual mistakes and in spite of the many possibilities of misunderstandings that are due to the lack of a common language among students of behaviour—that this work must be taken more seriously as a positive contribution to our problem than many critics have done. Lorenz is, in my opinion, right in claiming that elimination, through education, of the internal urge to fight will turn out to be very difficult, if not impossible.

Everything I have said so far seems to me to allow for only one conclusion. Apart from doing our utmost to return to a reasonable population density, apart from stopping the progressive depletion and pollution of our habitat, we must pursue the biological study of animal behaviour for clarifying problems of human behaviour of such magnitude as that of our aggression, and of education.

But research takes a long time, and we must remember that there are experts who forecast worldwide famine ten to twenty years from now; and that we have enough weapons to wipe out all human life on earth. Whatever the causation of our aggression, the simple fact is that for the time being we are saddled with it. This means that there is a crying need for a crash program, for finding ways and means for keeping our inter-group aggression in check. This is of course in practice infinitely more difficult than controlling our intra-national frictions; we have as yet not got a truly international police force. But there is hope for avoiding all-out war because, for the first time in history, we are afraid of killing ourselves by the lethal radiation effects even of bombs that we could drop in the enemy's territory. Our politicians know this. And as long as there is this hope, there is every reason to try and learn what we can from animal studies. Here again they can be of help. We have already seen that animal opponents meeting in a hostile clash avoid bloodshed by using the expressions of their motivational conflicts as intimidating signals. Ethologists have studied such conflict movements in some detail,[26] and have found that they are of a variety of types. The most instructive of these is the redirected attack; instead of attacking the provoking, yet dreaded, opponent, animals often attack some-

thing else, often even an inanimate object. We ourselves bang the table with our fists. Redirection includes something like sublimation, a term attaching
a value judgement to the redirection. As a species with
group territories, humans, like hyenas, unite when
meeting a common enemy. We do already sublimate
our group aggression. The Dutch feel united in their
fight against the sea. Scientists do attack their problems together. The space program—surely a mainly
military effort—is an up-to-date example. I would not
like to claim, as Lorenz does, that redirected attack
exhausts the aggressive urge. We know from soccer
matches and from animal work how aggressive behaviour has two simultaneous but opposite effects: a
waning effect, and one of self-inflammation, of mass
hysteria, such as recently seen in Cairo. Of these two
the inflammatory effect often wins. But if aggression
were used successfully as the motive force behind
non-killing and even useful activities, self-stimulation
need not be a danger; in our short-term cure we are
not aiming at the elimination of aggressiveness, but
at "taking the sting out of it."

Of all sublimated activities, scientific research
would seem to offer the best opportunities for deflect-
ing and sublimating our aggression. And, once we
recognise that it is the disrupted relation between our
own behaviour and our environment that forms our
most deadly enemy, what could be better than uniting, at the front or behind the lines, in the scientific
attack on our own behavioural problems?

I stress "behind the lines." The whole population
should be made to feel that it participates in the
struggle. This is why scientists will always have the
duty to inform their fellow men of what they are doing, of the relevance and the importance of their

work. And this is not only a duty, it can give intense satisfaction.

I have come full circle. For both the long-term and the short-term remedies at least we scientists will have to sublimate our aggression into an all-out attack on the enemy within. For this the enemy must be recognised for what it is: our unknown selves, or, deeper down, our refusal to admit that man is, to himself, unknown.

I should like to conclude by saying a few words to my colleagues of the younger generation. Of course we all hope that, by muddling along until we have acquired better understanding, self-annihilation either by the "whimper of famine" or by the "bang of war" can be avoided. For this, we must on the one hand trust, on the other help (and urge) our politicians. But it is no use denying that the chances of designing the necessary preventive measures are small, let alone the chances of carrying them out. Even birth control still offers a major problem

It is difficult for my generation to know how seriously you take the danger of mankind destroying his own species. But those who share the apprehension of my generation might perhaps, with us, derive strength from keeping alive the thought that has helped so many of us in the past when faced with the possibility of imminent death. Scientific research is one of the finest occupations of our mind. It is, with art and religion, one of the uniquely human ways of meeting nature, in fact, the most active way. If we are to succumb, and even if this were to be ultimately due to our own stupidity, we could still, so to speak, redeem our species. We could at least go down with some dignity, by using our brain for one of its supreme tasks, by exploring to the end.

FIG. 6-1: *Fighting male iguanas in threatening combat posture* (top) *and after the fight* (bottom), *with the vanquished lizard lying submissively in front of the victor* (according to Eibl-Eibesfeldt).

REFERENCES

1. A. Carrel, *L'Homme, cet Inconnu* (Librairie Plon, Paris, 1935).
2. AAAS Annual Meeting, 1967 [see *New Scientist* 37, 5 (1968)].
3. R. Carson, *Silent Spring* (Houghton Mifflin, Boston, 1962).
4. K. Lorenz, *On Aggression* (Methuen, London, 1966).
5. D. Morris, *The Naked Ape* (Jonathan Cape, London, 1967).
6. N. Tinbergen, Z. *Tierpsychol.* 20, 410 (1964).
7. R. A. Hinde, *New Society* 9, 302 (1967).

8. W. S. Hoar, *Animal Behaviour* 10, 247 (1962).
9. B. Baggerman, in *Symp. Soc. Exp. Biol.* 20, 427 (1965).
10. H. Kruuk, *New Scientist* 30, 849 (1966).
11. N. Tinbergen, *Z. Tierpsychol.* 16, 651 (1959); *Zool. Mededelingen* 39, 209 (1964).
12. ——, *Behaviour* 15, 1–70 (1959).
13. L. von Haartman, *Evolution* 11, 339 (1957).
14. E. Cullen, *Ibis* 99, 275 (1957).
15. J. H. Crook, *Symp. Zool. Soc. London* 14, 181 (1965).
16. D. Freeman, *Inst. Biol. Symp.* 13, 109 (1964); D. Morris, Ed., *Primate Ethology* (Weidenfeld and Nicolson, London, 1967).
17. H. E. Howard, *Territory in Bird Life* (Murray, London, 1920); R. A. Hinde *et al.*, *Ibis* 98, 340–530 (1956).
18. K. Lorenz, *Evolution and Modification of Behaviour* (Methuen, London, 1966).
19. T. C. Schneirla, *Quart. Rev. Biol.* 41, 283 (1966).
20. M. D. Knoll, *Z. Vergleich. Physiol.* 38, 219 (1956).
21. E. Cullen, *Final Rept. Contr. AF 61* (052)-29, USA-FRDC, 1–23 (1961).
22. W. H. Thorpe, *Bird–Song* (Cambridge Univ. Press, New York, 1961).
23. E. von Holst and H. Mittelstaedt, *Naturwissenschaften* 37, 464 (1950).
24. M. Konishi, *Z. Tierpsychol.* 22, 770 (1965); F. Nottebohm, *Proc. 14th Intern. Ornithol. Congr.*, 265–280 (1967).
25. E. M. Standing, *Maria Montessori* (New American Library, New York, 1962).
26. N. Tinbergen, in *The Pathology and Treatment of Sexual Deviation*, I. Rosen, Ed. (Oxford Univ. Press, London, 1964), 3–23; N. B. Jones, *Wildfowl Trust 11th Ann. Rept.*, 46–52 (1960); P. Sevenster, *Behaviour*, *Suppl.* 9, 1–170 (1961); F. Rowell, *Animal Behaviour*, 9, 38 (1961).

WOLFGANG WICKLER

Group Ties in Animals and Man

A flock of pigeons flying together or many hundreds of bees crawling about on a honeycomb is such a familiar sight that it hardly causes us to wonder what actually makes it possible. For there is nothing self-evident about it. One only has to put a bee from another hive among those hundreds to see how the outsider is killed by the other members of its own species. And when a young pigeon is put in an alien pigeon nest, it is scalped by the parent birds. The same kind of thing happens to many animals when they stray among others of the same species; on the other hand, there are species in which regroupings are accomplished without strife and which readily tolerate individuals from other groups of the same species.

It is possible to draw up a classification of social systems solely on the criterion whether or not the animals in question live socially with others of their own species, whether they are equally tolerant of all individuals of the species and by what method they distinguish the members of their own group from outsiders. Only, it must be borne in mind that one and the same species may, at different times, belong to different categories as conceived here. Young animals often behave differently from adults, males differently from females, the same individuals differently in the mating season than at other times.

In the first place, there are pseudo-societies, assemblies of animals of the same or different species, which arise from sharing a common aim or desire and are held together only by it. An example of this is afforded by vultures congregating on carrion; but a stork, too, is not so much "married" to its mate as to the same nest as the latter. Each bird will defend the nest against intruders of the same sex, and it reportedly makes little difference when one or other of the birds in a couple is replaced by another individual of the same sex.

Societies are to be distinguished from mere assemblies of individuals in that, in the former, there is an attraction between members of the same species. A large number of individuals may exercise a more powerful attraction than a small number (this is, for example, the case with shoals of fish); quite often, too, animals of the same age or the same size congregate together. These societies of animals, to which the adjective "social" is commonly applied, may be subdivided as follows:

A. OPEN SOCIETIES or "aggregations":

1. OPEN ANONYMOUS SOCIETIES: Typical examples are flocks of birds and shoals of fish; also certain migratory herds of mammals. The individuals in such groups are entirely interchangeable without causing any change in the behaviour of the flock, shoal or herd as a whole.

2. OPEN NON-ANONYMOUS SOCIETIES: These are exemplified by nesting and breeding colonies (consist-

ing of pairs, i.e., mating couples, in the case of gulls, or only of male individuals in the case of certain fish species, such as the painted perch, which hatch out the eggs in the mouth) whose members know at least their immediate and somewhat more distant neighbours. However, nothing changes in the behaviour pattern of the colony if some of its members are removed; newcomers who come to occupy places left vacant by departures are accepted after a short period of making acquaintance.

B. CLOSED SOCIETIES: These are characterised in that the animals living in them behave in a distinctly different manner towards members of the society as compared with their behaviour towards outsiders of the same species. Thus there are two kinds of individual: members of one's own society and non-members, i.e., insiders and outsiders. The latter are always attacked and driven out or even killed. According to the manner in which the individuals know and recognise one another, the following types of closed society are to be distinguished:

1. ANONYMOUS CLOSED SOCIETIES: Their members know one another by general, i.e., non-individual, characteristics—usually a distinctive tribal or nest smell. Typical examples are colonies of rats or insect communities. They are energetically defended against all intruders that are recognisably outsiders. However, non-member individuals can artificially be given the "badge of membership" and are then tolerated. Conversely, members can be "deprived of membership" by artificially removing or suppressing their distinctive smell, in which case they are treated as outsiders. In such experiments the members are freely interchangeable.

2. INDIVIDUALISED CLOSED SOCIETIES OR "GROUPS": The members of such societies know one another individually and are not interchangeable. Only in this category does it occur that removal of a member may change the behaviour of the other group members, who may, for example, start searching.

These categories have been listed in the order of increasing specialisation (in the sense of specific significance of the individual in relation to the society as a whole). This order also reflects an ascent to more and more highly developed species, both within the animal kingdom as a whole and within particular classes or families. It seldom occurs, however, that the next higher form of social behaviour evolves from the preceding one. This order of enumeration therefore represents progressively higher levels of development, but not successive evolutionary stages.

Of especial interest are those mechanisms which ensure the coherence of such communities. From animal sociology as a whole it is known that the group in which a species normally lives is in fact the smallest viable unit in which that species can survive; solitary individuals of such species usually soon die, either because they fall victims to enemies or because they are unable by themselves to obtain sufficient food, while furthermore they lack adequate opportunity to find a mate and thus propagate the species. On the other hand, however, the mutual inter-group repulsion of animals of the same species is advantageous to the geographical spread of the species. In higher animals this principle—probably a phylogenetically very old "invention"—manifests itself regularly in what is, in its most familiar form, known as aggression. Now if the group is the smallest viable unit of the species, it follows that groups as such must repel one another. For this the aggressive behaviour between members of the same species must, on the one hand, be preserved; but within the group it must, on the other hand, be suitably mitigated or suppressed. Also, the flight reaction in the presence of an aggressor must be suppressed with regard to members of the group. Flight and aggressive behaviour patterns are together referred to as agonistic behaviour. In the social life of the group there must therefore exist "anti-agonistic" or group-preserving mechanisms, i.e., behavioural elements which suppress aggression and flight reactions among the individuals of the group.

The smallest possible social community comprises two animals, normally of opposite sexes, and even within such a pair there exist the same difficulties. Species whose males and females must copulate in order to propagate the species but are too aggressive to permit mating must inevitably die out. Since the procreation of offspring in animal species living at the present time has certainly never been terminated for this reason, it follows that aggressive behaviour patterns can only have been built as a secondary phenomenon and then only to the extent that mating— be it but briefly—has remained possible. "Bad" aggression is therefore certainly younger, in evolutionary terms, than "good" peaceful living together in a community. But how does community life function in species which are aggressive in character?

MECHANISMS OF ANIMAL SOCIAL BEHAVIOUR

If, to start with, we simply observe how the partners in a pair behave towards each other as distinct from their behaviour towards other individuals of their species, we shall soon know which are the possible

anti-agonistic behaviour elements. Precisely which
one of these really has an aggression-suppressing effect will then be a matter for further investigation.

Quite often the partners of a pair are seen doing
something unitedly. In many animals these are reori-
ented aggressive actions. As a result of a slight reduction in pugnacity—e.g., due to flight or retreat
tendencies—the aggressive pattern of direct hammer-
and-tongs attack becomes directed away from the
object that initiates it; the slight tendency to retreat
from this object often manifests itself only if the creature turns its eyes away from it, often followed by
the head, until finally the creature turns its body at
an angle or presents it threateningly broadside on.
With such powerful flight or retreat tendency there
is—provided that the partner does not change its behaviour—no likelihood of attack. Often a mere suggestion of retreat causes the creature to overshoot the
"actually intended" object and instead attack a hitherto uninvolved "third party." In many species of fish,
but also in the grey goose, this pattern of threatening
behaviour that bypasses the creature's mate becomes
an action in its own right: a combined threat directed
at an—often non-existent—outsider; this joint threatening action is important in establishing the tie that
binds the two individuals together as mating partners. Between partners who already know each other
well, this behaviour is briefly indicated instead of
being actually performed in full, but is still recognisable.

The actions carried out unitedly may also derive
from nest-building activities (which perhaps only
in a remote past in the species' history were actually
done by the two partners together) or may be of as
yet unknown origin, such as the curious habit of

swans and geese of plunging their necks into the water.

A notable example of united action by mating partners is the singing of duets by birds. This is found in widely varying species, particularly in those which live in permanent monogamous "marriages." The partners sing the same phrase either alternately or simultaneously in unison or indeed even sing different parts of the same song. In the case of at least some species of shrike it is known that each of the two partners knows the whole melody and can sing both parts and that they decide only at the instant of starting their song which of the two will sing which part. Duets performed by mating partners are met with also in certain species which are not songbirds (see Fig. 7-1, for example) and even in mammals, such as the siamang, a species of gibbon monkey. The phylogenetic origins of these ceremonies have not yet been investigated. In the barbet, however, the male's part in the duet appears to have been derived from the young bird's cry for food: the adult male thus exhibits "juvenile" behaviour towards his mate. This would seem to be a more widespread habit than that of "bypass threatening," as described above.

The procedure of utilising united threatening behaviour by the two mating partners as a means of holding them together is not entirely satisfactory, inasmuch as the aggression is merely diverted but not compensated. This entails the hazard of needing the presence of a real threat from other individuals of the species in order to keep the pair together. There are indeed instances where mating pairs of fish have broken up their relationship by mutual aggression when isolated from other individuals of their species which served as scapegoats to keep the pair's aggressive instincts directed outwards, as it were.

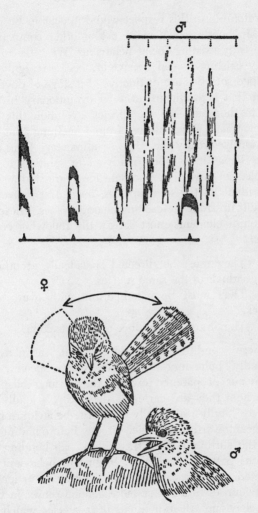

FIG. 7-1: *Mating duet of the barbet. Top: tone spectrogram showing the male (♂) and female (♀) bird's respective contributions. The female's wing movements are shown below.*

Preferable in this respect would appear to be partnership bonds which make use of other components of already existing social behaviour. We refer to "already existing" social behaviour, because highly developed societies are distinctive of a stage of development that is young in terms of evolutionary history, but in the course of the species' evolution this new development arises always from something that was previously already there, in a rudimentary form anyway. Thus there is no ready-made solution to the problem of how to compensate for aggression against individuals of the same species; instead, it is evolved or built up from pre-existing characteristics. These behavioural elements must satisfy the following conditions:

1. They must be directed specifically at other individuals of the same species.
2. They must be incompatible with overt attack.
3. They must not produce a flight reaction.

These conditions are in general satisfied by "friendly" behaviour towards one's own species. The behaviour of parents towards their young offspring for whom they are caring is decidedly "friendly" or indeed "kindly"; so usually is also the behaviour of sex partners towards each other directly before mating. As may be surmised from this, many pair-bonding behaviour patterns have their origins in behaviour associated with the care for the offspring or in mating behaviour, or in a rather more general sense: in family behaviour. All individuals of a species which are successful in being treated as members of a family can therefore, in the main, live peacefully together. Significantly, many—and perhaps even the majority—of the larger animal communities, in which a sub-

stantial number of individuals of a species live together in close proximity, have evolved from families
and sometimes form super-families with noticeable
inbreeding tendencies.

Some examples will serve to illustrate how mating
habits and parental care behaviour patterns have been
diverted into social behaviour channels. Examples
have been chosen in which the origin of the mode of
behaviour is quite clearly discernible even to the lay-
man and which moreover show how widespread this
principle underlying the structure of animal societies
is among widely differing species.

Insect colonies (e.g., termites, ants, wasps, bees
and others) originate from families, though only in
the case of termites does the male survive as "king."
In all these colonies the larvae receive mouth-to-
mouth feeding with special nutritive juices. In sub-
social wasps, for example, the adult insects feed their
mother—the founder of the group—as well as the larvae of the next brood. This group of adults is therefore, as it were, held together by the care for the
larvae. The latter excrete drops of juice which are
greatly appreciated by the adult wasps. In certain
social wasp species this larval excretion is so nutritious
that the larvae serve as a kind of food storehouse for
the colony. In the most highly developed social wasps,
but also in many other independently evolved social
insect species, the adult insects also practise mouth-to-
mouth feeding among themselves. This is perhaps the
most important bond that holds these populations together; as a secondary function, substances which are
important in connection with the formation of castes
(e.g., workers, drones, etc.) within the population are
passed from individual to individual together with
the nutritive juices.

In many bird species the begging or care-soliciting

motions of the young birds are incorporated into the mating behaviour of adults, as a direct invitation to copulation or as a greeting. Occasionally a male bird arriving with food will respond with copulation attempts to the begging of an older offspring—a clear indication that the birds are unable to distinguish between the two kinds of behaviour and can distinguish between the two different situations probably only by means of subsidiary signs. A well-known phenomenon is the mutual feeding practised by mating pairs of birds, more particularly in finches, also in pigeons, parrots and the crow family. In the case of gallinaceous birds (comprising domestic poultry, pheasants, partridges, etc.), and to some extent also in terns, it is a phenomenon of passing-on of food, not direct feeding, which is applied equally to the offspring and to the sex partner.

In some instances the practice of partner feeding, e.g., in bullfinches and some parrot species, has become ritualised into "billing," a kind of "beak flirting" in which no food is actually passed from bird to bird. Ravens similarly practise ritualised feeding. Gwinner has closely studied the pair feeding ceremony in ravens. The partners in a mating pair feed each other in exactly the same way as they feed their young. Some pairs, with beaks interlocked, were observed to push the food several times to and fro into each other's beak; later on, they "billed" also without food, and some pairs sat together with beaks interlocked for several minutes without passing food to each other or uttering feeding cries. But only some, not all, of the pairs modified the mutual feeding ceremony in this way, and from time to time all the pairs performed actual feeding in the "correct" way (see Plates 29 and 30).

A species of Australian starling (*Artamus*) has a

highly developed social life in which mutual feeding
plays a major part, for here the adults not only feed
one another as well as the young birds, but the latter
feed one another also, while furthermore there is
mutual feeding between adults not belonging to the
same mating pair, and sick birds are also fed. From
these habits a social greeting gesture has been
evolved: when a starling lands close to another bird
of the same species, it briefly makes begging motions
to the latter, which then in turn briefly responds
with begging and may even give food to the new-
comer. This begging performance is identical with
that of the young birds. Adult individuals of the
crested ibis (*Geronticus*), too, continue to make use
of the curious begging performance of the young
birds as a form of greeting between denizens of the
same nesting colony. The cuckoo (*Clamator jacobi-
nus*), which lays its eggs in other birds' nests and
does not itself do any feeding of its young, has retained the feeding habit only as a "social" function
in the mutual feeding of sex pairs in the mating season.

Comparable specialisation of behaviour is found
also in carnivores. Many of these supply their young
with food carried in the mouth or stomach. The cubs
beg for food by nuzzling the parent's lips with their
mouths, and the parent then drops the food or re-
gurgitates it. The cubs of the black-backed jackal (*C.
mesomelas*) may push their heads far into the parent's mouth if the food is not regurgitated quickly
enough. The parent animals, which form monogamous
mating pairs, greet each other by prods administered
at the corners of their mouths, but probably no food
is ever brought up on such occasions. The African
hyena dog (*Lycaon pictus*), on the other hand, lives
in closed groups comprising many individuals. It feeds

its young in the same way, but food is supplied also
to the adult animals—mostly females—which stay "at
home" to watch over the young. From the feeding
habit has evolved, phylogenetically as well as on-
togenetically, a form of greeting in which the animals
lick or bite each other's lips, but without passing food
from one to the other (Fig. 7-2). So far as is known,

FIG. 7-2: *Mouth-to-mouth feeding and greeting behaviour
in black-backed jackals (left) and hyenas (right).*

eared seals do not feed their young, but they do use
nose-prodding as a gesture of greeting, both between
mother and child and between adults. The male sea
lion (*Zalophus wollebaeki*) even uses this form of
caress to soothe quarrelling females. In these instances,
too, it is fairly certain that ritualised feeding or begging motions have been preserved as greetings, presumably derived from the practice of carrying food
to the young, as the ancestors of the seals used to do.

Mouth-to-mouth feeding of the young (with prechewed food) is done also by anthropoid apes, the chimpanzee's habits in this context being best known. From this practice the animals have derived the kiss as a gesture of greeting, in which no food is passed from mouth to mouth (Fig. 7-3). In view of all this it

FIG. 7-3: *Mouth-to-mouth feeding (right) and greeting behaviour in chimpanzees.*

can hardly be doubted that in man, too, the kiss (at any rate, the kiss on the mouth, possibly accompanied by tongue movements) is a ritualised form of mouth-to-mouth feeding drawn into the service of social life. As a matter of fact, mouth-to-mouth feeding of infants is still practised by various primitive races (Figs. 7-4 and 7-5).

In many vertebrates and invertebrates living in closed groups the mouth-to-mouth feeding of the offspring has thus evolved into a very important social behaviour pattern. In cases where the behaviour associated with the feeding of the young has been utilised also for the feeding of the adult mating partner, this latter function is in itself often merely of secondary importance; what matters more is that the partners thereby approach each other more closely and lose their mutual fear. None of the birds which, as adults, engage in mutual feeding as a preliminary to mating would die of starvation in the absence of such "social" feeding; but they would react so cau-

FIG. 7-4: *Human mouth-to-mouth feeding. From left to right: man and dog (ancient Mexican clay statuette, about three thousand years old), Papuan mother and child, Uruku Indian woman and piglet.*

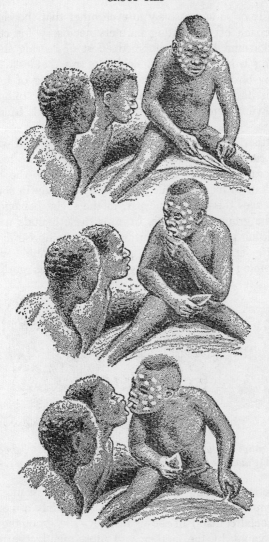

FIG. 7-5: *Ituri Pygmy distributing pieces of elephant meat by mouth-to-mouth transfer as a ritual action.*

tiously or so aggressively to each other that the close approach of the mating partners necessary for copulation and for the combined effort of rearing their young would be very difficult, to say the least. In many bird species there is no actual transfer of food from bird to bird in adults, and only the "billing" behaviour remains as the expression of social "friendliness."

Other behaviour patterns originally associated with the care for the young in the narrower or the more general sense may become incorporated into the behaviour of mating adult individuals and may in some instances thence become part of the social behaviour of the group as a whole. In birds these include nest-building movements; in primates they comprise more particularly the motion patterns associated with grooming ("delousing," Fig. 7-6). Whereas gorillas

FIG. 7-6: *Social grooming between adult female baboons (left); male baboon grooming a young animal (right).*

practise grooming only in the care of their young, in chimpanzees this activity has become mainly a means of social contact. In rhesus monkeys the grooming of the young by the mother, and subsequently the mutual grooming of parent and offspring, continues far into the latter's adult life and even undergoes further development into loose or more permanent "grooming communities" into which the mother's "acquaintances" are also admitted. This social grooming ritual serves as an outlet and a means of relaxation in a situation that might otherwise lead to an attack on members of their own species. Lemurs also groom one another (here done with the teeth) as an important social behaviour pattern that has evolved from these animals' care of their young.

When a behaviour pattern originally associated with parental care is utilised as a means of social pacification, it can perform this new function only if it is indeed available when needed. If begging motions were promoted only by a sensation of hunger, they would not be generally available for social purposes. It is therefore important that this behaviour should also be at the disposal of individuals for reasons other than hunger alone. The drive that is responsible for the occurrence of a particular pattern of behaviour is called motivation. When a behaviour pattern changes, we speak of a change in motivation. This implies that the same pattern will now alternately be conditioned by two different motivations—or, in the human, is "differently meant." As a further consequence of this, a behaviour pattern that serves two purposes will occur more frequently than before, and also in other situations.

In the process of parental care for the offspring there are, however, not only "juvenile signals" which call forth responses from the adults, but also the reverse. Quite automatically the female animal, which carries the eggs, becomes the parent that more particularly undertakes the care for the young. Especially in mammals the mother, who alone initially provides food, becomes the young animal's first important social partner. The mother's signals announc-

ing food will additionally come to signify safety and
protection, notably in species which continue to suckle
their young for a very long time, as some monkeys
do. Learning processes are bound to play a part in
this connection. Young kangaroos, which spend a number of months in the mother's pouch after birth, will
subsequently take refuge there when danger threatens, and will attempt to do this even when they have
grown too large for it. In fact, semi-adult kangaroos,
already sexually mature, are often still fed with milk
by the mother. In antelope herds living under natural
conditions it is observed that even quite large young
animals will, when frightened, run to their mother
and apply their mouths to her udders, though they
will suck only briefly or not at all. In one species of
antelope, whose males have a special system of territories, the buck licks the female's udders after mating; this probably helps to keep her near him, so
that she will not stray into another male's territory. In
any case the maternal source of milk here has a social
significance to the adult animals. Similarly, the adult
male dingo (wild dog) will lick the bitch's nipples as
a greeting and a friendly gesture of social contact.
Young monkeys can sometimes be seen asleep with
one or both the mother's teats in their mouth. In a
number of monkey species (woolly monkeys, rhesus
monkeys and other macaco species, baboons and
chimpanzees) young animals which have already long
been weaned will, when threatened by a real or imaginary danger, run to the mother, take one of her teats
in their lips and then look back in the direction from
which the danger threatened (Plate 31). Human children do the same when they have free access to the
mother's breast, e.g., among bushmen. The effective
"signal" character of the maternal source of milk
could therefore be expected to be susceptible of fur-

ther development as a social factor. In many animals this may well take the form of olfactory signals, which are difficult to study scientifically. Monkeys, however, are mainly visually sensing creatures. And indeed in the gelada, a species of baboon, the female's breast region acts as a social signal and has, to perform this function, been developed into a very conspicuous object. The parallel with the human species is obvious, for there, too, the female breasts have acquired the character of a social signal—indeed, to such an extent that in many races it is mainly a sexual signal, which is in fact superseding its original function, as is proved by the fact that many a mother feels embarrassment when other people, even quite good friends, are present while she is breast-feeding her child. Of course, fashion and education play a part here. But the human female is unique among primates in that her breasts permanently retain their very striking shape and do not become greatly reduced in size after the suckling period. This shape, which is largely due to the presence of connective tissue that provides support, cannot be explained solely in terms of the feeding function. It seems very likely that the social signal function plays an important part here (Plates 32 and 33).

Children in primitive tribes, who seek refuge with their mother, often confine themselves to seizing her breast in their hands or extending a hand towards it. When mother baboons and macaco monkeys stop suckling their children when the latter have grown to a fair size, the young monkeys may sometimes be seen "begging" for milk with hand outstretched towards the breast. In a zoo anyone can see how monkeys of many different species put their hands through the bars to beg food from the visitors; the animals soon learn to change the original grasping movement to an expectant holding-out of the hand, as this behaviour generally reaps a richer reward. More significantly, macacos living in freedom under natural conditions will normally make this typical begging gesture towards the individuals of their own species, while in chimpanzees living in freedom this has been further evolved into a greeting (Fig. 7-7)

FIG. 7-7:   *Begging gesture in chimpanzees.*

rather similar to the human counterpart. Young chimpanzees, as well as adults, thus extend the open hand, palm upwards, in a gesture of begging towards another individual, who has food. If the latter is willing to give some, he may place it in the outstretched hand or allow the other to help himself. As recently observed by Van Lawick-Goodall and Kortlandt, this same "begging gesture" is used also when a chimpanzee of low social dominance order wants to pass an individual of higher order to get to a tree with fruit: he may extend his hand towards his social superior and wait until the latter "consentingly" places a finger (or some other part of his body) in the "suppliant's" open hand. In stress situations, e.g., when an enemy is sighted or when engaged in battle with him, chimpanzees give one another signs of encouragement or assistance by extending the hand, handclasping, handshaking or placing the hand on some part of the other individual's body. It would seem that the gesture of extending the arm and hand towards some desired object in order to gain possession of it has, in these apes, been diverted to the individual who happens to have the object or can provide it and that this gesture has moreover acquired a wider meaning. According to the observations hitherto made, this gesture is aimed primarily at obtaining food, but it has, as a derived function, come to signify a request for consent or social support. In human language it would thus primarily mean: "I want food," then "Help me or allow me to get at the food" and finally just "Help me" or "Allow me to be with you." In these situations the gesture comes within the category of varied behaviour patterns which we call greetings.

The change or shift in the meaning of extending the hand can be observed not only in anthropoid apes but also in baboons. The present author saw young baboons, living in freedom, repeatedly snatch at food that the mother had in her mouth or was putting into her mouth. Sometimes they got something; but occasionally they put their hands on the mother's face while she was looking in another direction: she would then turn her face towards the young animals, gave them attention, or carried them away. An adult Arabian baboon in the zoo at Munich-Hellabrunn—besides using the usual "pasha" methods —would place his extended open hand on the ground as an invitation to his female partner to come to him or remain with him (Fig. 7-8). Even if this gesture

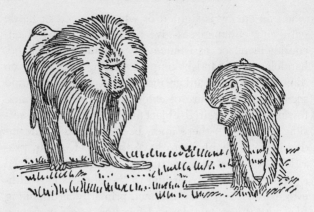

FIG. 7-8: *Begging gesture in Arabian baboons.*

developed from a begging movement directed at visitors, it would still provide an instance of the abovementioned shift in meaning.

For mating, too, the sex partners have to establish intimate contact without being thwarted in this by mutual aggression. It is therefore not surprising, and indeed only to be expected, that certain elements of sexual intercourse are utilised also for keeping the partners together beyond the actual mating or indeed to hold more than two individuals of the species together in larger groups (Plates 34 and 35, and Fig. 7-9).

Even among fish, the lowest vertebrates, certain species live in closed groups, e.g., *Tropheus moorei,* a cichlid which hatches its eggs in its mouth and is found only in Lake Tanganyika. Young fishes of these species may grow into the group or may establish new groups; but once the group exists, no outsiders are allowed to join it. If other fishes (of the same species) are artificially introduced into a group, they

FIG. 7-9: *Copulation (right) and mounting as a demonstration of social rank in Arabian baboons.*

are killed instantly or are starved to death; if they are females, they will never, in this situation, spawn again, even if they manage to survive in some protected corner: this is called "psychological castration"; it occurs also in monkeys under comparable conditions. Fights between individuals that are strangers to each other are very violent, but fights between members of the same group are avoided by an aggression-inhibiting movement on the part of the individual attacked. This movement, which is identical with the male courtship movement, is common to all allied species of fish. In *Tropheus*, however, it occurs many times a day, in both sexes, irrespective of the breeding cycle. The male fish can, by a special physiological process, in a matter of seconds produce a splendid display of colours which plays an important part in courtship during the breeding season. In that season the female is unobtrusively coloured, but at other times she can display the same brightly coloured finery as the male as a gesture of conciliation or pacification in the "social" context. It would appear that this conciliatory gesture, in the female anyway, is independent of sexual motivation.

A situation similar in principle is encountered in many old-world monkeys, notably the baboons. The conciliatory gesture within the closed group is the female invitation to copulate: presenting the buttocks, with the tail raised in varying degrees. Each individual of a lower social dominance order performs this gesture towards an individual of higher status, irrespective of the sex of either. In many species, however, the mating invitation of the female "on heat" is further accentuated by conspicuous swelling of the genital region. Associated with this is the phenomenon that the males of certain species of baboon likewise display sham genital swelling as a device for use in social intercourse, such as the prominent red buttocks of the Arabian baboon. They do not need this display for sexual courtship purposes any more than the female *Tropheus* needs her bright colours for mating, but it does have a function in social relations within the group. In both cases—*Tropheus* and baboon—the acquisition of the "signal" by the opposite sex shows how important a part is played by this derived or modified movement in the social life of the group.

Captive baboons kept in close confinement will, by force of circumstances, display the social conciliatory gesture much more frequently than baboons living in freedom. The assertion that baboons are oversexed is based on a misconception, for in these captive animals, too, the social gesture of "presenting the buttocks" is largely independent of any sexual intention. In birds the Australian weaver finches of the species *Poephila personata* show comparable highly developed social behaviour. Here the female invitation to copulate is used by both sexes as a gesture of greet-

PLATE 25. *Klaubauf revellers from Matrei in East Tyrol.*

PLATE 26: *Aggressive threatening behaviour as a distance-keeping manoeuvre: (top): a black-headed gull (Larus ridibundus) approaches with beak ready to peck and wings ready to beat. The brown facial mask, contrasting with the general white colour of the bird, serves to intimidate the would-be attacker. (bottom): Fighting male black-headed gulls. The bird on the right is qttacking; the other is facing away, thus showing its inclination to seek refuge in retreat.*

PLATE 25. *Klaubauf revellers from Matrei in East Tyrol.*

PLATE 26: *Aggressive threatening behaviour as a distance-keeping manoeuvre: (top): a black-headed gull (Larus ridibundus) approaches with beak ready to peck and wings ready to beat. The brown facial mask, contrasting with the general white colour of the bird, serves to intimidate the would-be attacker. (bottom): Fighting male black-headed gulls. The bird on the right is αttacking; the other is facing away, thus showing its inclination to seek refuge in retreat.*

PLATE 27: *Aggressive threatening behaviour in pairing of sex partners: (top): A male black-headed gull, as yet without a mate, reacts at first to a flying female bird as though to an intruder into his territory. (centre): As soon as the female (nearer the camera) has landed, both birds adopt a less aggressive threatening attitude. The parallel position side by side with beaks slightly raised and pointing forward indicates a mixture of "friendly" approach and diminished animosity. (bottom): After thus standing side by side the two birds raise their heads and face away from each other, as an appeasement posture, thereby removing the beak and facial mask from the partner's field of vision.*

PLATE 28: *Territorial fight in which the contestants do not harm each other: Mouth-to-mouth confrontation between fishes. Hippos engaged in a playful fight.*

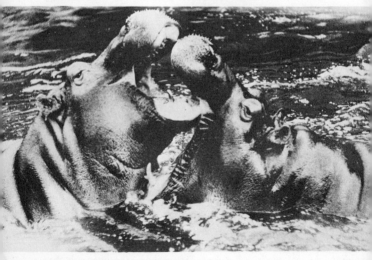

ing within the group, though between mating partners this gesture is reserved for the female alone.
Whether it serves also as a means of conciliation to
inhibit attack is not known.

Many more examples could be given. Again and
again we find behaviour patterns originally associated
with mating and with care for the offspring infused
with new meaning and incorporated into the social
structure of the species, where they regularly function
as an antidote to aggression and flight reactions directed at individuals of the same group or species.
"Juvenile" begging for food may pacify a would-be
attacker; "parental" offering of food may encourage a
timid individual to approach. The red buttocks of the
baboon probably combine both functions by serving
as a "female signal" and thus helping to neutralise
attacks from individuals higher up in the social dominance order and flight or retreat tendencies in individuals of lower order.

It is commonly supposed that "egoism" which manifests itself more particularly in the direct rivalry that
occurs within a species is older than "altruism," and
it is fashionable to think in terms of aggression towards
one's own species as being more fundamental
than kindliness—or, in short, that evil is older than
goodness, unpalatable though this may be to many
philosophers and theologians. However, the validity,
or otherwise, of this generalisation need not concern
us here. Suffice it to note that the aggression-inhibiting
mechanisms were not primarily invented as an antidote to aggressive behaviour that might endanger the
survival of the species, but are based on very ancient
procreative behaviour. From the earliest times creatures have lived and multiplied and have shown tol-
erance towards members of their own species. Intraspecific aggression is something that they may have

been able to indulge in as a secondary phenomenon, possibly in promoting the distribution of the species, but only up to a certain limit, stopping short of anything that would present a threat to mating or endanger the offspring or brothers and sisters. For what matters in the process of evolution is not whether any particular individual survives, but that those characteristics will be inherited whose bearers succeed in propagating them as widely as possible within a population. Hence the number of offspring is important, and anything liable to reduce the number must be suppressed. It can therefore be entirely compatible with the principle of preservation of the species that a mother defends her young to the point of self-sacrifice.

The more aggression develops, the more must the aggression-inhibiting mechanisms to compensate it of course also develop. So although social friendliness is certainly not a younger phenomenon than social enmity in terms of evolutionary history, the two have, in the course of higher social development of living creatures, jointly grown stronger and more abundant. This may even lead to new forms of pathological behaviour. For example, if in animals juvenilism is utilised as a means of warding off social aggression, it may occur under certain circumstances that a member of a community will, in consequence of social pressure, remain permanently locked in this juvenile behaviour pattern. The term *regression* is used to describe such a fall-back into juvenile behaviour in response to social stress situations. Regression in itself is not pathological, however, as a transient phenomenon (as such it is of regular occurrence in social animals and serves as a means of conciliating would-be aggressors), but only when in an individual it becomes a fixation with regard to the prevailing situation.

BIOLOGICAL ASPECTS OF HUMAN BEHAVIOUR PATTERNS

These considerations must inevitably lead to comparisons with human behaviour and indeed even to practical applications in the human sphere. Obviously, results of research on weaver finches cannot be directly applied to man. But it is possible to deduce from such comparative considerations certain working hypotheses for the study of man and his social behaviour. And this all the more so, when it appears that particular constitutional elements crop up again and again in animal societies, from the lowest vertebrates to the highest. This fact is indicative of a general "law" or recurrent pattern in the structure of vertebrate societies, which must thus also apply to human societies. Since we wish not only to give a correct classification of human behaviour, but also to arrive at a moral assessment, such "laws" can be quite important. We need not try to deduce moral standards from them, but we shall, in seeking to establish such standards, have to take account of these "laws," especially if it is desired also really to apply these standards.

This implies a purely practical approach, comparable to the efforts of medical science, which likewise engages in research into human physiology in order to make a corrective intervention should the need arise and which, for this purpose, also carries out comparative investigations on animals. In so doing, it does not set out to explain man in animal terms or to establish standards as to when intervention is justified, but it aims instead at improving the chances of success of such intervention.

General "laws" which are applicable to the behaviour of a large range of creatures including man can yield important clues to understanding human behaviour. When it is found that certain characteristics of social systems occur over and over again in the species hitherto investigated—ranging from the lowest vertebrates, fishes, to the most highly evolved vertebrates, anthropoid apes—we can expect to find them also in other social creatures that belong zoologically to the vertebrates, tend to form groups and are aggressive to members of their own species: i.e., including man himself. This being so, it is immaterial whether he is more closely allied to chimpanzees or to weaver finches or to fishes—in other words, our expectation or prediction is independent of the question whether or not man's systematic position among the vertebrate animals has been indisputably established.

What then are these expectations or predictions? Here are some examples:

1. We should expect that, in man, behaviour patterns arising from the set of functions associated with the care for the offspring have become functionally transformed and adopted into the relationship between sex partners or indeed between members of a larger social group. Such behaviour patterns could be, for example: mouth-to-mouth feeding or, if the actual transfer of food is abandoned, the practice of pressing one's lips against those of the other person; furthermore, holding on to the other, gently caressing each other (as is frequently done between mother and child), probably also uttering affectionate sounds and words of endearment.

2. We should also expect sexual elements, e.g., associated with courtship prior to mating, to be

utilised outside the direct procreative context as a means of establishing and strengthening the ties between mating partners and between the individuals in larger groups. Thus, for example, female signals which serve to attract the male could be directed, in "diluted" form, also at other members of the community and thus help to create a "friendly atmosphere"; or even that certain introductory movements in mating could be performed separately as an independent action, e.g., in a dance.

3. Furthermore, we should expect that for mating, procreation, care for the offspring and the establishment of ties with the other members of the community there also exist freely convertible behaviour elements, signals no longer bearing recognisable relation to their original purpose (such as smiling). The more numerous the functions that such behaviour elements have to perform, the more frequently should they occur, and perhaps in densely inhabited societies more than in thinly scattered ones. Since they largely preserve their form unchanged even when used with different intentions, the unsuspecting observer would at first be liable to overlook their functional diversity and perhaps—wrongly—be disposed to regard such a society as "sex-obsessed" (Fig. 7-10).

4. We should expect that physical features which act as such effective signals will have acquired particular prominence in the evolutionary process. The female breasts of various primates have already been mentioned as an example. In the process of technical evolution, man has acquired in cosmetics and fashions special means

FIG. 7-10: *The phallus as a social rather than sexual symbol, here more particularly in a guardian function: Korean stone phallic statue (about 5 ft. high); man-high straw phallic scarecrow on a rice field in Bali; carved wooden guardian symbol from Bali (about 17 in. high); wooden guardian symbol from Nias (about 5 ft. high); phallic symbol of rank worn on the forehead in southern Ethiopia; male baboon sitting on guard.*

of giving prominence to biological social signals (Fig. 7-11).

FIG. 7-11: *Characteristically enlarged buttocks of bushman woman and European lady's dress of 1882.*

5. We should also expect a society so fraught with signals and reactions modified away from their original functions to be susceptible to the abuse of biological social signals. By "abuse" we mean here the gaining of personal advantage by an individual at the expense of the community by exploitation of reactions called forth by such signals. In baboons the habit of "presenting the buttocks," already referred to, is sometimes applied as follows: one animal threatens another and at the same time "presents" to a third animal of higher social status. Socially superior animals often intervene in quarrels in order to pacify the contestants; in this particular case the higher-status animal has no alternative but to chase away the threatened animal because the other is "presenting" and thus safeguarded against attack. If the social life of human beings living together in a community is full of reactions functionally modified from those associated with the care of the offspring, we might, for instance, find that individuals of high social status will respond kindly to a "baby look" in social inferiors even in circumstances where that is hardly appropriate and that, in comparable situations, they will behave with greater kindness to fellow men or women with childlike faces than to those with more adult features. Natural selection can hardly be expected to remove this injustice, for any weakening of the reaction to juvenile care-soliciting signals would jeopardise the reaction ensuring proper care for the offspring.

These examples will suffice to show what possible functional interrelationships must be taken into consideration and how comparative research on animals can yield clues in studying and understanding human behaviour. This is not confined to the limited field of activities discussed here, for in the over-all behaviour of all organisms all sorts of activity fields are intermeshed. If biological ties binding numerous individuals together into coherent social groups are to function properly, this necessitates a degree of distribution of labour and individual specialisation for the good of the community as a whole. If these individuals can accumulate experience and also learn from one another, there will, in terms of selective evolution, be advantage in storing such experience; this is done automatically in the older individuals who have gained the experience. But, in addition, it is necessary to experiment, to gain new experience; and this is something best done by "unprejudiced," i.e., young, individuals, who, if they are unsuccessful, can still benefit by the experience of their elders, so that the community will not be at the mercy of utterly inexperienced and unsuccessful individuals. This conservative role of the older and experimental role of the younger individuals is encountered over and over again and would seem to be a consequence of the important part that traditions have played in the preservation and continuance of social situations, so long as there is no writing by means of which it is possible to store experience indefinitely. In societies where writing is still a relatively new invention we could expect the biologically established experience-storing role of the older individuals to have survived from the preliterate era and suppose that it must take time for a change to occur in this traditional role of the elders—perhaps in the sense that they, with the collected store of varied experience simultaneously at their disposal, engage in an open-minded scrutiny of the social system and, as a result of careful observation and reflection, discover entirely new interrelationships which nature does not reveal so obviously.

These are, of course, as yet mere speculations representing questions asked rather than results obtained. Since these questions are based on the results already yielded by behaviour study, there is reason to hope that this same line of research will one day also provide the answers.

OTTO KOEHLER

Animal Languages and Human Speech

COMPARISONS BETWEEN MAN AND ANIMAL

We wish to compare how animals communicate with one another and how people exchange information through the medium of speech. There are many who tend to reject any such comparison: human beings are to have nothing in common with animals. This attitude is indeed reflected in some of the terminology relating to basic functions: people "dine" and "make love," whereas animals "feed" and "copulate."

By the same token, only human beings are considered to be capable of speech; animals, on the other hand, merely "communicate" or are, at best, allowed "speech" only in a very watered-down sense. All such alternative mutually exclusive pairs of concepts (either-or, yes-no, guilty-not guilty), so common in our language, ignore the intermediate distinctions. Certainly 1 is not equal to 2, but in between them are many decimal values; and between white and black there are many shades of grey. Furthermore, every living creature possesses a large number of characteristics at one and the same time, and man is demonstrably a creature of animal origin. "To compare" does not mean "to equate," but merely to pick out points of correspondence or agreement, combine them into a wider concept, and also pay serious attention to the differences.

All life is a process of happening, advance, cycles, change, passing away, development. Alternative concepts are inadequate to describe it; what we require are injunctives which do not suggest unbridgeable gaps and boundaries but which, instead, do justice to the gradual transitions and the multiplicity of characteristics, many of which may moreover be eliminated anyway. Questions as to whether the chicken came before the egg, where a circle starts and ends, when an embryo turns into a child or when a boy becomes a young man, a man and an old man are all equally pointless. The old parrot which from sheer boredom has plucked out its last feather is nevertheless still a bird. Gnats and flies are classed as dipterous (two-winged) insects, but the "tetraptera" mutation of the fruit fly *Drosophila melanogaster,* a "four-winged dipterous insect," is really a contradiction in terms and yet it exists. To define injunctively means: to describe many characteristics, to demarcate their variability and to decide which items may perhaps be ignored.

The biologist seldom speaks of "the" animal, but mentions the species and has much to learn before he knows at what stage he can generalise and to what extent he can then permissibly do this. The genetic DNA code that we find in viruses occurs in all living creatures up to, and including, the human species. This fact alone suffices to prove that man shares his origins with all other forms of life. The electrophysiology of "the" nerve cell applies to all animals that have nervous systems, i.e., from fresh-water polyps (*Hydra*) upwards. Yet not every vertebrate must necessarily have a gall bladder such as man has; and in modes of behaviour the differences between one species and another play a decisively important part.

Thus, to the biologist, man is "an animal of a very special kind." The fact that in phylogenetic terms it is the apes that are our nearest relations is something that strengthens many non-biologists in their dislike of any suggestion that man is descended from animals. When they see monkeys at the zoo, they feel caricatured and affronted in their dignity. For similar reasons some people hide photographs of themselves as infants, so as to banish the thought that they once were such undignified little squallers.

In classical ancient times, according to K. Günther (1967), Anaximandros' hypothesis that man was descended from sharks apparently did not offend anyone. But, in the eighteenth century, Linnaeus—who at first upheld the doctrine of the immutability of species: *tot sunt species, quot initio creavit Infinitum Ens*—was criticised by the Stockholm theological faculty for having placed *Homo sapiens* at the top of the order of Primates (comprising man, apes and monkeys), a place that he has since continued to occupy. In later life, however, the great naturalist recognised that biological species can and do change. This view was shared also by Charles Darwin's predecessors: Lamarck, Erasmus Darwin and others. As long ago as 1830, the young Karl Ernst von Baer was already lecturing on phylogeny (evolutionary history) at Königsberg, but he applied this hypothesis only to each of the four divisions of the animal kingdom (as taught by Cuvier in those days), for each of which he presupposed a separate creation. In this view he long persisted; in particular, he was antagonistic to man's close phylogenetic relationship with apelike ancestors. This attitude was shared by some other important biologists until well into the twentieth century, such as Oskar Hertwig, who perhaps knew more about the evolutionary history of the mammals, and especially of man, than Charles Darwin himself, even though the latter's dictum still stands: "No science of life can be valid unless it has made its peace with evolution."

In Germany, Ernst Haeckel was the most prominent protagonist of the new doctrine. Although Darwin implored him not to, Haeckel as the originator of his theory of "monism," while not actually proclaiming himself an atheist, was not strict enough in preventing his followers from doing so. In consequence of rash utterances, he must share the blame for the now so widely held view that biology, and especially physiology, must be equated to materialism, irreligion and atheism and for the harmful consequences that this has had even to present-day research and science.

Altner (1966) rightly comments that Haeckel, despite his adherence to some of Goethe's doctrines, failed to understand the lesson taught by that poet: "Into the inner soul of nature, thou Philistine, no creaturely mind shall penetrate!," and failed to perceive how he distorted Goethe's immanent transcendental pantheism into a physiomonistic one. Actually, religion and science can never fight each other in a real sense but only in a meaningless manner with words; for they are talking about the same thing, each in its own language, and to mix these two languages is not permissible, as the philosopher Kant has pointed out. Nothing is so stupid as the so frequently heard phrase that faith begins where knowledge ends and that the progress of science spells the death of religion. No, religious faith covers everything, including the transcendental, whereas science is concerned only with empirical reality insofar as it is accessible to investigation. The statements "in the beginning God created heaven and earth" and *"omne vivum ex ovo"* are not contradictory; St. Augustine already referred to the natural process of renewal and rebirth of all life as "continuous creation."

An argument against Darwin which crops up again and again speaks of his "doctrine of blind chance," completely failing to recognise that mathematically defined quantities ought to be taken seriously. Scientific investigators normally try to find "rules and laws" (as K. E. von Baer has pointed out) and seek causes only in circumstances where something occurs with greater frequency than could be expected from the laws of probability. It is constantly being asserted that it is inconceivable how an eye could be formed "by chance"; after all, if you take a box containing all the parts of a watch jumbled together and shake it for all eternity, you will never succeed in making the parts fit together "by chance" to form a watch. If two gear wheels happened to become fitted together, continued shaking of the box would merely make them come apart again. Yet when a chromosome or a gene or a DNA filament is "identically replicated," i.e., exact copies of these unique and complex molecules are produced (which is something that no molecule of inanimate matter can do), and those parts which belong together do indeed come and remain together. With each addition of a small improvement due to natural selective causes the result becomes better. Thus, in the history of biological evolution the eye equipped with a lens for the focussing of images has emerged on no fewer than seven different occasions; and the compound eyes of insects and crabs also display parallel development of this kind (Koehler 1957), termed convergence. Besides, no scientific theory can seriously claim alone to explain everything and certainly not entirely from one standpoint only.

Much always remains shrouded in obscurity, and that is why research must go on.

Fortunately, it is being increasingly realised that the faster the human race multiplies, the greater becomes the importance of science, and more particularly biological science, as a vital necessity—as essential as food and drink. Science is establishing new links in all directions, including links with the arts, philosophy and religion. In this connection suffice it to mention the symposia organised by the Görres Society for the promotion of contacts between science and religion, F. X. Arnold's twice-repeated apology for the action of his Church in its dealings with Galileo, the lifework of Teilhard de Chardin and C. F. von Weizsäcker's *Geschichte der Natur* (*History of Nature*). The theologian G. Altner wrote in 1966: "We now know that Darwin's view was correct."

In his book entitled *The Expression of the Emotions in Man and Animals* Darwin laid the foundation for comparative psychology comprising the human as well as the animal world. The anthropomorphism of the earlier writers about animals, such as Brehm, who had no hesitation in ascribing human characteristics to animals, helped to popularise their writings, but soon called forth a reaction from scientists desiring a more objective approach. I have direct experience of my own consciousness, but not of that of any other creature, whether human or animal. I can observe only the behaviour of my fellow creatures and, basing myself on this and applying the principle that the simplest explanatory hypothesis that fits the facts is always to be preferred, I can try to conceive what I myself should feel and think in the same situation as the person or animal under observation. Accordingly, some ethologists (behaviour researchers) entirely rule out the problem of consciousness in animals and confine their attention to the animals' actions. For all ethologists physiology is the fundamental science; but even simple instinctive actions, let alone such processes as learning, thinking, comparing and all the higher mental functions, cannot as yet be explained in physiological terms. When we speak of mechanisms, this is to be taken more as a challenge to discover them and endeavour to give physiological objectivity to concepts derived from psychology. For the instincts and the innate trigger mechanisms (releasers) some tangible spadework has been accomplished; for the higher functional levels there yet remains everything to be done. Other investigators in the behavioural field—as indeed also every researcher in human psychology—do not let such epistemological objections stand in their way for practical purposes: the closer the animal species is related to us, the less we are disposed to doubt its conscious sensation of joy and sorrow, memory, expectation and indeed mental states that embody the rudiments of our own thought processes.

The system of concepts created by K. Lorenz, and called ethology, has turned out to be a useful one. It is certain that man has the following functions and properties in common with animals—always specifically different and yet always strictly comparable in the sense of homology or convergence:

1. The senses.
2. The fundamental features of neurophysiology.
3. The specific modes of locomotion.
4. The modes of orientation (the term *"taxis"* denotes an orienting response to a directional stimulus).

5. The instinctive behaviour, i.e., all innate activities that an individual needs to preserve himself and his species by his behaviour (such as attack, retreat reproduction, parental care for offspring, feeding).

6. Moods.

7. Affects (feelings or emotions).

8. The innate trigger mechanisms (releasers).

9. The capacity to learn, which is demonstrably greater according as the species of animal in question—from the earthworm upwards—is more highly developed and which, by virtue of innate capabilities, makes possible an increasingly high degree of freedom of action.

The tenth point in this list—the process of "thinking without words" (abstract thought) will be referred to later on.

As long ago as the Neolithic period man began to domesticate animals; by removing them from the processes of natural selection and mating them according to his judgment he increased their inherited variability, bred creatures to suit his requirement or taste and in the process of acquiring civilisation he domesticated himself also. But the more we get to know about innate behaviour and the capacity to adapt it even better to the environmental conditions by learning, the more awed and astonished we are by instinct—"that marvel of God," as Kant called it—which preserves existing species and changes with them into new forms.

THE ESSENTIAL NATURE OF MAN

No other creature is so helpless and so long in need of parental care as the human child, and yet the adult human being is, as the Bible puts it, lord of all the animals and of our whole earth. In exercising his power he too often disrupts the biological equilibrium and engages in the wholesale extermination of plants and animals in order to achieve his purpose.

This unique position or, in biblical terms, his creation in the image of God, man undoubtedly owes to the power of speech. It is this that has made him human and has created something new from all the above-mentioned properties that he shares in common with the animals and has inherited from them: something that we call mind and which, in this sense, includes all his highest spiritual attainments: responsibility, religion, art and science. And yet he would never have become human without a long line of animal ancestors who, in the process of natural selection extending through two or three milliard years, created his physical and mental entity. All the preliminary conditions and preliminary stages of his mind are already to be found in animals, though in no single species are they all present together. And if it should come to pass that man one day destroys all life on earth, it is hardly likely that new life will originate or indeed that the process of "humanisation" will be repeatable.

Ever since people began to have thoughts extending beyond their immediate needs, they must have speculated about the origin of languages and of speech in general. The ancient Greeks distinguished between θέσει, referring to words based on more or less arbitrary human conventions (the existence of many different dialects and languages was considered to bear witness to this), and φύσει, which denotes words which originated in man's vocal imitation of the sounds made by animals and by inanimate nature. In the biblical account of the Creation, God speaks to

Adam, who replies. God subsequently sends linguistic confusion to punish mankind for their hubris, their overweening pride, in building the Tower of Babel. In the tenth volume of *Dichtung und Wahrheit* Goethe makes the following comment on the subject of human speech and language: "Also, the question seemed a somewhat pointless one to me, for if God created man as man, then he must have been created with the power of speech from the outset, just as with the ability to walk upright; just as he must immediately have perceived that he could walk about and seize things, so he must also have perceived that he could use his throat for singing and that he could modify these sounds with his tongue, palate and lips. If man was of divine origin, then speech itself must also have been of such origin; and if man, on the other hand, considered within the context of nature, was a natural creature, then speech must also have been natural. Like soul and body, I have never been able to separate these two things." Nor has the present author. W. von Humboldt wrote: "Man is man only by virtue of the power of speech; to invent speech he must already have been human." He did not make any attempt to explain whence the power of speech was derived, but proceeded to concern himself only with comparative linguistic studies.

Two examples may serve to show how even modern investigators take their stand on the view that human speech is not derivable from animal origins. M. J. Adler (1967), who incidentally is not a biologist, starts off by laying down the law in defining "degree" and "kind" as alternative concepts, and thus, with inexorable logic, arrives at what he terms a "difference radical in kind" between the human and the animal. This is an instance of the time-honoured practice of juggling with words. According to such reasoning the infant who was baptised Johann Sebastian Bach would be "radically different" from the composer of some of the world's greatest music!

G. Révész (1964), who himself had studied methods of communication in animals, of course knew perfectly well that little children and parrots are able to imitate the words of human speech. But he compares such preliminary stages with an unmoulded lump of clay and forgets that without clay or marble it is not possible to make a statue. Although he does admit that there is some truth in all the hypotheses of origin of speech, he ends up by adopting his contact theory as the only valid one. By seeking to define everything "from one point," however, he fails to bridge the gap. "Speech is the expression of reason; the animal has neither," he asserts. But the same can be said of the human infant, which by the same reasoning would have to be classed as an animal.

Whenever it has been attempted to express the essential nature of man by an appropriate adjective, exceptions have always cropped up. Thus Linnaeus' nomenclature *Homo sapiens*, i.e., man designated as a creature possessing reason and judgment, is not really applicable to the imbecile or the infant or indeed the general mindless herd of voters in any political election.

For *Homo faber*, i.e., man conceived as a tool-using creature, the preliminary stages are already to be found in the insect world: the sand wasp *Ammophila campestris* conceals the entrance to its nest by patting and smoothing the earth with a tiny pebble gripped in its jaws. Weaver ants sew leaves together: in this operation a number of ants pull and hold the edges of the leaf together, while another gang of ants use their own larvae to spin threads for sewing up in the gap, these larvae being manipulated rather like a weaver's shuttle (Fig. 8-1). A species of Galápagos finch

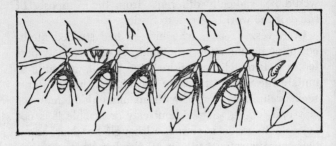

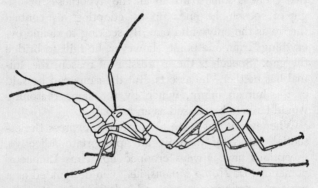

FIG. 8-1: *Weaver ants* (Oecophylla smaragdina) *holding together the edges of a leaf which will serve as an enclosure to the nest, while other ants sew up the gap with threads produced by larvae held in the adult insects' jaws* (bottom) (*according to Hesse-Doflein*).

breaks off spines of the *Opuntia* cactus to the appropriate length and uses them to prod insect larvae out of their holes in wood (Plate 36). The present author's own dog, a griffon, having found it very awkward to drag along an approximately 6-foot-long branch with twigs at a brisk trot, now always neatly bites off all the twigs before making off with a branch. The Californian sea otter dives for hard-shelled molluscs, sea urchins and snails; the animal lies on its back with a suitable stone placed on its stomach; with extended forepaws it then loudly hammers its prey on this stone as on an anvil, in order to crack the shells. Japanese short-tailed macacos for years used to pick up individual grains of rice scattered for them, until one group of these monkeys began taking up handfuls of rice and sand and depositing them in sea water, so that the rice grains were separated from the sand and were salted at the same time. Japanese researchers have made detailed observations of the emergence of dozens of such "work traditions" in various widely separated tribes of wild monkeys. Jane van Lawick-Goodall's wild chimpanzees used chewed leaves to make a "sponge," which they dipped in water-filled cavities in tree trunks and then sucked. Chimpanzees in other areas insert a hand or only a finger into the cavities; some species take the sponge and lick it. Nearly all species of monkey fundamentally dislike water, but the Koshima tribe of monkeys in Japan and a community of baboons on the coast of southeast Africa have developed typical bathing habits and compete with one another in diving for sea food. Such traditions, which usually derive from the inventiveness of individual animals, show—in contradiction of frequently repeated assertions—that animals have "history" in addition to their phylogenetic development.

As regards *Homo ludens*, i.e., man as a creature who indulges in playing, the picture offered by the world of animals is rather less clear. In the aquaria at Berne, Copenhagen and Fribourg certain species of fish (tapir-nose fish) have been observed to carry forked twigs playfully on their noses. The more stormy the weather, the more joyously do the various members of the crow family (rooks, jackdaws) ap-

pear to indulge in their flight games; and the playful
gambols of puppies, kittens, fox cubs and golden ham-
ster cubs are fascinating to watch. Even old male
chimpanzees join in the games in which young individuals, still lacking in due respect for their elders, occasionally involve them. Games of curiosity are real
preliminary stages of the exploration of nature.
N. Tinbergen describes how his twelve-month-old
grandson, not yet able to speak a word, crawled
around on all fours in the dunes and pricked himself
on a thorny thistle. He extended his leg again to touch
the offending thistle, then crawled to other plants,
which he handled with impunity, and then returned
to the thistle. Even the discovery of the DNA double
helix by J. D. Watson, who was awarded the Nobel
Prize, has rightly been described by him as a puzzle
game: "Trial and error take precedence over study!"

What is most characteristic of man, however, is his
aspect as *Homo loquens,* i.e., the creature capable of
speech. Where we score over all other creatures with
our word language is something that emerges very
clearly when we compare it with the methods of communication found in animals.

COMMUNICATION IN ANIMALS

When a phage (a virus that parasitises bacteria) lo-
cates a bacterium, when *Paramecium* (slipper ani-
malcule, a microscopic unicellular creature) finds its
conjugation partner, when a sperm reaches the ovum,
or when a male *Daphnia* (water flea, a small crusta-
cean) finds its mate in the confusion of plankton
among which these creatures live, these highly specific achievements, which we already understand to
some extent in physiological terms, are true prelimi-

nary stages of what we call social communication in higher animals: innate patterns of behaviour, which K. Lorenz has named "releasers" or trigger mechanisms, which call forth specific responses in other members of the species and whose communicative significance they understand as an innate function. Visual releasers are changes in colour, reddening, displays of plumage, attitudes and gestures, winking of glowworms and mimicry; audible releasers: calls, song or drumming noises. Similar functions are performed by odours, tactile stimuli or electric signals. Any textbook of ethology and comparative sensory physiology gives a vast number of examples drawn from all conceivable functional spheres.

The male stickleback, eager for mating and ready to defend his "territory," displays his red belly as a sign of his pugnacity to other males. He swims to and fro, brave in his own, but timid in his neighbour's territory; and when two male fish encounter each other at the boundary of their respective adjacent territories, they face each other with equal courage. An intruding female does not fear attack but, instead, shows the male her belly swollen with eggs. Now he tries to lure her to the nest by performing a kind of zigzag dance with her, shows her the entrance, tickles her by a vibratory motion of his nose, thereby inducing her to discharge her eggs (oviposition), fertilises the eggs with his sperm in the nest tunnel and then chases the female away. He repeats this performance with other females until enough eggs have been laid in the nest, and guards the spawn (Fig. 8-2). All the releasers involved are precisely known from experiments with dummies and are readily translatable into words of command. The sailor in a foreign port, too, can make the local girls understand what he wants even if he does not know a word of their language.

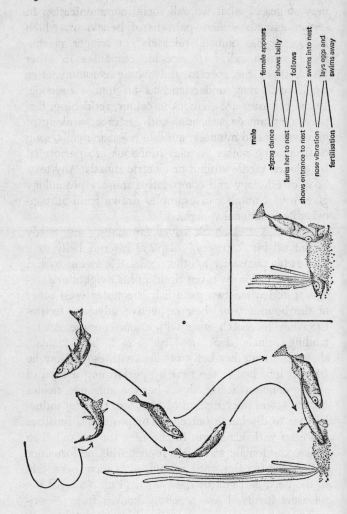

male
female appears
zigzag dance
shows belly
lures her to nest
follows
shows entrance to nest
swims into nest
nose vibration
lays eggs and
fertilisation
swims away

FIG. 8-2: *Mating and procreation behaviour of the stickle-back (according to N. Tinbergen).*

ents are performed by the scout bee on the vertical
omb in the darkness of the hive. The angle between
metrical (tail-wagging) path and the vertical line
the course that must be flown in relation to the sun
r to get from the hive to the source of food (flow-
he diagrams represent angles of o, 60, 120 and 180
s respectively. Centre: the abscissa in the graph rep-
the distance from the source of food to the hive in
the ordinate represents the number of tail-wagging
r quarter of a minute. Bottom: when the scout bee
ed the availability of food (F) at a distance of 800
thirty bees flew to that food; the other figures
he horizontal line in the diagram indicate the num-
bees which flew to similar sources of food located
same line of flight, but at different distances (e.g.,
, 400 m, etc.) (according to K. von Frisch).

e audible whirring of its flight muscles, indi-
he distance to the destination (source of nec-
On a horizontal surface the diametrical path
directly towards the destination. When the
is performed on a vertical surface, a vertical
tail-wagging run means: fly accurately sun-
if the run is in some other direction, its angle
he vertical appropriately indicates the correct
in relation to the sun. In this way the scout
orms the others what it has just experienced
hat they should do to follow the example. The
and the meaning of this language are innate.
uer took eggs from the nest of a species of
roat and allowed each of them to hatch in an
or in a soundproof room, so that each newly
bird could hear no sound other than its own
After six days three of the young male birds,
its own room, were uttering the "cheep" hun-
, and at the end of ten days they were also
"idat." Then the well-fed young birds com-
song from these two sounds, and the song be-

Just as the fish, with increasing pugnacity, successively exhibits quite different modes of attack (efforts
to impress the intruder, parallel swimming, tail
thrashing, ramming), so the human baby smiles when
he is gently swung to and fro, begins to laugh as his
sense of pleasure increases and finally crows with de-
light at the height of his enjoyment.

Of the thirty different sounds that a hen utters, one
serves as a warning against attackers from the air, another against attackers on the ground (Baeumer
1964). Jackdaws in a new and, to them, unknown
feeding ground call "kiah" (fly out) and "kiuh" (fly
home); after some hours of "debating the issue" the
"kiuh" call wins, and all the birds then unanimously
fly home to their roosting place (K. Lorenz 1965).

Male and female sandpipers live together monoga-
mously so long as both birds are alive. For example,
such pairs have been known to remain together for at
least eight years. Each takes turns to sit on the eggs,
while its mate remains on the lookout. The bird on
"guard duty" utters cries of warning which sound like
"tuwee" and whose tonal nuances defy our analysis.
But if the intruder is a harmless human being, the
brooding bird remains sitting on the eggs; if a fox approaches, the bird quickly leaves the nest and tries to
distract the intruder's attention by "pretending to be
lame" and lures it away from the nest; the bird's mate
and even neighbouring pairs give help. Are we to
suppose that the cries they utter are mere involuntary
sounds like our own "ohs" and "ahs," or are the birds
communicating with one another? The bee dances
only on the filled honeycomb. An old female bird in a
colony of jackdaws at Altenburg, on feeling abandoned by the other birds, spent hours calling "kiuh"—
instead of her usual "song" composed of all conceivable jackdaw calls—until the fugitives came back home

298 OTTO KOEHLER

with her again. The abandoned duckling "weeps" until its mother, or its brothers and sisters, or human help arrives. The spring song of male songbirds announces to unattached females: "You can marry here"; and to other males: "Keep out, you are not wanted." How much "intention" or "purpose" underlies such actions is not possible for us to decide; but in any case they achieve the desired result.

But is all animal communication really nothing more than mere transmission of moods? An insect, of all creatures, can do more than this; though admittedly it has perhaps the highest degree of social organisation in the whole animal kingdom, namely, the honeybee. When a bee finds a new source of nectar, it returns to the hive and communicates this information by performing a "dance" in which, by means of movements and tail-wagging, it explains to the other bees the direction and distance of the source, while the actual nature of the find is communicated through the sense of smell (Fig. 8-3). Equipped with this information, the bees will fly out and duly find the supply of nectar. At the edges of a swarm of bees hanging in a cluster in the open air each scout bee tells the other bees about the nesting place it has found, commending its good qualities: the more suitable it is, the longer is the dance that the scout performs, with other bees joining in: each participant goes to inspect the place thus indicated, and also other places indicated by other scouts. After days of "debating," the swarm then unanimously flies off to the best nesting place. In the behaviour of these insects one principal characteristic of our speech has been realised: the symbolic value of the word. The average time it takes the dancing bee to traverse the straight diametrical path in its pattern of movements, which it does to the accompaniment of tail-wagging

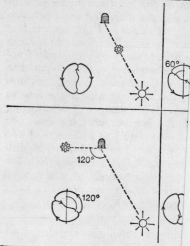

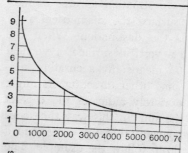

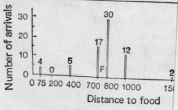

FIG. 8-3: *How the honeybee cates information on direction tional indication with reference*

move
honey
the d
shows
in ora
ers).
degre
resent
metre
runs
indica
metre
above
bers o
on the
at 75

and t
cates
tar).
points
dance
upwa
ward;
with
bearin
bee i
and w
words
F.
whitet
incuba
hatche
voice.
each i
ger ca
calling
posed

came richer and more varied with each new sound that the birds were permitted to hear—twenty-one in all. This so-called "infant song" has no more sense than the "babbling monologue" of human babies (from the age of about five months onwards); there is no lasting pattern in them, everything changes all the time; the nature of these sounds is recognisable only by their measure and timbre. Not until the next spring do the young songbirds form these sounds into short rigid motifs, either of their own composition or copied from other individuals. A bullfinch which had been reared by canaries sang like its foster father; in this way, a canary-like "family jargon" arose and was transmitted through several generations of bullfinches. As long ago as 1740, at Baron von Pernau's castle of Rosenau near Coburg, there was a copse in which all the chaffinches sang like tree pipits. The "language" of birds is learned by imitation of their own fathers, e.g., in the case of the chaffinch and the tree creeper, and quite often, in addition, the birds can recognise one another personally.

The chattering of young birds and the gurgling of infants are a form of play, without any specific motive or object, and in this respect they are comparable to our art; on the other hand, the song conforming to a strict motif, or pattern, has a serious purpose. Analyses of repeated tape recordings of one and the same bird-song motif recorded in nature showed them to be far more rigid and unvarying in respect of absolute pitch, purity of the intervals, time and rhythm than the best human musician could ever be without the aid of tuning fork and metronome. All birds, dogs and even fish (gudgeons) hitherto investigated with regard to this were found to have "absolute pitch," which is something that few people possess. To the others, who have only "relative pitch," transposing a

melody comes naturally; indeed, they are quite una-
ware that they are singing in varying keys. But with
birds, as with people possessing absolute pitch, it is a
special achievement. Parakeets were trained to distinguish thirds and fifths as such in arbitrarily varied
pitch (S. Knecht), and goldfinches which were every
day treated to a whistled song whose pitch was controlled with the aid of a tuning fork learnt to sing the
melody with the correct intervals and rhythm but at
a third higher tone (Nicolai, verbal communication).

The Californian whiteheaded bunting (*Zonotrichia*) also has local dialects. Already in the nest
and during approximately the first eight weeks of its
life the young bird memorises its father's song in every particular, although it cannot actually sing it until
after its "voice has broken"—and it can do this even if
it has been kept in a soundproof room from the age of
eight weeks onwards and has never heard the parent
bird's song again. It has therefore certainly remembered the song. If the bird goes deaf before the breaking of the voice, it will never be able to sing the
dialects that it once heard. But if it has even only
once correctly sung back what it heard in its infancy
and then goes deaf, it can nevertheless repeat this
song throughout the rest of its life (Konishi). Very
similar phenomena associated with loss of hearing at
different ages, with attendant consequences, have
been observed with regard to speech in man (Lenneberg 1967).

Mockingbirds can copy the song of other species of
bird, and some are additionally able to imitate all
sorts of noises. A crested lark had embodied the
whistled tune $c^4e^4g^4a^4c^5g^3$ in pure intervals into its
song; the five rising notes in major key were all of
precisely the same length, followed by a sliding descent from c^5 by an eleventh tone to g^3 (Fig. 8-4).

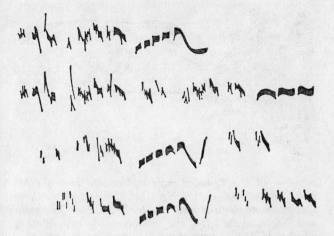

FIG. 8-4: *Tone spectrograms of the song of a crested lark embodying shepherd's whistled tune, repeated three times exactly in the middle (according to Tretzel).*

The example from which this bird had copied its song was a deplorably unmusical shepherd who, in whistling this tune to his dog, was unable to maintain key, interval, time or rhythm. From these unintentional variations the birds had produced a highly musical and strictly constant theme, to which the dog certainly listened. In addition, the tune developed into a crested larks' dialect. Something similar happened with blackbirds which imitated the tune whistled by a man to call his cat at Garmisch.

Whereas our cuckoo lays its eggs in the nests of many different species of songbirds, each of the many different African species of widow bird is a brood parasite on one particular species of host (Fig. 8-5). In addition to its own specific song, each widow bird is able to imitate the host species' song in every detail. In the course of nearly ten years' research Nicolai

FIG. 8-5: *The long-tailed male widow bird lures the female (below him, on the right) to the nest of the host species by uttering the male host bird's call note. The male host is seen on the left at the entrance to the nest, offering a leaf to his female partner inside (according to Nicolai).*

has, from a study of the singing of several brood parasites and host species, been able to predict which is parasitic on which and subsequently confirmed these predictions by observations of birds in natural conditions. In such cases the quality of the imitative capacity constitutes a contribution to the phylogenetic history of the species. When two European neighbouring male cuckoos hold a singing contest, the tempo increases, and the interval goes from minor third to pure sixth. Crowing cocks (Collias and Joos 1953) and quarrelling humans also go faster, louder and higher as they grow more excited; and in music a movement in brisk time (allegro) produces a lively and gay effect, whereas descending series of notes create a mournful impression.

Reinert (1965) trained a jackdaw to distinguish between triple and quadruple time, and the bird was then able, without further training, to distinguish between these two times in any tone and chord sequences and at any timbre or loudness, irrespective of tempo, even when the individual quarters were, for example, split up into eighths or triplets.

With monkeys these experiments should be tried on gibbons. Reinert found that an elephant easily learnt to distinguish between a three-tone melody played "up-down" and "down-up," respectively, and likewise generalised this principle, without further training, at least as well as the jackdaw did. In the zoo at Wuppertal a young Indian elephant turned the handle of a barrel organ, while another elephant beat time with his trunk through a number of tunes, both cheerful and sad. The "conductor" paused after each note and correctly indicated the time of the next note at once, or even in advance, while the "organ-grinder" maintained his speed of turning the handle accurately constant throughout—by no means an easy thing to do.

Just as birds can generalise what they have heard and reproduced in a "standardised" form, mammals are similarly able to form transposable visual patterns. Rensch and Dücker (1959) experimented with a mongoose which had been trained to distinguish between two concentric semicircles and two vertical parallel lines. From this basis the animal was to be able to form abstract notions in that it distinguished between "curved" and "straight" and also between "equal" and "unequal"; it applied this even to quite minor differences and was thus able at once to choose correctly between sixteen unknown specimen pairs. Lehr's rhesus and capuchin monkeys, trained with pairs of pictures, generalised the concept "insectlike" from among a random array of other pictures; also "flowerlike" from "stemlike to leaflike." The more

complex the pictures, the more unerringly did the
monkeys operate, and they sustained this performance even with quite abstract diagrams such as
"straight" against "somewhat dichotomous."

How splendidly birds, too, are able to generalise
what they have seen is evidenced by Herrnstein's
(1965) pigeon, which in one month learned to distinguish from among hundreds of small colour slides
only those on which people appeared, no matter how
dressed, how many, in what surroundings, and even
when half concealed. The bird was able to do this better than trained human observers.

THOUGHT PROCESSES WITHOUT WORDS IN ANIMAL AND MAN

The present author's experiments for studying the
counting capabilities of birds, over a period of more
than forty years, have brought him to consider the
"wordless" thought processes which are common to
animals and man. Under experimental conditions in
which the transmission of unintentional signs was
ruled out—in a self-recording experimental setup a
bird, left entirely to itself without the human investigator present, will work correctly—eight species
of bird (including pigeons and parakeets) learned to
distinguish between simultaneously presented sets of
points solely according to the numbers of points in the
respective sets. Also, they were briefly shown numbers and learned to respond to them successively: for
example, by picking up a corresponding number of
food morsels in succession. The birds performed both
types of experiment successfully in at least twenty
different arrangements. In all cases the two types of
ability were found to have the same upper limit:
pigons managed to score up to 5; parakeets and

jackdaws scored up to 6; grey parrot, Amazon parrot, magpie and common raven scored up to 7 (Lögler 1959). In the "successive" experiments the grey parrot even managed to score up to 8. Because of criticism—not all of a valid character—by Wesley, these experiments were largely ignored in the United States. But Zeier's (1966) best pigeon, in experiments carried out by means of Skinner's objective self-recording method, be it noted, scored as high as 8 in the "successive" series.

A jackdaw had been taught by Schiemann to "count" up to 5 in experiments in which it retrieved food morsels from a number of similar covered dishes, in which they were varyingly distributed from experiment to experiment. On one occasion, when the food morsels had been distributed in the sequence 1, 2, 1, 0, 1, the bird flew off already after the first three dishes had been opened, i.e., only with four morsels in its crop. After the observer had already recorded a "wrong" result, the bird returned through the still open trap door, nodded once to the first, twice to the second and once to the third dish, then opened the fourth, which it found to be empty, and finally opened the fifth, from which it took the fifth food morsel and made off with it. This behaviour is comparable with that of a child which gets stuck while reciting its lesson, starts again, quickly repeats what it has already said and thus, as a result of this second "approach run," succeeds in clearing the hurdle. Evidently the jackdaw "thinks" in terms of one nod for each unit: it can count in the abstract, the nods being the externally visible manifestation of this (Fig. 8-6).

The two abilities thus demonstrated, namely, to distinguish between groups of similar objects, and furthermore to respond to observed numbers and thus conceive a time relationship (although we all have a

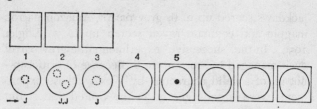

FIG. 8-6: *Experiment with the jackdaw (see text):*
*1, 2, 3=dishes opened in the first attempt (the squares
represent the opened covers, the dotted circles the morsels
of food taken); in the second attempt the bird nodded
once at 1, twice at 2, and once at 3 before passing on to
open the dishes 4 (empty) and 5 (containing food) (according to Schiemann).*

"mental clock," it does not mean to say that we possess a built-in time-sensing organ), have nothing in
common with each other in sensory terms. Only our
numerals in human speech (and then not even in all
languages) can count points simultaneously seen together just as well as they can count successive strokes
of a clock striking. To link the two abilities together—
i.e., to respond to numbers seen (the mother extends
four fingers; the child dips four times into the dish)
and to give a visual response to something already
accomplished ("How many cherries have you eaten?";
the child extends four fingers)—is something that
every normal child grasps instantly for any number
up to the limit of its counting capacity. On the other
hand, some mentally handicapped children learn this
only with considerable effort, as must also our experimental animals.

About twenty successful transposition experiments
that Lögler performed with a grey parrot included
one "successive-successive" transposition of a mixed
character: The parrot had learned to open the covers

of dishes, in response to two flashes of light, until it had found two morsels of food (these were placed in different dishes each time the experiment was repeated) and to look for a third morsel on seeing a third flash. It was then able to do the same thing when acoustic signals (whistled notes, or notes sounded on a flute or a tuning pipe) were substituted for the visual ones. It was even possible to obtain correct responses when visual and acoustic signals were arbitrarily mixed with one another, while no regular rhythmic pattern in presenting the signals was adopted, so that the bird received no help in this respect.

As long ago as 1935 Mrs. N. Kohts taught her chimpanzee to choose objects corresponding to specimens presented to it. Whenever she showed him a particular brick (from a child's box of toy bricks), the ape extracted a brick of the same shape from a heap on the table. If the bricks were, instead, placed in a deep bag so that he could not see them inside it, he was nevertheless able to pick out the correct one by relying on his sense of touch.

Thus two mixed (heteromodal) "successive-successive" transpositions have been conclusively demonstrated, namely, from visual to acoustic (grey parrot) and from visual to tactile (chimpanzee). When a creature is able to distinguish between shapes such as circle, triangle, square and rectangle both by its sense of sight and its sense of touch, it must be conceded that such a creature does indeed possess abstract concepts of shape; and a creature that can equate sequences of light flashes with sequences of acoustic signals (notes) and is at least able to learn "simultaneous-successive" transpositions in a variety of directions—and indeed achieves one of these spontaneously, i.e., without learning—must be rated as capable of abstract counting.

Mice learned to traverse a maze, from the start at A to the goal at E, where they were allowed to mount a wooden spoon and were returned to their case (Fig. 8-7). They were taught this with the aid of three

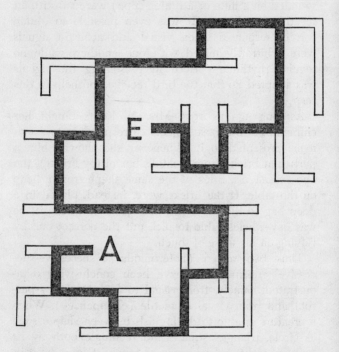

FIG. 8-7: *Maze used for experiments with mice. The correct path is marked by the heavy black line (start at A, end at E).*

special "clues" to help them and were able to go from start to finish without entering any of the twenty blind alleys. Small one-way trap doors were incorporated in the pathways in order to facilitate the

learning process. When these trap doors were removed, there was a setback in performance, and this
also occurred when the maze was cleaned so as to remove all traces of urine and other scent trails, or
when the whole maze was rotated after each run, so
that the echos from the walls sounded different. After
three months blind as well as normally sighted mice
were able to run unerringly through the maze without the three clues. But now if the maze was distorted in that the right angles were changed to angles
of 45 or 135 degrees, or the distance to be traversed
were doubled or the whole maze was transformed
into its mirror image or if, instead of a series of
straight passages, a maze consisting entirely of semi-
circular curved passages was used, none of the mice
had to be "re-educated." At first they did hesitate
sometimes, or retraced their steps for some distance,
and made a mistake or two. But then "the penny
dropped," and they ran unerringly to the goal: they
gave up the kinaesthetically determined running pattern acquired in the training maze and had in fact
learned a "path configuration" which was transposable
with regard to angles, distances and orientation—just
as a human being who can read is at once able to
read without difficulty a variety of handwritings or
printing types.

Any accurate observer of very young children who
as yet cannot speak or understand anything will confirm that they know exactly what they want. Also,
that when their range of vision becomes larger (looking out of the cot, standing in the playpen, crawling
and slithering, toddling, walking), they have a map-
like descriptive mental picture of the places they have
explored, together with all the possibilities offered by
them, and that even after several weeks' absence the
children at once utilise the possibilities just as they

had done before or restore old playing situations as they remember them. Furthermore, having subsequently learned to speak, they can give a correct account of things they had experienced before they were able to speak. The approximately nine-month-old son of Hans Honigmann, the former principal of the Birmingham zoo, was sitting on his mother's arm while being shown monkeys in a cage and was frightened when one of them put its arm through the bars and snatched away his mitten. A year later the boy, now able to walk and speak, was scolded by his father for being afraid of approaching the monkeys' cage. The boy defended himself by pointing to one of the monkeys and saying: "That one stole my mitten!" This is where man has a great advantage over the animal: both experience situations, form sensory impressions, demarcate their territory, classify fresh experience within the framework of old concepts, draw conclusions, learn and remember. But the animal will only in exceptional cases be able to concretise what it has learned and then only in a rudimentary fashion, whereas the human child learns it completely.

With its ability to babble a baby is born with the complete vocal range needed for learning any language in the world, as William Stern has pointed out; in addition, the baby, like the mockingbird, possesses the ability to imitate. Sometimes even ordinary birds will mock (imitate sounds) in specific situations. My grey parrot used to say "Hullo!" in imitation of his previous owner, when he picked up the telephone, and "Goodbye!," when someone left the room—which could be very helpful in cases where a departing visitor tended to prolong the conversation at the door. The parrot had also remembered the epithet "You sparrow!" and actually used it on one occasion when a sparrow had entered his cage to pick up some food that had fallen on the floor. A professor of philosophy who happened to be on a visit at the time was amazed at such "intelligence" and simply would not believe that it was a case of sheer coincidence. But saying "Hullo!" when the telephone is picked up, and "Goodbye!" when someone leaves the room, i.e., instances where words are imitated only in response to specific situations, are also the key to any understanding of words by a child learning to speak: the child associates the sound of the word with a long-familiar but unnamed meaning, and even a parrot is able to generalise and extend the scope of the unnamed concept, just as when the small child says "bowwow" to the dog and then says it to anything that walks about on four legs. For years we drank our coffee after lunch, according to an unvarying pattern, after which I went back to my office at the Institute. At first the parrot used to say "Goodbye!" when I reached for the door handle, but in due course he would say this a short time *before* I went to the door; at a later stage he would say it when I was taking leave of my wife, and still later he got into the habit of saying it as soon as I got up to go to her, but not when, for example, I went to fetch something from an adjacent room.

The first meaningful words uttered by a child also refer to things that are important to the child: mother, food, certain toys, to have. In accordance with the present state of knowledge, I have called this the "single-word sentence," meaning the limit of an animal's ability, whereas a child will, quite independently and unaided, form its first meaningful "two-word sentence" from words that it has learnt separately—e.g., it will say "cake gone" when the last piece of cake has vanished from the plate. When the grandmother says to the little boy who has not yet learned to speak: "Fetch Teddy," and he goes off and fetches his bear, the grownups will ask him to fetch other things; in this way they will find out how many names of objects he already understands, contrary to what they had expected.

Recently, however, this boundary has for the first time been crossed by an animal: Mr. and Mrs. Gardner (1968) managed to teach "Washoe," a female chimpanzee captured in the wild state when she was about ten months old, more than thirty words of the American sign language (ASL) for deaf mutes in a period of two years. Each mimic sign in this language denotes not a letter, but a word, as in Chinese. The ape used the sign for "flower" not only for actual flowers and pictures of flowers, but also for the to-bacco box and for the smell of roasting coming from the kitchen. Later on, she was taught the sign for "smell," and, with many setbacks, she learned to dif-ferentiate between the two within a few months. Washoe says "please come" to a calf and a dog, and correctly uses signs for "I," "me" and "you" in two- or three-word sentences; the grammatical ambiguity due to the absence of inflexions is overcome by the situa-tion in which the sentence occurs: Washoe makes a correct distinction between "I will tickle you" and "You must tickle me." In the eighty-third week of her training she responded to the words "let me kiss your doll" (in the sign language) by bringing her doll to the speaker. The results of further experiments, de-signed more particularly to eliminate possible un-witting transmission of signals by the experimenter to which the ape responds in a purely "mechanical" fashion, are awaited. Whether Washoe was able also correctly to understand sign-language messages trans-mitted to her independently of specific situations has not yet been consistently reported. To ask questions or to give a true account of something personally experienced—like the bee or the young child with its first two-word sentence—is as yet outside Washoe's range. It would appear, however, that the present author's surmise that the unmusical tarsier (a small arboreal mammal with huge goggle eyes) is much better able to learn, understand and use visual word signs than word sounds has been borne out.

For more and more species of birds and mammals it has been demonstrated that individuals recognise one another personally by the sound of their voices: for example, in a community of herring gulls the bird sitting on the nest can recognise amidst the general screeching the call of its mate approaching with food from a long way off. Young guillemots already learn to distinguish both parents' calls even before they are hatched (Tschanz). Parent martins can distinguish the voices of their offspring which have heedlessly left the nest for the first time from among the swarm of other martins wheeling and dashing about over the village pond and lead the young birds back to the safety of the nest at nightfall.

Some birds possessing imitative powers can do even better than this. Gwinner's male raven could bark like a dog; his mate imitated the gobbling of a turkey cock. When the male flew away, the female barked; when she was placed in a distant aviary, known to the male, he sat on the corner of his drinking tank and gobbled at her. Instead of the personal note of the original congenital call the acquired "foreign sound" becomes, as it were, a proper name with which individuals address each other.

In response to the ASL sign meaning "do that!" Washoe made the next sign in the sequence. To teach a parrot to say some specific thing in response to an order hardly ever succeeds. But the performing parrot

"Lora Eston" gave correct answers to more than thirty questions which her mistress put to her in a varying sequence in German. The bird also correctly answered a number of questions asked in French, English or Swedish. And this is by no means the only instance of such skill in a bird. But there is a trick which was disclosed to the present author by someone who had formerly trained it: the bird learns the question and the immediately following answer as a single unit, and then its response is narrowed down, by further training, to giving the answer only. Many a trained parrot which hears the beginning of a tune whistled in any key can take up the tune and finish it in the correct key. If the parrot joins in while the song is being whistled, it will be whistling in unison with the person. Thorpe (1967) discovered alternate singing in a species of African shrike under natural conditions, and a similar discovery in the case of another bird species was made by Albrecht and Wickler. Evidently such singing serves the purpose of strengthening the family ties.

Study of the sounds made by monkeys in captivity or living in the wild state has revealed that some species make upwards of thirty distinguishable sounds, though, so far as the present author is aware, it has nowhere been established that the animals can communicate personal experience independently of a specific situation by means of particular sounds alone. It would seem that many of the sounds are ambiguous as to any meaning they may convey. In addition, within the context of the specific situations, monkeys are apparently able to communicate excellently with one another by means of gestures and looks. J. van Lawick-Goodall (1967) describes how "Huxley," a chimpanzee, sat motionlessly looking at the trunk of a tree in the top of which a young baboon had taken refuge. Soon a group of chimpanzees which had been feeding quietly some way off came noiselessly running to the spot, and at once the hunt began, apparently in accordance with a well-thought-out over-all plan. Leyhausen (Lenneberg and Leyhausen 1968) reports an observation by Mottershead at Chester Zoo, Birmingham, where an electric wire had been pulled across the moat surrounding the chimpanzees' "island." An active male touched the wire and received two shocks in succession. Then he went to each member of the group in turn—scattered all over the island—and, putting his arms round him or her, appeared to whisper something in that member's ear. Having thus "got the message," the latter went to the place at the trench where the first male had had his "shocking" experience. When all the chimpanzees had gathered there, the biggest and strongest male seized a (wet) twig, waded into the moat and touched the wire, thus receiving a shock. After this demonstration no member of the group ever went near the wire again. Mrs. van Lawick is of the opinion, however, that in this instance the observer may, by staring at the offending wire, have attracted the various chimpanzees' attention to it.

In "thinking without words" it may be that apes in particular may be much in advance of even the most intelligent birds; but in the vocal imitation of sounds heard, even in specific situations, the birds are the winners. A certain parrot used to say "hoopoe" to birds of this species which it happened to encounter; according to another, older report, a parrot which frequented a garden would always call members of a family by their correct respective names. The present author's own grey parrot expressed a wish in a single-word sentence. He shrieked "koodooks" continuously at the top of his voice until his cage was covered up, the light was turned off and he was left in peace. Washoe, the chimpanzee, is reported to have formed two-, three- and four-word sentences in sign language. But no animal has ever yet, to the best of the present author's knowledge, ever asked a question, and only the honeybee (*Apis mellifica*) and another species of bee (*Apis indica*) are known to be able to communicate in minute detail something they have experienced. Information elucidating the evolutionary history of this ability has been provided by Lindauer's observations (1956) on the Indian bees *Apis dorsata* and *Apis florea*.

Animal Languages as Preliminary Stages and Preconditions of Human Speech

The animal inheritance of greatest importance to human speech is the capacity for "thinking without words," without which no child could begin to talk sensibly: it deduces the meaning of words heard for the first time from the situation in which these particular word sounds occur again and again, just as a parrot sometimes also does. While the child's unformulated desire for maternal contact, a toy, food, to be picked up, is being fulfilled it hears this particular emphasised word emerging from the general background of incomprehensible talk and associates it with the as yet nameless notion. It is only on account of the pre-existence of the notion that a word heard by a child learning to speak acquires its meaning, so that it is understood and is also (though this may be not until years later) repeated in a sensible context. When the child has grasped the meanings of some words, then it may in certain circumstances start telling about its own experiences, expressing wishes and, later on, also asking questions. During all this it quite automatically acquires the grammar of its native language. The fact that at first it tends to conjugate the irregular verbs as though they were regular ones are what W. Köhler has called "good mistakes."

How usefully human language, with the aid of increasingly comprehensive and generalised concepts, relieves us of the need for "wordless" rethinking, as would otherwise each time be necessary in all its details, is something that emerges, for instance, from a comparison of the "counting" achievements of birds with our own. When, under experimental conditions, we are deprived of the use of our numerals, our capacity for counting "in the abstract" is no better than theirs, and we can do a little better only with the aid of certain mental tricks. But as soon as we can use numerals and, to complete it, the decimal system (which was not known to the ancient Romans), the range of numbers and counting capabilities available to us at once expands enormously. Each new method of performing computations opens up explosively, as it were, new possibilities with tremendous savings of time and effort. Yet without our senses and the ability to co-ordinate the individual sensory perceptions—which is something that the young child does in its pre-speech stage just as any of the higher animals does throughout its life—without "wordless" thinking, we should have nothing to talk about in the first place. That this was not understood earlier is due, among other reasons, to the fact that only the human being possessing full powers of speech begins to think about the origins of language and retains no memory of his pre-speech infancy. And it is a surprisingly late realisation that the learning of a second language with the help of dictionaries and grammatical rules is an entirely different process from the learning of one's native language.

All through life our "wordless" thinking—i.e., our mental activities in obtaining sensory perceptions, remembering, comparing what we expect with what we are actually experiencing—is the touchstone on which the word is tested. Words are merely like a veil before the inner images, and these are by no means the reality either. In terms of human "common sense," and of science, words are "true" only insofar as they unambiguously and specifically interpret "unnamed" ideas, concepts and judgments. Mathematical axioms and aesthetic principles also derive from perceptions. To what extent logic and speculative and religious thought as intrinsic achievements of language itself are derivable from "wordless" thinking (in the sense envisaged here) is a question that could be profitably answered only by co-operation between all the various sectors of research involved, which is something yet to be achieved.

The happy ability of "picking up" not only our first words of speech but also all the subsequent peculiarities of dialect, intonation and subtle shades of accent, along with the whole grammar of the language, disappears at approximately the age of entering puberty. In learning a foreign language at school it sometimes still occurs that the new word "makes" the as yet unknown concept: we hear an unknown word and fully deduce its meaning from the definition accompanying it, without first having had to see, touch and smell the object represented by that word. In learning one's mother tongue, however, it is precisely the reverse: first the "unnamed" concept must exist. Fetch-bring, left-right, top-bottom, front-back (these three spatial co-ordinates are something that bees possess, just as we do), easy-difficult: without the underlying concepts such associated word pairs would be as meaningless to us as the names of colours to a person who has been blind from birth. Fortunately, the clear understanding of this is now spreading, be it very gradually (Koehler 1951, 1953, Count, Lenneberg and others).

But once verbal speech—thinking *with* words—exists, it transforms everything that we have inherited from the animals into something new, still with "unnamed" undertones, but with a meaning that is linguistically communicable with varying degrees of precision. Thus arises the new dimensions of the mind, which is forever closed to the animal: responsibility to oneself and to God, religion, art and science, and from this there emerge new degrees of freedom that far exceed anything comparable in animals. With the acquisition of speech and reason, man has lost the infallible instinctive certainty of the animal, and it becomes his duty to replace this, as far as possible, at the higher level of the mind by morality and ethics, together with reason applied to the examination and monitoring of their traditional forms. They make him both the most dangerous and the most endangered of all creatures. Nothing is obvious to him, everything becomes a problem. There is certainly no objection to calling attention to the fundamental significance of this great jump into a vastly larger dimension; but the fact remains that it is derived from preliminary stages already present in animals, as the development of any human child demonstrates. Everything that he needs for speech man owes to the "dumb" animals from which he is descended.

BERNHARD RENSCH

Basic Aesthetic Principles in Man and Animals

By means of a large number of observations and experiments it has, in recent years, been established that the anthropoid apes are capable of some astonishing mental achievements. Chimpanzees can learn to use such tools as spanners (wrenches), screwdrivers and wire cutters and to make meaningful use of these acquired skills in new situations. They can grasp causal relationships and utilise relevant experience. Also, they are able to weigh the effects of fairly long sequences of actions before starting. They therefore act with foresight and perhaps to a certain extent even with "insight" (B. Rensch 1968, B. Rensch and J. Döhl 1967, 1968).

But all their capabilities are subject to limitations because the chimpanzee, in contrast with man, has not evolved in its brain a "motor area" for speech. And it is the power of speech which has primarily secured for man his special position in the animal kingdom. It has turned *Homo sapiens* into a cultural creature, a creature that can link its conceptions to

words, that thinks in symbols and thus is able to identify logical and causal relationships. Also, it is speech
that makes it possible for us to report our experience
to our fellow men and to the next generation and
thus, by the formation of traditions, bring about the
rapid advance of our culture. Without speech no
ethics, religion, science, art, technology, administrative
patterns and meaningful social structures could have
developed. The origins of human ethics are, however,
already discernible in primitive instinctive form in
our animal ancestors, as K. Lorenz has strikingly
pointed out in his widely read book *Das sogenannte
Böse* (*So-called Evil*).

But what about artistic perception? Can higher
animals be credited with possessing certain aesthetic
feelings? In general this is regarded as most unlikely.
Yet Darwin did assume it. His theory of sexual selection (1901 and 1951) is based on the assumption that
female birds, for example, are able to appreciate the
beauty of male plumage. This view was, however,
disputed by A. R. Wallace (1889) and K. Möbius
(1906). Both these authors pointed out that we are
here dealing with an instinctive congenital response
to certain male "signal stimuli." The correctness of
this view was subsequently confirmed by numerous
animal psychological experiments. But complex bird-
song patterns and the scribblings and paintings of
apes and capuchin monkeys, on the other hand, suggest that certain basic aesthetic feelings can indeed
be assumed to exist in higher animals. Also, the already relatively high level of human pictorial art manifested in the middle Palaeolithic (Stone Age) suggests that an aesthetic sense extends far back into our
ancestral line of descent and possibly even into the
animal predecessors whence we have originated.

BASIC AESTHETIC PRINCIPLES IN MAN

If we are to find the answer to the question whether
the possession of aesthetic feelings by higher animals
is to be inferred from their behaviour, we must first
find out what, in man, is to be regarded as belonging
to the corresponding basic factors of perception and
judgment. The ancient Greek philosophers who concerned themselves with art and aesthetics were
already seeking to establish this. Since the eighteenth-
century aesthetics has evolved as a branch of philosophy and as a special subject of scientific investigation. However, it was not until much later that the
fundamental scientific principles were established
with greater precision by the more thorough empirical
investigations and aesthetic experiments conducted
by such researchers as G. T. Fechner (1876), T. Lipps
(1903, 1906), O. Külpe (1921), T. Ziehen (1923,
1925) and others. It was shown that in aesthetic effects the important aspect is always the feelings that
are produced and, more particularly, positive—i.e.,
pleasurable—feeling-tones which may occur as properties associated with many of our sensations and conceptions. Usually, in such cases, several feeling-components become merged together. For judging the
forerunners of aesthetic feelings in animals we must
consider only the "pure" components, i.e., those directly eventuating from perceptions, not those which
Kant has reckoned as belonging to "appended" beauty
and which, in man, are also very important, such as
may be caused by the spiritual content of a work of
art or by the natural beauty of a scene. On co-ordinating the available information concerning the aesthetically active feeling-components which have been
established particularly from experiments on the aes-

thetic preferences of children and from analyses of primitive cultural products we can state the following basic principles:

1. In the visual field certain colours and colour combinations have aesthetic appeal. Children and "primitive" tribes which have had little contact with modern civilisation usually prefer colours to shades of grey, black to white, and especially like intensive degrees of colour saturation (i.e., strong colours rather than pastel shades). Furthermore, the pure colours red, yellow, green and blue are more highly appreciated than mixed colours such as violet, yellowish green, brown or olive green. The fact that red is often most highly prized as a "warm" colour could be attributable to its powerful stimulative effect, but its contrast with the predominantly green shades of colour found in nature may also contribute to this.

When two colours are combined, children and primitive people usually show a preference for more or less complementary colours, i.e., red and green, yellow and violet, blue and orange. With two pure colours which are physiologically linked by simultaneous contrast, there is presumably an increase in clarity and therefore of perceptibility, while complexity is reduced, this being attended with positive feeling-tones. Correspondingly, combinations of colours which are only slightly different from each other are felt not to be beautiful, e.g., yellow and greenish yellow or violet and mauve. According to the "principle of disappointed expectation" the negative feeling-tone associated with such colour perceptions is produced by the fact that the two colours are not sufficiently distinct from each other and that it therefore demands some effort to perceive the difference.

Of course, the adult civilised human being, accustomed as he is to the works of art and the art fashions of many cultural periods, often reacts quite differently. He also assesses shades of colour, mixed colours, delicate tints and combinations of non-complementary colours. It is, however, quite typical that artists have again and again "rediscovered" the effect of pure bright colours and complementary colour combinations —more particularly such painters as Van Gogh, Gauguin, Matisse, Vlaminck, Derain and others. Henri Matisse, a leading figure in the group of artists who were called "les Fauves," once wrote: "This is the starting point of Fauvism: the courage to rediscover the purity of the media . . . A blue, for example, enhanced by its complementary colour, affects the senses like a powerful gong."

2. In the case of shape figurations a pleasurable sensation is produced more particularly by the repetition of stripes or dots, for example; or by measure and rhythm in music; or by regular alternations of stress, lines having equal numbers of syllables, rhyming or alliteration in poetry— makes for easier comprehension and reduces the complexity. This again is associated with positive feeling-tones, i.e., it produces a pleasurable sensation due to recurrence (T. Ziehen). In the case of primary bilateral symmetry, which is likewise experienced as pleasurable, the significant element is apparently the once-only mirror-image recurrence of similar components.

3. An easing of comprehension and its associ-

ated positive feeling-tone is also experienced on looking at the continuous curvature of a line or the outline of an object. A circle, a spiral, an S-curve, a wavy line, but even merely a straight line, are in general primarily experienced as more pleasurable than irregular or jagged lines. In these examples it is the "principle of the good shape" that is active. Similar positive feeling-tones are generated by the precision, the clarity, of a shape or configuration, especially the clarity with which it stands out from its surroundings, e.g., because of its sharp, clear-cut outlines ("principle of clarity").

4. In the case of more complex representations such as drawings and paintings an equilibrium between the left-hand and the right-hand side of the picture is, to the unbiased viewer, primarily more pleasurable than the predominance of one half of the picture. A balanced effect of this kind may, in the simplest case, be produced by a high degree of symmetry in the arrangement of individual components. If the two halves of the picture are very different from each other, the sense of equilibrium is obtained only if the intensity of the visual stimuli for the two halves approximately counterbalance each other. Correspondingly, when visual elements are presented in isolation within an enclosed area—e.g., a small cross or a solitary flower on a large square or circular area—a central position is primarily felt to be more pleasurable than an off-centre arrangement.

5. Finally, in the case of more complex material or immaterial representations, as also in music and poetry, a certain harmony is experienced as

being aesthetically more agreeable than disharmonious visual arrangements or sequences of notes or words. Such "unity in multiplicity" (eurhythmic or isodynamic quality) facilitates comprehension by its repetition of identical or similar components.

AESTHETIC PRINCIPLES IN THE BEHAVIOUR OF HIGHER ANIMALS

In animals the existence of positive feeling-tones, corresponding to basic human aesthetic feelings, can be inferred only from their behaviour, more particularly their preferences. Investigations in this connection have hitherto been carried out by two different methods. One of these consists in giving higher animals a choice of playthings in various colours, colour combinations or black-and-white patterns (Plates 37, 38 and 39). In the other method, monkeys are given chalks or pencils for scribbling or brushes and paints for painting (Plates 40 and 41). Both methods presuppose the animals to be in a relaxed condition and that their actions are not influenced by human beings.

SELECTION TESTS WITH MONKEYS, BIRDS AND FISHES

Tests for determining colour preferences can be carried out in various ways. Animals which have been shown to possess colour vision more or less similar to that of human beings may be offered small variously coloured cardboard discs or coloured wooden blocks for selection as playthings, or the animals' normal food may be offered to them in dishes with different colours or be placed beside or under variously coloured mats. The number of first choices made by the animals in fairly long series of experiments are counted. With monkeys it is moreover possible to let them actively form colour combinations by means of objects that can be stacked on top of one another or be fitted into one another (Plate 39).

If such experiments are repeated a sufficiently large number of times, they often reveal definite preferences whose relevance can be verified by means of statistical significance calculations. However, such results must not lead us at once to conclude that the animals' apparent preference must necessarily correspond to an aesthetic appreciation. Most animals are born with a positive or negative feeling-tone for particular colours or patterns. In the majority of cases these relate to distinctive markings or signs which are characteristic of the animals' species or which function as releasers in triggering their responses to one another. Thus a red-bellied male stickleback in search of a mate and defending his territory will respond to an elliptical piece of cardboard with its lower half painted red with the same attack movements as when confronted with another male stickleback invading his territory. On the other hand, the males of many songbird species show a preference for the distinctive colour of their own sex in experiments in which they can take food from differently coloured boxes equally distributed in octagonal cages, as has been proved by G. Dücker (1963) for a number of species, especially spotted weaver finches. A green long-tailed monkey (*Cercopithecus aethiops*) in selection tests with coloured balls showed a preference for white ones, a colour which also occurs in the bare skin around these creatures' eyes and is evidently a signal stimulus for the recognition of their own species.

When such innate "colour triggers" are eliminated from the experiments, higher animals are still found to show some preferences which correspond to the basic

aesthetic feelings in man. Several thousand tests performed with two species of monkey by the present
author yielded, among others, the following results
(B. Rensch 1957). In the selection of coloured cubes
the capuchin monkey and the green long-tailed
monkey showed a distinct preference for bright colours over shades of grey, just as human children do.
The probable reason for this preference is that the
stimuli which are associated with the sensations of
colour and which are generated in the cones of the
retina are more powerful than stimuli generated in
the rods, which respond only to varying degrees of
light and dark, i.e., to different shades of grey. Besides, colours usually stand out more distinctly from
their background than greys do and are therefore
more easily discernible.

In our monkeys there was no ascertainable preference for pure as opposed to mixed colours. In experiments involving the fitting together of coloured cubes,
however, there was statistically a significantly larger
number of instances where cubes of the same colour
were combined with one another than would correspond to the basic probability. As a result of so combining the cubes there is again a reduction in complexity, i.e., discernibility or comprehensibility is
enhanced, which presumably gave rise to positive
feeling-tones. When the monkeys were offered cubes
showing transitions from chrome yellow to dark red in
seven stages, while each particular colour was thrice
represented in the cubes all jumbled together, the
capuchin monkey more frequently combined either
those cubes out of the twenty-one which were of the
same colour or otherwise cubes of distinctly different
colours than cubes having directly "neighbouring"
shades of colour. The tendency to avoid sequences of
"almost equal" colours points to a behaviour pattern

conforming to the "principle of disappointed expectation" in that an apparent, but not sufficiently realised, similarity and at the same time a not sufficiently distinct difference would be created.

In order to investigate the existence of colour preferences in birds, we confronted a jackdaw and a carrion crow with six square pieces of cardboard which were arranged in a ring and which alternately displayed two different colours or were alternately one-coloured and two-coloured. After having overcome some initial distrust of the coloured cards, the birds playfully seized them with their beaks. In each case the first choice was observed and noted. There was found to be a statistically significant preference for grey and black over bright colours. Hence we are here evidently confronted, not with an aesthetic, but a congenital preference. Furthermore, in most cases, two-coloured cards were very much more frequently chosen than those provided with only one of the two colours, which is attributable to the greater stimulative power of the colour combination. Later supplementary tests with five jackdaws by M. Tigges (1963) showed that in many instances there is nevertheless a preference for bright colours rather than grey or black. Possibly such differences are caused by "moods," e.g., by a change of the reactions to a procreative mood as distinct from a purely playful mood. In experiments in which the birds were only offered cards in varying shades of grey there was a general preference for the darker of the two shades in any particular instance.

What can, however, be regarded as a manifestation of an aesthetic sense in jackdaws is their statistically significant preference for pure colours as against mixed colours, e.g., carmine red rather than lilac or light brown, and green rather than olive. Furthermore, Mrs. Tigges's jackdaws chose shining gold plates much more frequently than dull gold ones, and shining silver plates more frequently than dull silver ones. These results confirmed the well-known fondness that birds of the crow and raven family display towards shining objects. It would appear that the shining appearance attracts by its higher stimulative intensity.

Selection experiments with black-and-white patterns proved even more informative. In these experiments, too, pairs of patterns drawn on cards were laid out in a circular or a checkerboard arrangement or in rows (Fig. 9-1). Each pair comprised a symmetrical or rhythmic pattern on one card and an irregularly shaped pattern (but containing about the same quantity of black) on the other. After many thousands of individual tests it was established that, with relatively few exceptions, a capuchin monkey, a long-tailed monkey, a carrion crow and five jackdaws definitely preferred the regular patterns to the irregular ones. This result certainly cannot be explained in terms of congenital responses to particular signal stimuli. Three parallel black bars, three concentric squares or a semicircle cannot constitute innate "trigger patterns" in monkeys and birds. A much more likely assumption is that in these creatures, as in man, the recurrence of similar components in a symmetrical or rhythmic arrangement is more readily intelligible, less complex and therefore associated with positive feeling-tones, i.e., more "pleasurable." The reactions of these four species of creature differed somewhat in other respects, however. The capuchin monkey and the jackdaw usually looked at the patterns more attentively than did the long-tailed monkey, which seized the cards in a much more indifferent manner, so that in the case of four out of ten pairs of patterns the regular

FIG. 9-1: *Cards provided with rhythmic and symmetrical black-and-white patterns (right-hand row) between which the experimental animals had to choose. Of each pair of patterns six or eight individual patterns were offered for choice, laid out either in a circle or a row.*

and the irregular pattern were chosen with equal frequency.

Then, at the present author's suggestion, Mrs. Tigges offered her jackdaws also a choice out of three different pairs of patterns: two circles of equal size side by side, two circles nearly equal in size, and two circles clearly different in size; also, three pairs of squares corresponding in arrangement to the circles were used in these experiments. Analysis of the results of one thousand tests of this kind shows that a significantly smaller number of choices were made in favour of the combination of nearly equal circles or nearly equal squares. Jackdaws, just like people, therefore acted in accordance with the "principle of disappointed expectation"—i.e., they tended to avoid the combinations in which the difference between the two circles, or the two squares, was not directly and distinctly apparent; instead, they preferred the combinations in which the two circles or two squares were of equal size or were clearly different.

It now seemed reasonable to consider whether vertebrate animals of more primitive types do not also prefer patterns which in human beings, and apparently also in the above-mentioned monkeys and birds, generate a basic aesthetic pleasurable sensation. For example, it seemed that such experiments could suitably be carried out with fishes. In these creatures, however, the visual sense centres are located, not in the forebrain, but in the top wall of the midbrain. Rather different experimental methods had to be employed here. A fish cannot be expected to play with specimen cards or plates. We accordingly put a fish (of the species *Macropodus viridiauratus Lac.*) in a round enamel dish at the centre of which was placed a round glass jar, so that the fish had an annular "swimming track" at its disposal. Along the encircling wall of the dish it could see black-and-white patterns, which were so arranged that two rhythmic or symmetrical ones alternated with two irregular ones, and so on. The fish appeared to look fairly attentively at the patterns, which indeed were the only features that could attract attention in the basin. The number of times that the fish spent more than thirty seconds stationary in contemplation of any particular—regular or irregular—pattern were counted. The results obtained with two fishes of this species tested in succession were definite: both fishes looked substantially more frequently at the irregular patterns; the percentages relating to the majority of pairs of patterns were statistically significant.

In other experiments performed with fishes of a different species (*Carassius carassius gibelio*) they had to learn to swim up to a circular rotatable synthetic-glass disc to which six white paper squares were affixed, on one of which a small worm was presented as food. Once the fishes had got into the habit of regularly swimming up to the disc, the white squares were replaced by regular and irregular black-and-white patterns, but were offered no food. Instead, each fish was given food as a reward only when it had touched a pattern with its nose and then turned away. Again a count was made of the number of times that a regular or an irregular pattern was thus selected (Plate 40).

The tests were performed with four *Carassius* specimens and subsequently also with four fishes of yet another species (cichlids)—nearly fifteen thousand tests in all. These yielded clear-cut results: with few exceptions, the fishes showed a statistically significant preference for the irregular over the regular patterns. It thus appeared that the fishes instinctively chose patterns which more closely resembled the irregular shapes of objects encountered in their natural habitat, e.g., water plants or stones. I felt almost a sense of relief at this result: it would surely be somewhat uncanny to suppose that even a fish should have "basic aesthetic feelings," though this could well have been possible, because these creatures, too, could have experienced a sense of easier comprehensibility in the regular patterns and perhaps have overresponded to the more powerful stimulative effect of the irregular patterns.

SCRIBBLINGS AND PAINTINGS BY MONKEYS

Painting experiments were conducted by N. Kohts with a chimpanzee in Moscow since 1913 (the results were not published until 1935, however), and in 1915 W. T. Shepherd reported that a chimpanzee drew lines with a pencil. Since then numerous publications dealing with the scribblings and paintings of chimpanzees, gorillas, orangoutangs and capuchin monkeys have appeared, and D. Morris even wrote a whole book on the subject (1962). Analysis of these reports makes it possible to shed some light on the question whether apes and monkeys possess basic aesthetic feelings. Besides, in 1957, the Institute of Contemporary Arts, London, held an exhibition of paintings by monkeys, and since then various other similar exhibitions have been held in America, Holland, Belgium and Germany. As there is a recognised form of abstract expressionism in human painting called "tachisme" ("action painting"), it is justifiable to apply the term "painting" also to these monkeys' productions.

If a monkey of one of the above-named species is given a pencil, a piece of chalk or a paintbrush and is shown how, by pressing it on paper, it can produce a visible mark, the animal will nearly always at once begin scribbling a painting (Plates 41 and 42). This is a game that the animals usually indulge in quite attentively at least for a time. The results they produce in this way are rather variable. Of major importance are the size, shape and position of the sheet of paper to be painted (whether vertical, sloping or horizontal on the table or the floor of the cage), thickness of the pencil or brush, interest or indifference of the animal and the experience and practise it already possesses.

In the simplest case, more particularly with "uninterested" or "untalented" chimpanzees, the results are scribblings very similar to those that an eighteen-month-old human infant will produce (Plate 43). They consist of slightly curved, more or less parallel, inclined groups of lines which are drawn by moving the hand to and fro sideways. The underlying urge appears to be no more than the pleasure felt in performing "motor" movements and making visible marks. Aesthetic factors certainly do not enter into it.

Much more often, however, and especially when apes are given paintbrushes, fan-shaped patterns are produced which express a certain rhythm and also, in consequence of the convergence of the lines towards the base, a certain dynamism (Plate 44). Whether primitive aesthetic feelings play a part in this connection is hard to decide. But if the ape is successively given, in a scheduled sequence, brushes dipped in paints of different colours, so that it is possible subsequently to know in what sequence the lines and daubs were produced, there is in many instances undeniable evidence of a certain harmony in the "painting" (Plates 45 and 46). The centre or, rather, the "centre of gravity" of the picture is located roughly in the middle of the sheet, the lines are more or less equally spaced and thus display a certain rhythm and the right-hand and the left-hand half of the picture are sometimes relatively well balanced against each other. In some cases this is more particularly manifested in the fact that the ape marks out the whole width of the "fan" with the first brush, while with the second and the third brush (if any) it starts less far over to the left and ends correspondingly less far to the right. When the choice of colour was left to the apes themselves, there was usually no noticeable preference, and not infrequently they smeared all the colours on top of one another. In other cases chimpanzees used chalk merely in an attempt to apply a uniform layer of colour to the paper, to part of the wall or to the floor of the cage. The present author experimented with "Pablo," a capuchin monkey which painted long, more or less vertical straight or somewhat curved lines on sheets of paper pinned to a vertical surface.

In the chimpanzees studied by D. Morris there was found to be a certain development towards improvement in the animals' achievements. The present author observed the same effect in "Julia," a chimpanzee kept at the research institute. When she was about three years old, she painted chiefly "fan" patterns; rather elaborate combinations of curved lines (Plates 45 and 46). Although some of these paintings may appear aesthetically pleasing to the human observer, it is nevertheless difficult to decide to what extent the apes or other monkeys were inspired by primitive aesthetic feelings.

The results can be more reliably judged when experiments are conducted in which individual aesthetic factors can be somewhat more specifically analysed. P. H. Schiller (1951), experimenting with a chimpanzee named "Alpha," had drawn various diagrams in blackdots on sheets of paper (a circle, a cross, a triangle or several squares) by way of demonstration and then let the ape "have a go" with crayons. He found that the ape usually confined its scribblings to the interior of the diagrams, though sometimes it drew right across them. Similar behaviour has been observed in other chimpanzees and also in capuchin monkeys. A diagram drawn in advance nearly always presents a temptation to scribble on top of it or to fill in the empty space inside it.

D. Morris found that when such a diagram, e.g., a grey triangle, was placed off-centre on a sheet of paper, so that it was near an edge, the chimpanzee named "Congo" did not paint over the diagram but, instead, often scribbled on the vacant area of the sheet in such a manner as to produce, it seemed, a certain amount of over-all equilibrium. In similar experiments with a female chimpanzee and with a capuchin monkey the present author was unfortunately unable to repeat Morris's results. Both animals nearly always scribbled or painted across the rectangles, crosses or circles that the experimenter had drawn for them in advance; they drew lines extending also into the vacant half of the sheet, but not in such a way as to establish a balance.

It proved possible to test the principle of centralisation more definitely. Two chimpanzees at the Münster zoo were successively given some circular sheets of paper 4 inches and 3 inches in diameter. After the apes had scribbled on them in pencil for about two or three seconds, the sheets were taken away from them. It was found that the animals had almost invariably started scribbling fairly accurately at the centre of each sheet. In tests where apes were allowed to paint and draw on large rectangular sheets (usually 12 inches by 18 inches) it was also often observed that they started at approximately the centre of the sheet.

There was also very clearly a certain degree of adaptation of the lines to the size of the paper. When the apes were given circular sheets (12 inches and 5½ inches in diameter), they were tempted to produce more sharply curved lines; narrow rectangular sheets caused them to produce correspondingly elongated sets of lines; and very narrow sheets resulted in lines drawn almost parallel to the edges of the sheets (Plate 47).

Contrary to our expectation, black circles, double crosses or broad parallel lines (about ⅜ inch wide) drawn in advance on large sheets of paper (12 inches by 18 inches) tempted two chimpanzees and our capuchin monkeys only occasionally to produce similar sets of lines. Often the animals casually painted over the so very conspicuous diagrams that they found on the paper. Different results were obtained when we offered the chimpanzees (two zoo animals and one kept in the research institute) patterns formed by strips of white paper (½ inch to ⅞ inch wide) stuck on to grey cardboard. The patterns were in the shape of a ring (6¾ inches diameter), a triangle (7 inches base length), a square (6 inches side length), a wavy line, a zigzag line or a spiral. In these experiments the three chimpanzees nearly always tried to keep the black brush strokes on the white strips, i.e., to be guided by or indeed to "reproduce" the white diagrams in black paint (Plate 47).

Such results must not, however, be rated as first steps towards the copying of examples. True copying has not hitherto been observed in experiments with any of the anthropoid apes. With our institute's female chimpanzee we had tried to achieve this by drawing a triangle or a square in chalk on a black-

board and, in addition, marking the three or four
corners in chalk beside each diagram. The ape soon
learned to connect these points by a continuous line,
so that something approximately resembling a triangle or a square was drawn. Next, we proceeded to
make the corner marking points fainter and fainter.
When they had become almost invisible, however, the
ape merely painted an irregular roundish diagram,
irrespective of whether the example next to it was a
triangle or a square. The animal had therefore only
learned to draw some sort of outline, but had not understood that a diagram had to be copied.

MONKEY'S PAINTINGS AND HUMAN ART

Summarising the results described in the foregoing, it
can be said that the behaviour of monkeys and birds
(more particularly of the raven and crow family)
points to the existence of basic aesthetic feelings in
these creatures in that they prefer rhythmic and symmetrical patterns to irregular ones, sometimes also
prefer colours to grey, and in many cases, when confronted with combinations of colours or patterns,
avoid acting in accordance with the "principle of disappointed expectation." Many of the drawings and
paintings produced by monkeys also show this to some
extent: these efforts produced in play often reveal
rhythm, dynamism, adaptation of the strokes to the
shape and size of the sheet, centralisation and some
degree of balance between the right-hand and the
left-hand side of the sheet.

The achievements of monkeys must not be over-
rated, however. Nothing indicates that the animals
have a conception of what they want to depict, and
only in a small number of instances do they of their
own accord stop painting away on a sheet of paper.

Human tachistic painters do, however, assert that they, too, by no means always have a preliminary conception of the composition that they are about to produce, but that, instead, they let themselves be inspired by any initially emerging colour and shape elements to continue working in particular directions. Nor is it always clear whether a picture, on reaching a particular stage of development, is "finished" or whether further components need to be added to complete it —or whether, alternatively, any such additions would merely "spoil" it.

Yet it is undeniable that many paintings produced by monkeys—and not just specially selected exceptional ones, but sometimes whole series of such paintings—are aesthetically pleasing to human beings. It has indeed occurred that competent art experts, on being shown monkeys' paintings without being told who had painted them, sometimes enthusiastically praised the dynamism, rhythm and sense of balance. In so doing they have not made fools of themselves, but simply confirmed what the experimental biologists had already also established. Of course, when the art historians, museum directors or architects who had thus been led into pronouncing opinions on such paintings were afterwards told who the "artists" were, they were always rather put out and sometimes even offended at the deception that had been practised upon them—as the present author has himself had occasion to experience. In view of this it is hardly surprising that in cases where, at modern art exhibitions, a surreptitiously included monkey's painting has received acclaim from the critics, subsequent disclosure of the deception has produced something of a scandal, as has occurred in Sweden, for example.

Human pictorial art usually also has quite different aims, however, which can in no sense exist in connection with monkeys' paintings: it wants to make "statements." For this the content of the picture is generally of decisive importance in one way or another in that it arouses certain associations of ideas in the viewer. Every naturalistic picture has such an effect. But in general we attribute a higher artistic value only to those pictures in which, in consequence of concentration or transcendence of the depiction, and in consequence of the composition, the expressive power is intensified—i.e., in cases where we are confronted with an expressionist representation, for once using this term in its literal and widest sense, so that it embraces the works of Giotto and El Greco as well as those of the twentieth-century expressionists including semi-abstract paintings and even also works of the impressionists, who have given us intensified representations of light and air and the sparkle of sunshine.

Surrealist painting, too, has transcended nature to an almost limitless extent and has given rise to entirely new concepts. These developments were, however, often exposed to a danger due to an innate human biological characteristic, namely, that we tend to react with a negative feeling-tone when confronted with a picture that seems too "unorganic." The exaggerated distortion of familiar proportions in the objects, plants, animals or human beings depicted by the artist may indeed be carried very far in order to strengthen the impression that it is desired to produce. Blue horses, green faces, fanciful plants and unreal landscapes may have a notable artistic effect. An artist can go amazingly far in the chimera-like combination of totally heterogeneous and incongruous components, as is manifested in many surrealist paintings, such as those of Max Ernst, for example. We are, however, very sensitive with regard to human faces or bodies. Just like all other higher animals, we are born with the instinct to react positively to a particular normal appearance. Major deviations from these inherited "trigger characteristics," which in animals—and also in man's remote ancestors—are essential to recognising the animal's own species or members of the opposite sex, are felt to be pathological or in some other way repulsive. It is therefore a highly questionable artistic experiment to paint a human face with eyes on its cheeks, as Picasso has done, or to represent a head as a mere knob on a piece of sculpture, in the manner of Henry Moore. Also, the sense of pity or horror aroused by extreme pathological deformations of a human body or by the picture of a giraffe on fire imposes a limit upon the degree of admiration that we can feel for a picture. What the average viewer dislikes about such pictures is not that they are too unrealistic but that their individual components are in fact still too realistic. Only the rhythm of structural or coloral elements that is nearly always present is able to elevate such dubious pictures into the sphere of art.

As already stated, the only human paintings with which the paintings produced by monkeys can validly be compared are those belonging to the category of tachisme, in which the pictorial content is of very little or no effect. In any case the amount of "statement" contained in such paintings is very slight. Usually it is a matter of perceptional effect, a pleasurable sensation produced by rhythm, tension, movement, harmony or colour combination. But quite a few present-day artists want to ban all demands that art should have an aesthetic content. However, if rhythm, harmony and pictorial balance are completely eliminated from tachistic art, there remains nothing but a meaningless jumble, to which many a quite pleasing monkey's painting would be preferable.

AESTHETIC PRINCIPLES IN THE ACOUSTIC SPHERE

Suffice it merely to point out briefly that some of the songs and sound imitations of birds make it seem likely that these creatures experience auditive aesthetic sensations. In human musical appreciation the basic aesthetic factors are more particularly: time, rhythm and harmony. It is possible, though difficult to prove conclusively, that birds which can utter widely different patterns of song—e.g., blackbirds and mockingbirds (*Mimus*)—have pleasurable aesthetic sensations. This is suggested by the fact that these species, as well many others, including parrots, ravens, beos and lyrebirds, habitually imitate the sounds, calls or songs of other species or incorporate them into their own sound sequences (W. Craig 1963, E. Tretzal 1965, 1967). Craig also pointed out that the songs of many bird species are rhythmic and are composed of sounds, not of noiselike tones such as are characteristic of many of the warning or threatening calls of birds. J. Kleinbrecht (1968), who studied under the present author, was able to prove by exact methods that hens are able to learn to solve visual problems, and to remember them longer, when they simultaneously hear periodic tone sequences than when the tones of equal character and frequency follow one another aperiodically. Important also are J. Reinert's (1965) discovery that jackdaws, after being trained to certain rhythms, are able to recognise them even when played by different instruments, i.e., with a different tone quality (timbre), or when the tempo, pitch or intervals are altered. They can also learn to distinguish in general between two-four and three-four time.

HANS-GÜNTER ZMARZLIK

*Social Darwinism in Germany—
An Example of the Socio-political
Abuse of Scientific Knowledge*

The history of the natural sciences can be dealt with in isolation by considering only their objective logical interrelation through the ages. But if we extend our range of vision, this apparently separate and self-contained field is seen to become part of the history of the sciences in general. These have more and more become instruments in mankind's conduct of practical affairs. They have released man from the tyranny of natural conditions and enabled him to become master of the earth. It is now no longer possible to gain a proper understanding of general history if the part played by the sciences in shaping it is ignored. We must therefore concern ourselves with interrelations which constitute the links between the scientist's striving for knowledge and the politician's more mundane aims. In most cases such links have been established through a number of intermediate stages. For this reason the belief in the innocence of disinterested science as contrasted with the questionable character of politico-sociological practices has managed to survive. It is a kind of self-preservation of those who adopt scientific careers and are now more than ever dependent on the state and the community —a useful regulating factor. For it not to become a factor of self-deception, it must not be forgotten how often already a seemingly harmless theory has been made subservient to inhuman practice. Social Darwinism and its effect in Germany affords an impressive example of this.

Everyone knows how callously human dignity was disregarded under the Nazi regime in the Third Reich. One may ask oneself how a nation which was second to none in its level of civilisation and humanitarian achievements was induced to follow a leader who, under the motto: "You are nothing, your nation is everything," radically rejected the individual's claim to freedom in pursuing his own aims and instead humiliated him to a mere unit of human material whose sole function would henceforth be the fulfilment of collective aims. In seeking explanations, we encounter, among the many underlying causes, certain ideological factors that emerge more prominently: a dogma of inequality based on certain theories of racial biology; moral nihilism based on the supposed universal validity of the "struggle for existence" as a law of nature; and finally—as a corollary of the two— the conviction that the weeding-out of racially or biologically inferior, and the selection of superior, individuals is necessary to a strong and vigorous nation and therefore entirely justified.

"Struggle for existence," "weeding-out," "selection" are terms that owe their origins to Darwinism; and this is by no means accidental: anyone who spends a little time browsing in *Mein Kampf*, the book in which Hitler set forth his political views and philosophy, will at once perceive how strongly a social-Darwinist form of monism helped to determine the intellectual horizon of the National Socialist leadership. And the historian must add that this vulgarised Darwinism is among the few ideological elements which Hitler did not manipulate arbitrarily to suit his power-political tactics but which instead governed his mental attitudes throughout his career as a politician and demagogue. In the context of the history of ideas it is for this reason necessary to investigate the origin and significance of this type of Darwinism. It does not matter greatly, for the present purpose, to know precisely where Hitler and his followers got their ideas. More important is the question whether these perhaps belonged to the primitive category of conceptions which are to be found in politically right-wing bourgeois circles. For this would help us to understand why the inhuman mentality and actions of Hitler and his party did not, in these strata of society, meet with the opposition and rejection that one would really have expected from people of their intellectual and ethical status.

But this extension of our range of vision is not sufficient either. If we are to understand the historical importance of social Darwinism we must not narrow down the question merely to the previous history of the Third Reich. We will therefore examine the social effects of Darwin's doctrine from the very beginnings.

EARLY EFFECTS OF DARWIN'S THEORY

The significant year for our present purpose is 1859, when Darwin published his most important book: *On the Origin of Species by Means of Natural Selection, or the Preservation of Favoured Races in the Struggle for Life*. This book was eminently opportune. Within a few years it had not only revolutionised the science of biology but had also fired the imagination of intellectuals far beyond that field. In the title Darwin, with characteristic precision, formulated the essence of his theory: it links the idea of the evolutionary interrelation of all living organisations—an idea which had repeatedly cropped up since Buffon and Lamarck but for which no sound basis had hitherto been established—with a theory of natural selection, i.e., the doctrine that changes in species are brought about as the result of a process of selection applied to varying descendants in the biological struggle for survival.

What tremendous explosive power is locked up in this scientifically cold statement of the doctrine becomes evident when we call to mind the intellectual horizon of Darwin's contemporaries. Pre-Darwinist biological thinking based itself, broadly speaking, on two metaphysical premises: the assumption of general prototypes (a concept that had found its most thoroughgoing expression in Plato's philosophical doctrine of ideas) and the conception of individual directed potentialities in the manner of what Aristotle called "entelechy." Though in modified form, they governed all attempts at interpreting the rich store of empirical data that had been assembled in zoology, botany, embryology, palaeontology and allied sciences in the first half of the nineteenth century. As opposed to these "ideal" doctrines, which regarded all events in living nature as conforming to some predetermined spiritually conceived pattern and detected a shaping and guiding hand behind the phenomena—a purposeful, planning and directing force, or in short: a higher unity in the multiplicity of empirically established phenomena—Darwin formulated his causal-mechanistic explanation which was able to dispense with any metaphysical or supernatural factors. The wonderfully "purposeful" or "functional" character of living organisms, the way they appear to fit so meaningfully into the pattern of biological relationships, had previously been regarded as the manifestation of some supreme directing principle, or in Christian terms: the revelation of God's creative power in nature. Under the new interpretation, however, the functional efficiency of organisms would no longer be dependent on purposeful causes but would instead be conceived as resulting from a mass of in themselves non-purposeful adaptational possibilities which are selected or rejected according to whether or not they are able to reserve or enhance the viability of individuals or groups at any particular time. The biological design of organisms would henceforth be conceived as the total outcome of a series of improvisations, far removed from any ideal "grand scheme." By the same token the whole natural universe must be the product of blind chance.

In this way Darwin took the metaphysics and the "magic" out of natural phenomena by reducing them to scientifically explicable functional relationships. He "naturalised" biology and adopted a realistic-historical approach to the phenomena, i.e., he replaced the hitherto generally assumed constancy of biological species by an all-embracing evolutionary relationship which, emerging from previously unsuspected depths of time, interrelated the whole multitude of forms in animate nature into a process of gradual ascent from the simplest to the highest organisms—a proposition which Darwin conclusively supported with an amazing array of factual evidence.

As a result, the evolutionary conception received an unprecedented impetus. This in turn had profound effects on the sciences as a whole, with repercussions on the over-all social pattern. However, such indirect

PLATE 29: *Common raven feeding its young.*

PLATE 30: *Adult ravens engaged in billing.*

PLATE 31: *Young long-tailed monkey seeking refuge at its mother's breast.*

PLATE 32: *This Masai woman leaves one breast bare—an example of a "maternal signal" which has lost its original function and become a "social signal" of wider scope.*

PLATE 33: *The breast of the female gelada, a species of baboon.*

PLATE 34: *Male courtship behaviour which has been adapted to serve as a conciliatory gesture in a species of perch.*

PLATE 35: *Female copulatory invitation serving as a social greeting among Arabian baboons.*

PLATE 36: *Galápagos finch (Cactospiza) using a cactus spine to prod insect larvae out of their holes.*

PLATE 37: *Jackdaw choosing between single-colour and two-colour cards (B. Rensch 1958).*

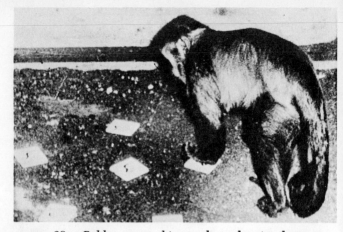

PLATE 38: *Pablo, a capuchin monkey, choosing between cards with a regular pattern (semicircle) and an irregular one (B. Rensch 1957).*

PLATE 39: *Pablo fitting together cubes of different colours.*

effects will not be considered here. Directly and most distinctively the dynamic social implications of Darwin's doctrine manifested themselves in the violent controversies that at once broke out between the Darwinists and the champions of the Christian religion. What particularly offended the latter was the fact that the evolutionary principle was applied not merely to the vegetable and animal kingdoms, but also to the human species: it explicitly and unavoidably presented man as having evolved from animal ancestors. Although this concept contained no definite assertions about the origin and character of those particular qualities that give man his special position as a creature that is conscious of itself, the obliteration of the border line between man and animal as a result of the demonstration of their natural interrelation produced an extremely severe shaking-up of man's conventional image of himself and contained a latent temptation to slide into a naturalistic anthropology.

It would certainly be appropriate to the present discussion to examine the ways in which theologians and biologists have come to terms with one another in the course of time. After the polemics of the first few decades, they eventually arrived at greater objectivity in their discussions, so that nowadays each side graciously concedes to the other its own well-defined legitimate territory, although full clarification of the problem has not yet been achieved. But we must leave that as it is and, instead, take a look at those attacks which, going outside the bounds of disciplined scientific discussion, have been levelled against the credibility of Christian doctrines by the exponents of a Darwinistically inspired monism. Such attacks can be shown to have occurred in the Western cultural sphere in the eighteen-sixties and -seventies. In Germany they assumed the most outspoken forms. In this

country, biblical criticism and philosophical materialism had, even before Darwin's time, provided food for
scepticism about the credibility of the Christian doctrine of divine revelation. All the more inexorably did
popular liberal thinking, in the then following period
of German history referred to as the *Kulturkampf*
(characterised by the struggle between the state and
the Roman Catholic Church), seize upon the arguments that Darwin's theory offered. One of the main
protagonists in that struggle was Ernst Haeckel, a
professor at Jena, whose undoubted eminence as a
zoologist was equalled by his naïvety as a philosopher. His controversial assertions and those of his
supporters appeared to constitute so serious a threat
to established religion that in the eighteen-eighties
the teaching of biology in the upper forms of grammar schools and other secondary schools in Germany
was discontinued—a measure which (with some exceptions) remained in force for more than three decades.

Another prominent symptom of the importance acquired by Darwinism distorted into a "philosophy of
life" was the tremendous success of Haeckel's book
entitled *The Riddle of the Universe* (*Welträtsel*).
Published in 1899 and intended as a compendium of
a monistic "natural religion" based on Darwinism, it
was translated into more than twenty languages and
had by 1914 sold upwards of 300,000 copies in Germany alone. By then, however, Haeckel's readers
were no longer the upper-middle-class *Kulturkampf*
liberals of the late nineteenth century. Instead, they
were now drawn largely from the lower middle and
the working class and from young people of all social
strata, who obtained from this turbid source the
knowledge that their schools had denied them.

To what extent these readers were receptive to

Darwin's ideas as a lasting influence is something that admittedly cannot now be ascertained. But there are many indications that the fascination of Haeckel's theories lay not so much in what was propounded in detail as in the fact that the established authority of the Church was assailed most virulently and apparently with the full weight of science to support the attack. For this reason Haeckel's "philosophical Darwinism" became part and parcel of a more comprehensive stream of mass enlightenment whose advocates were committed to a scientific interpretation of the universe and to an anti-Christian or, at any rate, an anti-clerical attitude of mind. In this way he helped to prepare the ground for a materialistic-naturalistic anthropology. Insofar as this is concerned his activities come within the scope of the present article, but in an unspecific manner. For the criticism here levelled against the Christian doctrine left the accepted socio-ethical standards unscathed. It was particularly on the basis of Darwinistically interpreted evolutionism that the free self-realisation of the individual under the motto "Let man be noble, helpful and good" was indeed supposed to become fully possible. Evolution was conceived optimistically—entirely in the spirit of the liberal creed—as continuous progress to higher and higher moral perfection, a pre-established harmony between individual self-interest and public welfare.

Something similar can be said of the leading British propagandist of a monistic synthesis on a Darwinistic basis, Herbert Spencer, whose influence was widely felt particularly in the United States, but who also had followers and imitators in Germany. He, too, believed in a process of evolution which proceeded automatically to higher things as a fundamental law governing social as well as natural phenomena and which was urged along to unceasing cultural and moral progress by the competitive struggle of the individuals. Thus Spencer was in complete agreement with the laissez-faire ideology of the Manchester School of economic liberalism which exercised considerable influence in his day—but not with Darwin's theory.

The central feature of Darwin's theory is an essentially undirected and (in terms of value) neutral selective process. Although Darwin, in referring to the "improvement of most organisms with regard to their fitness to survive," admitted to a certain degree of direction of the evolutionary process to higher and more efficient types, he nevertheless avoided deducing value criteria from this. Being the uncompromisingly keen observer that he was, he had found that not every evolutionary change in nature must necessarily be a change for the better, a development to something higher. Strictly speaking, his doctrine stated that success in the struggle for existence could signify no more than biological suitability under the given conditions of life. But those who exalted Darwinism above its actual field of application into a universally interpretative principle projected their belief in progress and their liberal ideology into it—with the result that they came to regard Darwinistic evolution as the royal road to higher and higher levels of humanity. They failed to perceive that any attempt to apply Darwin's explanation of biological phenomena to social evolution must lead to a naturalistic degradation of the human image and that the presupposed universal validity of the principle of the struggle for existence must have inhuman consequences. They did not see that any kind of social Darwinism must inevitably lead to conflict with the socio-ethical standards that regulate the relationships within human societies.

This manifested itself more clearly when, in the period of imperialism, the emergence of the middle classes and nationalistic conflicts in eastern central Europe, faith in the automatic upward progress and in pre-established harmony of the over-all social process evaporated. This basic change in the climate of the times, which began to appear all over western Europe in the eighteen-seventies and achieved a general breakthrough some twenty years later, was characterised by a brutalisation in political style. What previously could still be regarded as free competition of individuals exercising their skill in aspiring to moral improvement now appeared as a perennial struggle for self-assertion and greater power—and no longer as a contest of individuals but of whole groups: social classes with the same interests to protect, nations, races.

Now the theory of natural selection, which had hitherto remained in the background behind the conception of evolution, acquired decisive importance in the sphere of social-Darwinistic ideas. From the fundamental law proclaiming the struggle for existence a system of Darwinistic social ethics was developed which assigned a central role to self-preservation and self-assertion. The right of the strongest was postulated, and in this way the power egoism of the group, the nation or the race to which one belonged was sanctioned. As a logical consequence, Christian ethics and the principles of "natural law" and humane behaviour—an inheritance from the late eighteenth century, the Age of Reason—were assailed and rejected as a flabby morality of compassion for the undeserving or indeed mere dabbling in humane sentiments for

their own sake: attitudes no longer suited to the new
and harsher times that had now arrived.

There were various reasons why such ideas came to
be widely accepted, more particularly in the United
States, in Britain and not least in Germany, where the
Alldeutscher Verband (Pan-German League) and
other nationalistic activist groups within the educated
middle class very loudly and insistently proclaimed
the struggle-for-existence ideology. But, as a rule, they
used slogans without any explicit social-Darwinistic
basis. The latter was to be found more strongly represented at a lower social level, namely, where lay the
origins of the popular movement whose notions
helped to shape the ideological outlook of German
national socialism.

RACIAL ANTHROPOLOGY AND RACIAL HYGIENE

In the foregoing, two aspects of social Darwinism
have been referred to: the optimistic doctrine of evolutionism and the brutal struggle-for-existence ideology. In Germany a third now emerged, which could
be described as "later social Darwinism." It began to
assert its influence around the turn of the century and
was distinctly different from the earlier ideologies.
The earlier social Darwinists had applied the supposedly all-embracing laws of nature in bulk to human society. Their successors looked down from the
heights of Neo-Kantian philosophy disdainfully upon
such monistic aberrations. They drew a distinction
between what is and what ought to be. They stated
their objective more precisely: to show the existence
of interrelationships between man's biological constitution and the social phenomena. In principle, this
was a promising field of investigation.

The later social Darwinists' efforts were, however,

from the outset burdened by the desire not simply to analyse and interpret empirically ascertainable phenomena, but also to derive therefrom a set of precepts for a future reordering of society, and they felt called upon to prepare the way for this. This attitude reflected an increased will to take action, which had widely manifested itself since the end of the nineteenth century. In attempting to characterise the "over-all picture of cultural development" shortly before the First World War, a contemporary described this as follows: "The gigantic development of technology and industry has . . . not only brought about a radical change in the external world, but has produced a new type of man, in whom the most vital conception is that, as Marx . . . has expressed this, it is essential not merely to interpret the world differently but also to change it. In other words: as a result of the upsurge of technology and industry, theory and practice have entered into an entirely new relationship. So also have past and future. From people of the past we have become people of the future. Comte's phrase: 'Savoir c'est voir pour prévoir' is the watchword of our time."

This attitude of mind arose not only from the sense of power engendered by the tremendous growth in scientific and technical resources, but also from criticism of the present time, i.e., a purpose which made the future its responsibility because confidence in tradition and in the automatically beneficial functioning of evolution was vanishing. With the Marxists it had primarily been a question of criticism of a false mental attitude, an attempt to bring about, with the help of the rightly guided consciousness of the masses, the final breakthrough of the trend that was asserting itself in the process of history anyway.

To the later social Darwinists the problem pre-

sented itself in a much more radical form. Their starting point was that civilising development presented a
deadly peril to the racial and biological substance of
society—a viewpoint that derived its full weight from
the conviction that man's social qualities were the direct products of his inherited biological equipment.
Hitherto—it was argued—natural selection had, in the
main, ensured that the biologically valuable forces
had retained the upper hand. But now this regulator
was being seriously upset. Hence it had become necessary to supplement natural selection by socially controlled selection. Thus, to the later social Darwinists
it appeared vitally important to go against the trend
of the times and achieve the planned application of
social-biological measures. The alternative would inevitably be a general "proletarisation" of society, i.e.,
the qualitative deterioration of the human material,
with catastrophic consequences to cultural creative
power and to the capacity for political self-assertion.
This second aspect, the political factor, became increasingly important in this context—at first borne
along by the nationalistic thirst for power of the early
years of the twentieth century; after the military and
political disaster of the First World War it was
goaded on by the passionate desire to bring about the
political resurgence of the beaten and weakened
German nation.

There was, however, diversity of opinion as to the
methods and criteria to be applied in order to achieve
that purpose. Two main directions can be distinguished: racial anthropology and racial hygiene. The
anthropologists based themselves on racial differences. They endeavoured to provide a scientific foundation for the speculative racial theories of the nineteenth century, particularly Gobineau's, and to
develop them further. With the aid of cranial and

body measurements and pigment determinations they defined and described certain racial types. Underlying these different external forms were assumed to be different intellectual and psychological qualities, and these differences were duly sought and supposedly established. The Nordic-Germanic race was given the highest qualitative rating and thus the natural claim to social leadership. Biological care and the preservation of racial purity therefore appeared as the most essential obligations, and it was considered by the advocates of these theories that public opinion should be re-educated on these lines. The outcome of this was the attempt to derive—with an appeal to the authority of science—a rigid dogma of inequality from the empirically demonstrable diversity of human groups. Thus the individual's claim to social and political equality of opportunity was denied, and the trends towards social mobility in the modern industrial society were stifled.

It is evident that the racial anthropologists' claims purporting to provide a scientific foundation for their theories were based on gross self-deception. This was because, among other reasons, the concept of race that they adopted was of such a kind as to involve an unjustifiable oversimplification of the complex relationships between phenotype and genotype, as though external characteristics must always be rigidly associated with distinctive psychological and intellectual characteristics—quite apart from the fact that the influence of environmental factors was greatly underrated. By conceiving the races of mankind as though they were self-contained, sharply separate blocklike units and then proceeding, on this sort of basis, to "explain the military and intellectual achievements of the nations from the physiological characteristics and inequality of the races of which they are composed," the racial anthropologists were obliged to misinterpret the biological and social phenomena and distort the facts to fit their theories. Indeed, these pundits were self-taught amateurs with inadequate basic scientific training. However, their efforts were opportunistically convenient to the cause of nationalism, which, in accordance with the teachings of men like Lagarde, Langbehn and Chamberlain, aspired to renewal and resurgence from the "primitive Germanic essence" and its racial basis. This brand of nationalism flourished in those same politically right-wing circles of the German-Empire-minded bourgeoisie which had shown themselves to be particularly susceptible to the struggle-for-existence ideology. In these circles the theories of the racial anthropologists found an eager response. And this even increased after the First World War, as is evident from the success achieved by Hans F. K. Günther's writings, which continued to propagate the racial anthropological theories, though in a differentiated form and in closer relationship with the views of the racial hygienists. By 1932 his book entitled *Ethnology of the German Nation* (*Rassenkunde des deutschen Volkes*) had sold more than 50,000 copies, and by the end of the Third Reich close on half a million copies of his various writings had been sold in all. Thus the racial anthropological manifestation of social Darwinism must be reckoned among the forces that helped racial ideology and biologically oriented ways of thinking to come to the fore—with momentous consequences.

Now let us take a look at the second main trend in social-Darwinistic thinking: racial hygiene. The exponents of this doctrine compared favourably, in the professional sense, with the amateurism of the racial anthropologists, for here the leading experts were university-trained scientists. They made a serious at-

tempt to confine the interpretation of social phenomena from the Darwinistic point of view to scientifically demonstrable facts. They could establish a
linkup with the tremendous progress that the science
of genetics had made since Darwin's time. This had
shown conclusively that the process of heredity takes
place independently of the changes that an organism
undergoes in reacting to its environment. But if individually acquired properties are not hereditary
(Lamarck had held the opposite view, and Darwin
had not ruled out the possibility), then—so the racial
hygienists reasoned—everything that individuals have
attained by education and social achievement must
remain ephemeral if the substance of inheritance is
not protected from deterioration. Such protection was
now, according to the racial hygienists, no longer as-
sured, for the achievements of modern civilisation
and the claims of Christian-humanitarian ethics con-
spired to act in a manner detrimental to the nation's
biological welfare. For example, constitutionally weak
and hereditarily inferior individuals, who in former
times would not have survived to sexual maturity,
now not only survived, thanks to modern medical science and social security, but procreated numerous
offspring, whereas the most gifted and socially superior strata of society were inclined to limit the number
of children they brought into the world. The social
conditions as well as the prevailing ideas were, it was
asserted, permeated with extreme individualist conceptions, criminally ignoring the dictates of the preservation of the species, the biological duty towards
the nation as a whole.

Observations of this kind were, at the time, being
made in all industrialised countries and led to a
deeper concern for, and involvement in, bio-social
problems. The racial hygienists, too, made valuable

contributions to this. But, regrettably, all their scientific discipline was unable to save them from falling into the same trap that had claimed the other social-Darwinistic school of thought for a victim, namely, the error of taking the scientifically demonstrable principles relating to certain aspects of man and applying them to man as a whole. In spite of all readiness to discriminate, these investigators nevertheless assigned to the inherited biological equipment such overriding importance with regard to man's social qualities that the fulfilment of racial hygienic requirements loomed large as a "matter of destiny" that towered above all other considerations. Thus, for example, Fritz Lenz, professor of racial hygiene at Munich University, declared in 1930: "The question of the genetic quality of the coming generations is a hundred times more important than the struggle of capitalism versus socialism and a thousand times more important than the struggle of black, white and red versus black, red and gold." Many other statements of similar tenor could be cited. They all imply a rethinking of outlooks on life in terms of racial hygiene.

Furthermore, bound up with this approach, the same critical attitudes towards civilisation as those displayed by the racial anthropologists emerged here, too, though admittedly at a much higher intellectual level. The modern industrial society was disparaged, and its political concomitant, democracy, was rejected as a harmful levelling influence, whereas the rural way of life and the social structure based on the recognised existence of distinct classes were held up as admirable examples. The conviction that the Nordic-Germanic race is the most valuable factor in European culture and more particularly in the German nation was also part of the mental make-up of the adherents of these doctrines. Under these circumstances the ethical content of these later social Darwinists' ideas was doomed to debasement. They seriously and subjectively wanted to protect their own nation from the pernicious influences of people with "modern" ideas, which they regarded as dangerous. In fact, however, their attitude and activities brought on far greater dangers than those they had sought to avert.

We thus come up against the question as to what assessment we can make of the part that the racial hygienists have played in history. Their actual members were small and their range of direct influence was limited. It was not until after the First World War, which so obviously underlined the importance of "human material" and which moreover, in defeated Germany, produced a receptive psychological climate for the idea of biological renewal, that interest in population policy and genetic care was revived. Thus, racial hygiene received greater publicity, even in respected periodicals such as the *Süddeutsche Monatshefte*. But as yet this was of little importance in achieving practical application of its ideas. Only at the extreme right wing of the political front, where racial consciousness and anti-Semitism were central factors, the demands expressed by the advocates of racial hygiene were seized upon, though as yet hardly as ammunition for popular agitators. Thus, until 1932, racial hygiene played only a relatively minor role on the fringe of events.

THE PERVERSION OF THE HUMAN IMAGE

With the take-over of power by the National Socialists the doctrine of racial hygiene suddenly leapt into prominence, along with a general focussing of interest on racial studies in Germany. The National Socialists' hazy ideas about "race" and "social biology" found some measure of support in the theories of later social Darwinism: the authoritative backing provided by a supposedly scientific basis, together with a to some extent cut-and-dried doctrine essential for "educational" purposes. Also, these theories offered concrete starting points for the carrying-through of socio-biological measures. In this sense the preparatory work done, and the assistance rendered, by the later social Darwinists helped to make possible the practical application of the socio-biological doctrines in the Third Reich. They confirmed and promoted the conviction that biological-racial status constituted the only true yardstick for determining the quality and historical rank of individuals and nations and that the systematic use of scientific and technological resources could provide the means of regulating and modifying this status. Thus the later social Darwinism came to have an important historical effect, not so much in consequence of any direct widespread influence, but because it provided certain convenient thought patterns and indications for action aimed at reordering the social relationships on a biological basis.

Just how that was done is only too well known. It started with official measures to prevent genetically defective individuals from having children. Here the principle of voluntary co-operation of those affected by such measures was indeed already abandoned, but at least they were fairly strictly limited to a scientifically well-defined circle of pathological cases. But it did not stop at that. These doctrines led on to the mass extermination of so-called "worthless life," and eventually to schemes, and experimental preliminary work, aimed at the sterilisation of whole nations. It was only the defeat and collapse of the Third Reich that prevented the execution of those schemes. And even more sinister was the line of reasoning by which,

starting from theoretical postulates about the "alien-
ness" of the Jews as a national menace, they became
the victims of social discrimination culminating in
their physical destruction by means of a highly organised system of deportation and mass murder.

It would, however, be a gross oversimplification to
seek an explanation for this descent into barbarity
solely in terms of social-Darwinistic origins. A host of
other factors were also involved, not the least important of which was the tremendous pressure that the
events of the Second World War brought to bear on
moral standards. This may indeed provide the key to
explaining the eventual breakdown of all inhibitions
which hitherto had stood in the way of safeguarding
the "nation's biological purity" by such nakedly primitive methods, so that racial hatred and arrogance
were given free rein. But the question how such ideas
about biological or racial purity arose and found ac-
ceptance, and how people came to be distortedly
viewed as mere exponents of their racial-biological
origins, could not be adequately answered without an
understanding of the principles of social Darwinism.
It can be conceded that the theoreticians of this doctrine did not desire the way in which events were
subsequently to develop. At the same time, however,
it would be dodging the truth to regard them merely
as the innocent victims of an historical process in
which their basically quite moderate and genuinely
well-intentioned aims were grossly abused.

What those aims were has been outlined here. So it
is hardly surprising that before 1933 the majority of
the racial hygienists—not to mention the ethnologists
—wished the political victory of national socialism.
They did, it is true, object to its primitive radicalism,
but these objections did not outweigh their sympathy
with its fundamentals. The later social Darwinists

proceeded from the same basic ideological positions
as did the popular National Socialist movement. They
were in agreement on a number of issues, such as
their opposition to the industrialised society and to
democracy, their esteem for a social order based on a
class system culminating in an elite, their disparage-
ment of a materialistically technological civilisation
and praise of an organically evolved culture, and their
criticism of individualism of the liberal-minded variety, against which, for example, they upheld the ideal
of a nation-oriented communal spirit. In short: they
found their common meeting ground in resentful protest against the social remoulding processes that had
been started by the political and industrial revolutions
of modern times. Thus they also shared the conviction that the future of the German nation could be
made safe only on the basis of natural inequality, i.e.,
by virtue of a reordering of social life in accordance
with socio-biological and racial principles.

No wonder, then, that the *Archiv für Rassen- und
Gesellschaftsbiologie,* the leading journal of the racial
hygienists, openly acknowledged as far back as 1931
that Hitler was the only German politician of any importance who showed a proper understanding of the
signs of the times. Any misgivings (and there were indeed misgivings, as must emphatically be noted)
were relegated to the background by the hope that
here at last was someone who would enable the principles of racial hygiene to be applied on a large scale.
Hitler's assertion that, in dealing with these matters
which purportedly affected the whole future existence of the German nation, he would not let himself
be deflected by petty bourgeois scruples, was at the
time regarded as a promise, not as a sinister warning.
The racial hygienists fondly imagined that Hitler
would heed the advice of dedicated experts such as

themselves. And they personally were quite disposed to put their ideas into practice—in a properly humane manner, be it understood. But in actual fact their enthusiasm for their own cause blinded them to the dangers lurking in the means that were to serve the end (namely, the application of socio-biological measures). Thus, even after 1933 (when Hitler had come into power), they could still bring themselves to act in public as apologists for repressive measures which in private they deplored. Typical of this state of mind is the reasoning with which one prominent member of the Society for Racial Hygiene, the scientifically respected anthropologist Eugen Fischer, in 1934 commented on such measures:

"Many worthy and well-meaning people will be harshly and cruelly affected. But can any sacrifice be too great when it is a question of saving a whole nation? Was it not particularly this nation that lost infinitely more of its most valuable genetic stock in the war? Ethnical renewal, deliberate racial care pulls a nation back from the abyss to which the so-called culture of the last few decades has brought it."

In short: the biological-racial concept of the nation proved to be stronger than all humanitarian scruples in favour of individual human rights. The German people were on a slippery slope, and when common sense and better judgment eventually began to emerge, it was too late.

Viewed in this light, the later social Darwinism is seen to be of symptomatic importance with regard to the problem from which we started: why was it in Germany, of all countries, that such biological-racial theories were put into practice, and why was it here, in particular, that the experiments dreamt up by the social Darwinists were brought to such barbaric reality? An examination of specifically social-Darwinist thinking fails to provide the answer to this question. For in Germany this doctrine was not sufficiently widespread for that, and it was not confined to Germany anyway. It has already been pointed out in this article that social Darwinism in its two earlier forms manifested itself throughout Western civilisation, and it must be added that this is largely true also of later social Darwinism.

Yet only in Germany did that uprooted social stratum of lower-middle-class origins, which has ever provided the most fertile soil for the proliferation of biological-racial ideas, come to power. Important reasons why this should have occurred must be sought in many directions. From the viewpoint of the present article, concerned as it more particularly is with the history of ideas, it is a notable and—viewed from this distance in time—puzzling fact that the primitive biological-racial elements of National Socialist ideology did not have a more repellent effect upon those middle-class "fellow travellers" who, not so much by active participation as by passive toleration, opened the way to Hitler and thus to his regime's inhuman practices. Examination of later social Darwinism does provide clues to this. These have exemplary value because behind the actual socio-biological aims—but corresponding to them—we can discern motives which were active far outside the circle of the social Darwinists in the German middle classes. While to them racial hygiene may have been a remote concept and ethnology something that concerned other people, yet they had some important basic attitudes in common with the exponents of those doctrines (and therefore also with the National Socialists). There was a widespread belief that only the most uncompromising application of the power of the state, both at home and in international politics, could safeguard Germany's right to exist and her political future and that considerations of upholding constitutional government, international law or humanitarian scruples were of secondary importance in comparison with these all-important aims. The democratic principle of equality was emphatically rejected. Who could indeed be expected to make a resolute stand against this all-pervading dogma of the natural inequality of individuals and races? Even in circles that disapproved of the anti-Semitism and bogus racial theories of the National Socialists and abhorred any assault upon human dignity there no longer existed, in such circumstances, the conditions for a fundamental rejection of that biological-racial ideology, and so there was no basic standard that could have shown that adoption of the National Socialist ideas of running a country was tantamount to a vote against humanity.

From such considerations the doctrines of the later social Darwinism emerge as part of a more comprehensive trend of ideas, in which a number of forces of different origins were acting in the same general direction. From our present-day standpoint it can be described as an obliteration of the boundaries of the individual's sense of his own worth, his personal dignity, which society had hitherto recognised and respected. It led to the degradation of the human individual to mere material subservient to the future of the species. This ultimate step was not the logical consequence of the over-all process, but it was made possible by it. In it the later social Darwinism found its special direction and room for expansion. Thus it was at once a propelling force and a symptom of a trend of thought and behaviour which eventually swept like a tide of inhumanity over the protective barriers that had hitherto safeguarded decent human behaviour.

But also the earlier forms of social Darwinism developed in the course of such interaction with predominant trends of the times: as such they were the expression but also the propelling force, first of the liberalistic and later of the imperialistic era. In all these changes and transformations we may look for a constant factor that will enable us to characterise and understand the pattern of social-Darwinistic thought as a whole and to determine its special unmistakable share in the over-all evolutionary development. With regard to this aspect the situation can be described as follows: Here the personal entity of the human being is placed in a causal or final relationship with natural evolution (or, to be more precise: evolution interpreted in a scientific sense). His personal value is here primarily traced back to his biological origin and then reduced to his biological functional effectiveness. Thus human dignity is transformed from something inviolable and indivisible into a concept that admits of various qualitative gradings which are measurable against the yardstick of what is desirable in the interests of "the nation's biological health" and which can be regulated by appropriate planning and corrective measures. Proceeding along this path, the border line of what is biologically utilisable or expedient must ultimately coincide with the very border line of man's basic right to live.

These trends acquired historical importance as forces arrayed in the struggle against the teachings of the Christian religion and the principles of the liberal-democratic ideal of the constitutional state based on the rule of law. Thus the various brands of social Darwinism (of which only the three most important have been discussed here) can be described as impelling forces in that destructive process whereby the social guiding power of Christian and enlightened humanitarian ethics is being broken down and perverted—a process which has gone ahead with particular rapidity in the last hundred years. Thus our subject becomes a matter of topical importance. It brings us up against a set of problems that is not confined to the antecedents and history of the Third Reich. For there is plenty of evidence that this process has gone further and is continuing.

Admittedly, social Darwinism no longer has any share in this: not only because it was carried to extremes in Hitler's misdeeds, but also because empirical and epistemological progress in biology have deprived social Darwinism of every shred of credibility. It is no longer seriously possible to conceive biological evolution as a progressive rectilinear process; in the light of present-day knowledge we are compelled to draw a fundamental distinction between biological evolution and psycho-social evolution. Also, it is now recognised that the principle of selection, important though it remains, merges into more complex relationships in which, besides natural selection, other factors such as mutation and heredity play their parts in shaping the course of evolution.

And, finally, the tremendous increase in genetic knowledge that has been achieved in recent decades has conclusively shown how shortsighted it would be to regard the genetic constitution of the human being as socially all-important or indeed to seek a genetic interpretation for the rise and fall of nations. Besides, considering the vast complexity that the present-day scientist discerns in the biological natural phenomena, and the correspondingly refined methods of research (including mathematical analysis of the results), modern biology no longer presents any obvious easily visualisable patterns that could be manipulated as providing an interpretation of human history in a manner that could appeal to the general public.

THE SOCIO-POLITICAL RESPONSIBILITY OF THE SCIENTIST

In the light of present-day biological knowledge, social Darwinism is an historical phenomenon in the full sense of the word. At the same time, it provides an approach to the perennial question as to the modern biologist's position and attitude with regard to the community, social ethics, humanity.

And what has this social Darwinism really to do with scientific biology, and more particularly with Darwin and his theories, anyway? This question raised by the biologists cannot be evaded. And they are indeed entitled to ask it, not without some resentment, inasmuch as attempts have been made, by criticising social Darwinism, to strike at Darwinism itself.

Yet there is no valid ground for any such real or feigned confusion of the issues involved. Already during Darwin's lifetime the social Darwinists indulged in some inadmissible and vulgar generalisations of his theories. But even the most scientifically disciplined exponents of racial hygiene failed to keep within the limits of the strictly established genetic knowledge of their day. Therefore it follows that social Darwinism is bound to act as a distorting mirror when it is attempted to use it as a basis for an assessment of Darwin's theories. On the other hand, however, it focusses attention on conflicts which exist between scientific biology and the social world and which cannot simply be attributed to neglected transgressions across the border line between the two.

What this implies can suitably be illustrated by reference to the activities of the racial hygienists. Their starting point had been the existence of demonstrable hereditary biological defects which are liable to emerge and survive under the environmental conditions of modern civilisation. In adopting this approach, they had taken up a challenge which science could not simply ignore, once it had become aware of its existence. In actual fact, however, they wanted to achieve too much with too little knowledge—misled by extraneous unscientific aims and pressures. In the upshot they contributed to the triumph of inhumanity. But even if we eliminate from this picture what we now know to be scientifically bogus and politically wrong, the danger is still there. For we have not thus disposed of the problem, namely: how can knowledge and methods evolved within the detached and rational context of a specialised discipline, which must necessarily base itself on scientific biological criteria, be applied to human sociology? For they are thus transferred to a sphere which, although it cannot afford to ignore biological considerations of health and hygiene, nevertheless regulates its activities on the basis of behaviour standards which, if the criteria of what is biologically desirable are consistently applied, must inevitably be violated. This is so because the standards that have hitherto determined modern civilised man's conception of himself and the patterns of his social behaviour are shaped by "transcendental" values embodying the tradition of two and a half millennia. They are challenged and called in question by the results of empirical biological research which has, in the last hundred years that have passed since Darwin's time, penetrated so deeply into the principles and functional relationships of living nature that its previously undreamt-of possibilities of influencing man's physical and psychological existence have increased apace, with a correspondingly unprecedented increase in the means of manipulating human social life.

This conflict is ever at the problematical core of the erroneous conclusions into which the social Darwinists let themselves be trapped under the influence of particular situations. In other words: even in cases where scientific biology remains strictly within its legitimate boundaries it nevertheless calls in question the validity of the conventional social and ethical standards. And this applies not only to biology but to the natural sciences generally. With each new addition to scientific knowledge there is a corresponding increase in man's power to intervene according to his schemes and wishes in the social and biological phenomena of his existence. Urged along by the competitive pressure of international power politics and social competition, compelled by pressing problems in this age of political, economic and technological revolutions, but also attracted by tempting possibilities of controlling individual development and aspiring to the manipulation of procreative processes, man seizes and avails himself of the means that science offers. And with each step that he takes along this path he himself, as well as the functioning of his social machinery, becomes increasingly dependent on the achievements of science.

So it is hardly surprising that man's understanding of himself and of the world in which he lives is becoming more pragmatic and rational, that the metaphysical dimensions of his existence are tending to fade away and that the objective logic of controllable planning is gaining more and more control over the social and the individual sphere.

Darwin's theory, too, was a world-shaking breakthrough on this path of progress. Who would deny that it, like modern scientific development as a whole, has brought about a tremendous gain in freedom, in emancipation of mankind in terms of understanding and potentialities for action. Social Darwinism, however, shows—grotesquely but unmistakably—where the dangers lurk in this trend towards "scientification" of the world. It reminds us of the debit side of the balance sheet of scientific and technological achievement. Thus we find ourselves confronted with a situation that Aldous Huxley has characterised in the following words: "Technically we are supermen, but morally we are not even human. That is the main problem of our present time."

It is not the time to deplore this situation—nor is there any reason to. It constitutes the historical challenge of the twentieth century. To come to terms with it is our task. This we cannot achieve by criticising Darwinism or indeed condemning modern science as a whole for having given rise to dangers. And to suggest that man's progress along the path of rational scientific research should be slowed down in order to contain and diminish those dangers is merely to indulge in self-delusion. It signifies a failure to realise that there is no turning back, that the time is past when even the biologist could at some point along his line of research calmly sit back and venerate "the unknowable" with appropriate awe. By present-day standards such an attitude would hardly be compatible with serious research aims. Only by proceeding in a professionally "irreverent" manner, led by the working hypothesis that there must be no "impossible" in pursuit of scientific knowledge, can we discover possibilities of curbing the dangers of today by means of the deeper insight and better means of tomorrow. It has been pointed out earlier on in this article that modern biological science has in this way definitely rendered any form of social Darwinism obsolete. In

addition, its progress has released theoretical thinking about social problems from all sorts of shortsighted biological interpretations with which it has
hitherto still been riddled. In his summing-up of man's
present-day biological knowledge the zoologist and
1960 Nobel Prize winner P. B. Medawar states:
". . . we can cast out the conception . . . that all
changes in our society take place in the manner, and
under the pressure, of normal genetic evolution. Furthermore, we can abandon the idea that the direction
of a social change is determined by laws different
from those which once used to be subject to human
decisions or acts of will. That competition between
people constitutes an essential element of our social
life, that human societies are organisms that grow
and must inevitably perish, that the laws of genetics
can claim absolute authority, that social evolution
must move in a direction which is determined by
powers outside human control—all these are biological evaluations . . . wrong judgments based on bad
biology."

"Better" biology, which is more rigorously conscious
of the limits of validity of its judgments, will therefore
be disposed to view the historical world as an imperfect system full of makeshift arrangements, an open
process whose future is not predetermined but is instead placed under the control of man himself.

This of course places greater responsibility on all
of us for the future course of social and political evolution. We must realise that salvation from the dangers
that face us must be wrested afresh from changing
patterns of facts and situations. Methodically controlled empirical science pursued with a genuine desire for knowledge will help to achieve this, is in-
dispensable, but not in itself sufficient. The scientist
who, basing himself on the division of activities and

specialisation in human society, remains totally immersed in his research work is placing more confidence in the harmonious combining of all individual efforts into a meaningful whole than would appear to be justified by mankind's experience. Besides, there is no such creature as the "exclusively scientific man." He is, whether he likes it or not, also a contemporary of his fellow men and a citizen of his country. With his conscious and subconscious value judgments he is inescapably involved, drawn along in the wake of political and intellectual developments. What this may mean in the most unfavourable case is shown by the example discussed in this article; and by the same token the scientist also has a social and political responsibility under more favourable conditions. The strict discipline and rationality to which he has been trained in the practice of his science are not a sufficient guide. Without critical reflection on his own social standpoint and on the interrelationship of science and society he cannot rank as a fully conscious and informed contemporary man, and without this background even present-day science is no safeguard from folly.

GEROLF STEINER

Manipulation of People by Mass Persuasion

Commercial advertising, political propaganda or any other form of persuasive publicity acts upon people in two ways: through associations and through congenital behaviour patterns. A simple example will make this clear: A poster shows a glass of beer covered with condensed moisture, which in places has merged into drops that have started to trickle down. The viewer experiences the following association of ideas: cold beer—warm, sultry weather—thirst. Thus an appeal is made to an instinct and thirst behaviour is induced or suggested, so that, when next an appropriate situation arises, the mental images will quickly "click," and the viewer, remembering the poster, will order beer. The poster will then have achieved its object: the viewer has become a paying consumer of the product advertised.

Nearly all mass persuasion operates on the same principle. As a rule, a chain of association is initiated, which leads to a motivating factor, a so-called releaser, or trigger of action, that brings about the action that the advertiser wants. This "creation of needs or desires" is a standard feature in the advertising of consumer goods. In similar fashion propaganda may be designed to arouse curiosity, fear or aggression, if the aim is to make people engage in some particular form of social action—e.g., as demonstrators, voters or warriors.

MECHANISMS OF COMMERCIAL PUBLICITY

The sequence: "association—trigger of action" can be reversed by putting the trigger first. Another example: A poster shows juicy ripe oranges many times larger than natural size. The picture has a fairly direct action in arousing an appetite for these fruits and now leaves the viewer to seek out the corresponding objects, which are perhaps available from a market stall or barrow under the poster. No long chain of association is needed here. The oranges illustrated on the poster act directly as triggers because of their size and their visibility from a distance.

Comparable posters showing, not fruit, but desirable girls are not often used in such a direct context. Those posters do indeed arouse (sexual) appetite, but now this appetite is "put on the scent" like a bloodhound. The poster contains, either in pictorial form or in accompanying texts, hints which initiate chains of association. The viewer can thus be led along this associative path until he arrives where the advertiser wants to lead him and where fresh triggers can then be offered to him. These will vary according to what it is intended to sell: a snow-covered landscape suggests a winter sports holiday resort, or text and additional details get the viewer interested in some brand of soft drink or other refreshment, none of which has primarily any connection with the pretty girl in the picture.

The success of such advertising methods will depend on whether the associations of ideas are sufficiently compelling and therefore—among other factors —on the mental background and psychological preparation of those at whom the advertisement is aimed and also on what is the obvious choice in those particular circumstances. The various triggers offered must moreover develop a powerful cumulative effect and generate appetites acting in approximately the same direction and focus the instincts whereby the desired consumer behaviour is induced. In psychological language: strong hopes must be raised and desires which can be fulfilled only by the advertised product must be aroused.

Thus the pretty girl becomes associated with, say, a winter sports holiday resort. The desire for recreation becomes linked to the hope that, on such a holiday, there will be opportunities for flirting with such a girl. If the poster is sufficiently suggestive, it will continue to exercise its effect even when the viewer is no longer actually looking at it. This is important, since the two instinctive mechanisms brought into play by the poster (sexual desire and the desire for recreation) cannot immediately be gratified, i.e., the action has to be deferred and thus become a delayed action. The lasting effect of the advertisement must thus provide continued stimulation of these desires. In the end, the man buys a ticket to the holiday resort advertised in the poster and books a hotel room there. Something very similar happens in the case of the soft drink poster; for here, too, the appetite aroused by the pretty girl becomes merged with the suggestion of thirst. The advertised drink thus acquires a sexual overtone and will be regarded as correspondingly more desirable and, when drunk, correspondingly more satisfying by the consumer. Sexual desire is of course not satisfied in this way, but is instead utilised as a selling force which, as it were, attaches itself to the product and finds a kind of outlet in the quenching of thirst.

It is more particularly in advertisements for drinks and refreshments of all kinds that the sex image plays a major and well-established part; the human desire to impress one's fellow men is also similarly exploited. A high proportion of all drinks and refreshments is consumed in the company of other people. Conversations between self-styled connoisseurs of wines or cigars are often amusing to an outsider as specimens of humbug and show-off. The need to impress is such an important component of social behaviour in animals and people (more particularly in their dealings with rivals and sex partners) that it can be activated with almost absolute certainty, provided that the right trigger is employed. In the case of mass persuasion by advertising the same visual image or the same set of words may even function both as a sex image and as a trigger actuating the desire to impress. The example of the soft drink advertisement, already mentioned, can serve to illustrate this point, too: while it affects the male viewer in the manner described, the girl on the poster has her clothing, hair styling and make-up in accordance with the latest fashion affected by the majority of the female viewers, or, at any rate, within the range of what they could afford if they felt so inclined. The triumphant smile of the girl on the poster, her gestures and everything about her conform to the conventional ideal of girlhood or young womanhood that the female viewers have been conditioned to emulate. They can thus identify themselves with the girl and her sexual allurement—and associated with this desirable image is, of course, a glass or bottle of that particular drink at one's mouth or in one's hand!

Further triggers can be added by showing the girl on the poster in the company of some charming young men. They, too, function as larger-than-life sex images for the benefit of the female viewers of the poster and as images for self-identification by the male viewers. Besides, the whole scene comprising the pretty girl and the young men presents an idealised picture of how charming, attractive people behave—again with the advertised drink as an aid to social "togetherness."

The attentive observer can hardly fail to notice how neatly such advertised scenes fit in with pre-formed social behaviour patterns: gestures and expressions while smoking or drinking, and the way in which girls move about in "sporting" or "feminine" garments, are daily exhibited in stereotype patterns to cinema or television audiences. Teen-agers of both sexes, whether consciously or unconsciously, tend to copy these socially standardised and idealised patterns in naïve imitations. And such copying is by no means confined to the teen-age group. Commercial advertising consistently and methodically takes advantage of this tendency by offering the consumer goods that go with these supposedly admirable behaviour patterns. The compulsion thus brought to bear on the mass of the buying public is almost inescapable.

The example of the soft drinks advertisement was chosen to illustrate these principles on account of its relatively uncomplicated structure and its obviousness. It is representative of a very wide range of consumer goods advertising, and it exercises its effect more particularly in a relatively prosperous society whose basic necessities of life in terms of food, drink, shelter and security have largely been provided for.

There are, however, many other pre-programmed human behaviour patterns that can be brought into play for mass persuasion purposes. Thus, for example, the two opposing principles: curiosity and the desire for security. Every animal capable of some sort of independent action possesses a desire for safety, or security, such as expresses itself—as extreme instances —in the timid flight of the hare or the self-protective curling-up of the hedgehog. In man the precautions that ensure safety and security are more elaborately differentiated; but the "basic urge" is the same. This desire for security manifests itself on every occasion as an elementary force. When it cannot be satisfied, it gives rise to marked feelings of uneasiness, whereas "comfortable security" produces a sense of happiness. The antithesis to security is curiosity, which is something that man does not have in common with all animals, but only with those species that possess in the true sense a capacity for learning, such as ravens, parrots or monkeys. Curiosity, is also the manifestation of a congenital program, a desire to learn, whose probable purpose is to increase the creature's store of experience. Non-learning animals, possessing no such desire, avoid unusual situations, whereas learning animals tend to seek out such situations. Man also does this, and he takes pleasure in novelty and in change.

That this tendency is exploited to the full in commercial advertising is a well-known fact. "Let's have something new!" is the kind of approach widely used in the advertising of consumer goods which perhaps have nothing to recommend them other than the fact that they are "new." That this sort of advertising is aimed more specifically at those younger people who are still in the exploratory stage of life is obvious. The older a person grows, the more his need for security outweighs his curiosity. The kind of slogan more likely to appeal to the "established" citizen is: "no experiments"—particularly in situations that involve a certain amount of risk. People who feel they have more to lose than to gain are inclined to be suspicious of "experiments," and anyone offering them novelty with the suggestion "have a try" is more likely to arouse their distrust than gain their good will.

In such circumstances advertisers prefer not to publicise a new and therefore—to this category of consumers—"dubious" product simply on the merits claimed for it, but will instead adopt a more indirect approach. They will exploit the more disagreeable aspects of the old by first disparaging it as "old-fashioned," "obsolete," etc., thus confirming what the consumer—who, in spite of everything, shares the general human urge towards novelty—may already have secretly felt for some time: that he really is a bit fed up with the old and would like a change. When the advertisers have thus "softened up" their potential customers, they can almost unnoticeably introduce the advertised commodity (whether of a commercial or a political character) into the gap they have thus created. Even the initially suspicious members of the public have thus allowed themselves to be manipulated.

There are a number of such oppositely directed patterns of behaviour which, like curiosity and the need for security, can readily be played upon by mass persuaders. For example, thrift is another human urge which acts in opposition to curiosity, just as the security urge does, and thus puts a brake on the desire to spend money on new consumer goods or just try a change. Thrift, the urge to economise, is a behaviour pattern controlled by instinct—as is clearly demonstrated by its morbidly exaggerated form, miserliness. In any newspaper we can find advertisements tempting us to buy all sorts of consumer goods side by side with advertisements exhorting us to save and invest our money. Although we can rationalise our attitudes, there is no denying that the two sides in this tug of war both appeal to our deeper emotions in some form or other.

Cruder methods may occasionally be applied to make us spend our money. It is a very old trick first to paralyse or at least weaken the potential victim's rational and critical faculties. It is a well-known fact that when people are in a state of euphoria (elated well-being) they can more readily be induced to part with their money than when they are under the control of cool common sense. The euphoristic state of mind—which may be fairly unspecific, as it need merely be a basic mood serving to "make the soul receptive" to the temptations offered—can generally be induced by a display of luxury and splendour. In many a business deal a glass of wine can have this effect. The inhibitions against giving away money or letting oneself be parted from other possessions are more readily removed by such methods of persuasion even if the rational arguments that may be used to back them up are weak.

All this goes to show that, basically, the rational arguments and the sequences of mental associations used in mass persuasion techniques are at best merely a prelude to getting at the instinctive desires and fears which ultimately determine the decisions of the persons thus manipulated.

Of course, this does not mean that the prelude can be entirely neglected. It is quite appropriate to draw attention to the practical and technical advantages of a refrigerator or a motor car as arguments in selling a particular model. We all know, however, that the attractive metal casing of the refrigerator or the in-

scription "de luxe" on a car often exercises greater
persuasive power than the technical advantages, or
that, for equal technical excellence, the decisive part
is played by factors which stimulate the prospective
purchaser's vanity or his desire for something different, or which enhance his social prestige or, if he is a
male, appeal to his urge to display his finery and
thus impress the female of the species. Very often it
is these or similar motives that prompt the consumer
to buy. Primitive instinctive behaviour patterns, not
reason, decide the issue.

Having thus called attention to the active part
played by such congenital patterns of response and
behaviour, we shall now take a closer look at the associative side of mass persuasion for purposes of commercial advertising. An example is afforded by the
excellent slogan "Persil remains Persil." Formally it
is very nearly the statement of an identity ($a=a$),
except that it says "remains," not "is"—and at least
three different chains of association at once link themselves to this and in turn set three different important
instinctive mechanisms in motion:

1. If a product remains unchanged, this directly
generates a sense of security and dependability
and thus exercises an attractive action that comes
before any rational considerations as to the technical merit of such constancy of quality.

2. If a housewife thinks she possesses a certain
amount of experience with the product recommended in the advertisement, the advertising slogan will confirm her belief that she is on the
right track, and she will wish to continue in this
way. This gives her a direct sense of satisfaction
and is closely related to, though not quite identical with, the first argument. Besides, the house-

wife, thus appealed to, will feel she is in good
company, namely, that of other evidently experienced housewives; this is something that gratifies
her social self-esteem as an expert or at least
someone who knows what is what.

3. The housewife who has not yet tried Persil
has her curiosity roused by this product which
can so confidently advertise itself in this way, not
even drawing attention to particular qualities,
but simply emphasising its sameness. Curiosity,
especially when it appears rationally justifiable,
is—as has already been pointed out—one of the
most powerful inducements in promoting the sale
of merchandise.

Thus, from three words, almost the grammatical
minimum for forming a sentence, a whole group of
associative chains extend and speedily link up with
important instinctive mechanisms. What more could
one wish?

But the slogan has other advantages, too: it has
symmetry, rhythm and a clarion-like ring. These
things appeal to primitive aesthetic values and therefore stamp themselves very vividly on the consumer's
mind. So this very cleverly devised slogan exercises an
appeal even by virtue of its verbal form, and it is
therefore not surprising that it has continued to be
effective over the years. It is in fact a cunningly contrived assembly of highly active signals which actuate
a number of psychological mechanisms in the consumers at whom they are directed. So striking a result can seldom be achieved with such—one might
say—elementary simplicity. More often, advertising
has to rely on more complex associations of ideas
whose appeal and driving power must measure up to
the over-all situation in any particular case. But al-

ways they lead to the built-in congenital response
patterns. If these are not activated, all the effort put
into the advertisement will have been in vain. It is
impossible to discuss the vast number of combinations
and connections potentially available. Each category
of consumers, depending on educational level and intellectual outlook, has its own particular "responsive-
ness," and each commercial product has its own particular niche and affinity with certain desires and
instinctive mechanisms. On these matters there exists
a massive and, in the main, practically oriented literature in which, however, the theme highlighted here
is manifested over and over again in ever different
variants, while at the same time there is a marked
reluctance to bring the basic psychological mechanisms out into the open.

POLITICAL PROPAGANDA

Propaganda—publicity conducted for political purposes—is understandably a fiercer and more truculent
business than commercial advertising. The aims of
the latter are not of a compelling kind; for ultimately
it is not a matter of fateful significance to a man
whether he smokes cigarettes brand A, B or C. On
the other hand, it needs no advertising to persuade a
hungry man to buy bread. Political propaganda, however, strives to persuade the public at which it is directed to make important decisions, the consequences
of which will be of a much more important and lasting character.

Yet political propaganda makes use of the same
psychological principles, except that the behaviour
patterns to which the commercial advertiser likes to
appeal are in part different from those which the
propagandist primarily exploits for his purpose. The

politician is not simply aiming at getting people to pay him their money, but he wants to gain power over the whole person of each member of the public. There are only two groups of instincts through which this can be achieved through the medium of mass persuasion:

1. The propaganda is designed to appeal to the instincts that control the patterns of social life even in the animal world—e.g., the urge to imitate or to adopt an attitude of submission to authority or power; or people are assigned socially esteemed "plum jobs," on condition that the recipients of these favours acknowledge the bestower thereof as their superior. Wherever mankind has created artificial distinctions of social rank—not only in politics—it has been possible for propagandists to fall back upon the primeval willingness to accept a grading of society into ranks or classes and to utilise the inducement of aspiring to high rank and office as a tool of political propaganda.

2. Whole groups of people can be persuaded to hazard their lives and property in the service of some cause only if the primeval urge towards self-preservation and security is overruled by powerful instinctive mechanisms which cause the individual in some measure to give up his own independence of action in favour of action by the group as a whole. A mechanism of this kind is found in group aggression, which may manifest itself in its mildest form when a number of people join with one another to hurl insults and abuse at others who have incurred their displeasure. In a more virulent manifestation it may

take the form of bitter struggles between social groups or indeed lead to all-out war.

Group aggression in man can be sparked off with alarming ease. Even the mere deviation from conformity with accepted fashions by an individual may cause him or her to be treated with suspicion and perhaps even ostracised by the community at large. The "conforming" majority thus collectively turns against the "non-conforming" individual, just as hens sometimes turn against one particular hen and drive it out or kill it. It is quite easy for a demagogue to seize upon some "peculiar" characteristic of a "foreign" group and represent it in propaganda as something hateful: dialect, speech, religion, professional or other social status—any of these can by itself function as a "trigger" which can, in a suitable over-all situation, instigate people to engage in group aggression. The manipulator's "art" here again consists in linking the over-all situation to the chosen trigger of aggressive action by means of skilfully contrived associations of ideas. As in other action-triggering situations, the trigger need not be "real." An appropriately chosen simulacrum, a deceptive substitute, can equally serve the purpose; and history offers examples enough where "popular anger" was inflamed by quite arbitrary factors chosen to serve as grievances.

To the bellicose politician the activated group aggressiveness may be attractive in circumstances where a nation, already filled with truculent jingoist nationalism, is to be led into a war with a neighbouring nation. However, in the majority of cases such demagogue politicians do not really want war but only the noisy preliminaries—the threats and abuse that unite their people against the enemy. The unity achieved in this way is not an end in itself, but a means, because when people are in the grip of the group-aggressive mood they are more obedient to their leaders than in other circumstances. Even in primitive wild tribes at Stone Age cultural level, in those situations which are associated with the mood of group aggression, the leader and the led are very closely interdependent. This unity, this cohesion of the group, is brought about by a congenital behaviour mechanism which human beings retain even at a high level of civilisation and which continues even then to act in the same manner. "Strong men" and power-hungry political groups are, for this reason—in order fully to taste the delights of wielding their power—prone to avail themselves (often irresponsibly) of the possibilities of group aggression as a means of furthering their ends.

More than any other innate behaviour pattern, however, group aggression entails a danger which can best be illustrated by means of an example. Anyone who has heard howling monkeys in the depths of the primeval forests of South America is unlikely to forget this "concert": high up in the mighty trees a widely resounding shriek is heard, as though a human were screaming in horrific crescendo: "Ahoo ahoo ahoo ahoo aoooooo!" Then a second monkey joins in, then two or three more and then more and more—and within a minute or so the whole forest is resounding from every direction with this many-voiced sinister howling which only gradually dies away. The first monkey started a kind of avalanche of howls. In this particular case all this noise is harmless: these monkeys work off their group-aggressive urges almost entirely in howling. They live in large families which move about the forest in the treetops, and their outbursts of howling give warning to other families, so that they keep their distance and do not become directly involved with one another.

"Howling" is indeed also a common form of behaviour in sparking of human group aggression. But it does not stop at that; it is too often followed by belligerent actions: scuffles, shootings, organised rioting, war. Just as with the howling monkeys, so also in man the "avalanche principle" acts ("sow the wind and reap the whirlwind"), and this is something that, once started, can hardly be stopped. Thus revolutions have usually escaped from the control of their instigators, who started by exploiting the group aggression of the people they were going to lead. Many a war started almost "unintentionally," because the demagogues who, in order to strengthen their position of authority, at first played a coolly calculated propaganda game with a nation's group aggression were subsequently no longer able to restrain it and moreover had meanwhile aroused similar feelings of mass antagonism in their adversaries. Or, alternatively, the group-aggressive mood got the instigators themselves in its grip and clouded their vision, so that they were no longer able to see the situation clearly and objectively.

THE DUAL CHARACTER OF MASS PERSUASION

Particularly with regard to this most dangerous form of manipulation of people by propaganda it would be important to know whether we are completely and inescapably at its mercy or whether it can be bypassed. At least the "manipulator" who knows the psychological tricks of mass persuasion whereby he makes his puppets dance should—one would suppose—be immune from his own poison. But in general this is not so. For one thing, his really expert knowledge is (on account of the often complex associations of ideas involved) confined only to his one specialised field in the so highly differentiated domain of mass persuasion, so that outside his own narrow field he is first and foremost a human being himself and, as such, is trapped by deceptive mass-persuasive images almost as easily as the most gullible of his contemporaries. This state of affairs can be illustrated by another example: When we look at pictures in a stereoscope, we know that the two almost identical pictures in the apparatus are perfectly flat, and yet we are compelled to see them as a three-dimensional image. An understanding of the physiological principles whereby this "deception" is achieved in no way changes the situation. Something similar applies to the critical faculties of those who are themselves experts. And if this is true of those who "know the ropes," how can their uninitiated fellow citizens be expected to resist the influence of mass persuasion?

Besides, people are becoming more and more susceptible to the increasingly perfected techniques of publicity; for the mass media that are so important in the industrial society—especially television—synchronise the lives of a great many of them. Thus the advertiser soon discovers what points can serve as link-ups for chains of association and in what circumstances an appeal can be made to particular innate patterns of behaviour. The only "antidote" that may enable people to resist the lure of mass persuasion is to explain to them the methods and principles on which it operates. As already stated, however, its counteracting influence is at best only limited. Yet it is desirable to enlighten as many people as possible about the nature and perils of group aggression, so that they can take timely steps to prevent the build-up of an "avalanche."

Mass persuasion does not, however, necessarily always involve sinister temptations to purchase certain consumer goods or embrace certain political views and aims. In the modern "mass society" it may more appropriately be practised as the gentle art of coordinating the thoughts and actions of millions of people, without having to resort to brutal coercive or repressive measures. An appeal to reason seldom meets with a widespread response, as experience has proved. Besides, it is possible really to convince only those people who are sufficiently educated to make at least something approaching a true assessment of a situation. With the complex economic and technological structure of a modern society, however, it is hardly possible to fulfil this requirement on a significantly large scale. So instead of convincing people, attempts are aimed merely at persuading them—and this is achieved by advertising and propaganda, using means such as those described here.

In conclusion, an unfortunate nexus must be mentioned: it is precisely the highly dangerous spirit of group aggression, capable of leading to the extermination of the whole human race, which—in a different manifestation—enables people to make vast combined efforts in peacefully tackling major problems. The enthusiasm to perform great deeds and the willingness to devote one's efforts to the benefit of the community belong to the same group-aggression complex whence arise the war cries and bellicose attitudes. Mass persuasion therefore cannot do without people's readiness to participate in group aggression! This increases the hazards, since it is not possible to impose an outright ban on all appeals to this instinct, so that it may in certain circumstances be too late to stop attempts at abusing it. Thus the manipulation of peo-

ple by mass persuasion encounters the frightening dual
nature of man, which Sophocles characterised 2400
years ago in the words:

> "Much is terrifying—and nothing
> more terrifying than man."

GÜNTER ALTNER

The Human Creature?

"PARANTHROPUS" LIVES

"The human creature"—who or what is he? This was
the question that prompted the French author Jean
Bruller, who wrote under the pseudonym of Vercors,
to write his *Juridical, Zoological and Moral Comedy:
Zoo or the Humane Murderer* in the nineteen-fifties.
In this story a journalist joins an anthropological expedition to New Guinea and witnesses the discovery
of *"Paranthropus,"* a genus of primitive man long believed to have been extinct but now found to be alive.
This creature presents his *Homo sapiens* contemporaries with some almost insoluble problems of definition. Is *Paranthropus,* who lives in caves, grinds pebbles for use as missiles and prepares pieces of smoked
meat for food, still merely an ape, or is he already
human, or is he something in between—*Pithecanthropus* in the true sense of the word? The journalist compels his contemporaries to decide: he successfully has
a number of *Paranthropus* females artificially insem-
inated with human sperm, kills one of the babies born
as a result of this and thus provokes legal action
against him. The jury arrive at the following verdict:

Man is essentially the creature who is in revolt against nature, the "rebellious spirit," and in his rebellion he poses many questions of all kinds—including the question about God. Since *Paranthropus*, too, already shows the rudiments of such rebellion, this creature must be classed as belonging to the human species. The journalist is therefore guilty of murder, but he must not be punished for his crime, because in committing it he broke a law which did not yet exist at the time.

Vercors makes his point very aptly and gets down to fundamental problems which also come within the scope of the subject matter of this book. It may well be doubted whether a jury of laymen can, after hearing some expert opinions, properly be expected to give a ruling on the nature and essence of man. Yet in the last resort there is, in dealing with this problem, no alternative but that people should get together to discuss and decide, according to the best of their knowledge and ability, what the concept of man comprises and thus arrive at an approximate definition.

That is the approach adopted in this book. Its title, *The Human Creature,* is not meant to embody some indisputable pretension to knowledge. Instead, it is meant to signify a multiple awareness of the problem, an acknowledgement of multiple dimensions, leaving it to the individual authors and to the reader to decide just where they stand with respect to these. Although the scientific authors are in the majority, the subject matter has not been confined to a discussion of specialised problems within their field of science; the universality envisaged in the title *The Human Creature* has been deliberately highlighted, even though it has not been possible to deal exhaustively with the subject.

PROVISIONAL DEFINITIONS

The Human Creature—the contrasting concepts embodied in this title point to the old and indeed obsolete, but nevertheless still acute, controversy about
creation and evolution. "Creature" denotes the living
organism which owes its existence to the action of a
Creator outside this world and which, in the case of
man, is able to give thanks to him. "Human," on the
other hand, relates to the genus *Homo* and more particularly the species *Homo sapiens,* which according
to the biologists is to be regarded as the product of a
process of natural development extending back
through millions of years. *Creatura* is a concept which
comprises more than *physis,* which signifies "that
which has grown," and *natura,* meaning "that which
has been born." But the concept of "creature" may
also—like the concept "human"—include the despicable and degrading things that people do to one another and expect from one another. "What a sham is
man!" said Blaise Pascal. "What a marvel, what a
monstrosity, what a piece of chaos, what a bundle of
contradictions! Judge of all things, stupid earthworm,
custodian of truth, concentration of uncertainty and
error, glory and excrement of the universe!"

Between the two extreme concepts of man as a
"creature," i.e., a creation of the Divinity, or as a
product of an evolutionary process are numerous com-
promises and transitions which, on careful examination, may turn out to constitute progress in our knowledge and understanding of these matters. Thus Karl
J. Narr, already at the start of his article in this book,
emphasises the creative qualities of *Homo sapiens*.
Before an attempt is made in this section to establish
the over-all essential nature of the human species,

some notable views and conceptions expressed by
earlier thinkers on the subject of man will be re-
viewed. Thus alone will it be possible to make contradictory aspects understandable and to penetrate
the meaning of new information. It is, however, in no
way the intention to attach undue weight to the
"creatural" side in the sense defined above, or indeed
within the framework of any particular religion, philosophy or outlook on life.

FEUERBACH'S PASSIONATE IDEAS ABOUT THE NATURE OF MAN

For centuries the human being has been the exclusive
subject of religious and philosophical thought. Present-day scientific knowledge of man also derives from
such roots, more particularly from Greek and Christian traditions. But in recognising these relationships
we do not necessarily have to make a specific choice
one way or the other; for the apparently unbiased
observer there is always Feuerbach's position. To con-
template religion critically as a decisive stage of human consciousness, to assess it as a statement by man
about himself, is something that might also be expected from the "modern" atheist, unless he has already come to regard Feuerbach's preoccupation with
Christianity and his too optimistic and too subjectivis-
tic estimation of the human species as too narrow a
view, and has therefore discarded it. But there remains something compelling about Feuerbach's concern with the essential nature of man, about the manner in which he has expressed it, however much one
may want to extend one's vision: "The consciousness
of God is man's consciousness of himself; the perception of God is man's perception of himself. By his
God you know the man, and by the man his God; the

two are one. Whatever is God to man, that is his
mind and soul; and whatever is man's mind, his soul,
his heart, that is his God: God is the manifested in-
ward nature, the expressed self of man; religion is the
solemn unveiling of a man's hidden treasures, the
revelation of his intimate thoughts, the open confes-
sion of his love secrets" (from: *The Essence of Christianity*, 1841).

Ernst Bloch calls Feuerbach's atheism an "inspiring
reversion of theologically applied limitations into fi-
nite human terms." Ignoring all mechanistic and materialistic considerations, Feuerbach conceives and
preserves the essential nature of man as a mystery to
be unravelled, while at the same time he neither over-
nor underrates his animal nature. This is what makes
his approach to the problem of man so up-to-date
and compelling—at any rate for those who seek to
solve the problem of the human creature within the
context of, for example, psychoanalysis and the Marx-
ist critique of religion, i.e., without recourse to a Creator. Thus the religious conception of God must retain its place in the discussion of man, either in that
it is understood to constitute an early stage in man's
consciousness of himself or, alternatively, in that it is
adopted in the direct sense. Vercors is right. It is part
of human nature "to make symbols and myths" and
"to recognise God." Only if this situation is duly appreciated is it possible to present a proper treatment
of the problem of the human creature.

THE INTELLECTUAL CLIMATE IN THE NINETEENTH CENTURY: "PLATONISM" EVERYWHERE

Although the people of Darwin's day were to some
extent already prepared for the idea of evolution,
the publication of his book *On the Origin of Species*

by Means of Natural Selection in 1859 caused a general storm of indignation. The explanation for this outcry must be sought not so much in the religious conservatism that still predominated at the time—though this is often asserted to have been the case—as in a Platonic-idealistic attitude of mind which still exercised considerable influence in the nineteenth century. For Plato—and this applies also to the views held by prominent philosophers of Darwin's day—any notion of "change" in the true sense is inconceivable, because for him all reality can be no more than an image of the externally existing Ideas. If the all-determining external Ideas come before everything that manifests itself in what we call reality, then it signifies that every object must essentially have pre-existed always and that any change it undergoes can be no more than a manifestation of something that was already there.

This view had been strikingly expressed a century earlier in the principle enunciated by Carl von Linné (Linnaeus) (1707–78), who achieved fame as the founder of modern systematic botany and introduced the system of classification and nomenclature of plant and animal species which is still in use: *Lot sunt genera et species, quot ab initio mundi creatae sunt* ("There are as many genera and species of living creatures as were created at the beginning of the world"). Linnaeus presupposes the constancy of species, i.e., he bases himself on the assumption that each species has become what it was destined to be in all eternity, independently of other species. To man he gave the name *Homo sapiens* and assigned him his place at the top of the order of the Primates, the highest order of mammals, which, in addition to the genus *Homo,* was in those days considered to include the monkeys (*Simia*), lemurs and bats (Vespertilio).

Thus classified and yet separate from his nearest
relations in the animal kingdom, *Homo sapiens* continued to occupy his special position until Darwin's
observations led to a fundamentally novel interpretation of the natural system and shed new light on the
descent of man. How greatly the thinking of those
days was dominated by the Platonic conception of
Ideas and how revolutionary was the impact of Darwin's theory of evolution can be judged from the fact
that Linnaeus, in enunciating his above-mentioned
principle as an article of faith (though, incidentally,
he changed his mind about this in his later years),
knew this to be in harmony with the then popularly
held religious belief in the creation. Admittedly, this
view does not leave the Creator very much creative
freedom, if he is conceived as the Platonic demiurge
who can only arrange what has already been predisposed in all eternity. Nor is there much freedom in
it for man, if he can be only what he has in fact already always been. This is good Platonism but not in
the true sense a biblical religious belief. In actual fact,
the Platonic attitude was an impediment and a delay-
ing factor in achieving the long-overdue breakthrough
in knowledge both in theology and in biology. If evolutionism and creationism, in their approach to the
problem of the true nature of man, both felt the influence of Platonic philosophy as a restrictive force in
the last century, one might suppose that the two opposed views must have features in common in their
respective thought patterns and might seek points of
correspondence between them. (The notions of "evolutionism" and "creationism," basing themselves upon
the theory of evolution and upon the biblical concept
of creation, designate the traditional ways of thinking
representative of two classic directions of thought. In
the present context they are not to be regarded as

representing rival ideologies inviting an invidious comparison.) In the following discussion of the subject it will indeed be attempted to make a comparison in which, on the one hand, new knowledge and insight in the domain of theology, which were only beginning to emerge in the previous century, will be given proper consideration, while, on the other, the historical interpretation will be further elaborated. This may provide the starting point for a comprehensive interpretation of the essential nature of man as embodied in the notion of the human creature.

WHAT THEOLOGY HAD FORGOTTEN IN DARWIN'S TIME

Fully committed as it had been to the static conception of a supernaturally acting external Creator, theology has latterly had to learn once again to appreciate the creative dynamics in everything that happens in the world, leaving aside the question—for the present—whether God's action in the world's affairs is more of a transcendentally controlling or more of an immanently impelling character. In any case the Hebrew and early Christian insistence on God the Creator whose future-directed actions manifest themselves through human history provides a clear alternative to Graeco-Platonic thought which views the divine demiurge merely as the natural Orderer of a cosmos that is self-existent and eternal. The comparison calls for details, but it will here be pursued only to the extent that attention is called to the personal, historical and ethical categories, by means of which Scripture has untiringly and hopefully striven to present the familiar conceptions of divine promise, human disobedience and divine redemption, since the beginning of creation, as tending towards something new and something final.

According to Greek thought, the true can exist only in the timeless and the eternal; biblical thought, on the other hand, seeks truth in the coming of the new, which God has promised and which he effused in an ever new and uncompleted fashion during the period of time between Adam and Christ. Thus the biblical history of creation has by no means been fully told in the first chapters of the Bible; it extends, instead, through all the books of the Bible and ends in the visions of the Apocalypse. It is a history of salvation with a universal purport and an awaited end, continuous in the unswerving character of divine fidelity, discontinues in the reassertion of divine action at any particular time. Accordingly, the biblical conception of man essentially aims, not at an "idealistic" separation of him into two parts—the uncreated and indestructible soul in the transient body—but at the creatural wholeness of unique and non-interchangeable human individuals, who, in the course of history, must maintain their responsibility towards God in constantly new ways. As the Bible sees it, the creature who is man possesses the quality of being human, because in him something new is accomplished in accordance with the undeflectable will of God. Here evolution is specifically taking place, not just the realisation of possibilities that have already always existed. Admittedly, this is conceived as something that happens through external causes and not from within, spontaneous and not as a continuation of predetermined circumstances; yet in such a way that the New finds its starting point in the Old. Michael Landmann, who has very carefully studied the biblical and the Platonic traditions in present-day thought, writes:

> Let us compare creationism and evolutionism. In the former, the New is introduced by supernat-

ural means, discontinuously, from nowhere, not from God but solely by God; in the latter, it emerges continuously from within, in the process of time, coming forth from the changing self. To that extent the difference between the two remains immense. Evolutionism is fundamentally much closer to the old notions of birth from chaos, the fashioning of the world by some super-craftsman, etc. than it is to creationism. Yet both can be grouped together as opposites to eternal-static Platonism in that they let the not previously existent New emerge, as something qualitatively transcending it, from the Other in which it was not previously contained, and affirm this. From creationism it is at any rate possible, by modification in the light of Greek immanentism, to build a road to evolutionism; from Platonism no such possibility exists. To that extent one might say that modern thought is based on a long-range action of biblical notions and that it is really this which, in a subsequent transformation and itself rendered capable of this by a transfusion of Greek thought, can overcome Platonism. (Landmann 1966.)

If Landmann's thesis as to the affinity between creationism and evolutionism is correct, then it should be possible at least to derive some clues to that effect from the history of human thought. In Herder's philosophy of history and in Goethe's pantheistic morphology we do indeed have examples of "evolutionary thinking" which biblical creationism has had a share in shaping and which endeavours to link the special, the particular, in man with the world of physical generalities. Haeckel, for that matter, felt Goethe's morphology to be a congenial philosophy and singled it out as being conducive to Darwinism. True, Haeckel utterly failed to realise that Goethe's thinking was concerned, not with the successive emergence of particular series of forms in the history of the species, but, rather, with their mentally conceived interrelation. The unity in the changing pattern of forms, the co-operation of matter and mind, the uniting and the separating principle in the idea of metamorphosis —the terms one chooses hardly matter: what Goethe is always aiming at is an immanent-transcendental interpretation of history, with the object of putting new content into the biblical creationism that has been handed down through the ages. At the end of this chapter we shall have occasion to re-examine this statement from some new viewpoints and carry it a stage further. But to Darwin, in whose mental background the Goethe traditions had no place, must go the credit of having found his own way to solve the problem of creation versus evolution—a way which was to play a decisive part in the subsequent controversy between evolutionism and creationism.

DARWIN'S DISCOVERY AND DARWIN'S LEGACY

Darwin's theory as the causal explanation of the evolution of living organisms considers heredity and natural selection (and furthermore: random chance and isolation) to be the deciding factors in the general process of change occurring in plant and animal forms. The great multiplicity of forms, in which man himself is included, is not—as the theologian Paley had once taught Darwin to suppose—due to the dispositions of a divine Creator at the beginning of time, but to the constant interaction of heredity and selection. The preformation of species by the Creator gives place to the continuous process based on genetic variability which is controlled by the non-survival of the more poorly adapted offspring because of the selective action of their environment. The divine dispositions of a supernatural Creator give way to the self-controlling process of natural selection. Cautious as Darwin was, he had at first entirely avoided discussing the position of man within the context of his theory. It was not until twelve years after the publication of his original "bombshell"—*On the Origin of Species by Means of Natural Selection* (1859)—that Darwin carried the results of his anthropological studies in *The Descent of Man* to a tentative conclusion. Having already long rejected creationism of the traditional kind as envisaged above—"We can, for example, no longer maintain that the beautiful lock of a bivalve mollusc must have been made by an intelligent Being just as the lock of a door has been made by man"—Darwin is now concerned with assessing the special position occupied by man within the general framework of the other organisms. Darwin's method in dealing with the problem is to pose the question "whether the human being is subject to variations, however slight, in physical structure and mental ability; and, if so, whether such variations are transmitted to his descendants in accordance with the same laws that govern heredity in lower animals." Darwin's researches, which extend far into the domains of adjacent sciences such as behaviour study, cultural anthropology and comparative history of religion, always arrive at the same conclusion, namely, that man cannot possibly be "the work of a special act of creation" but must instead "be descended from some less highly developed form" and must thus "along with the other mammals be the descendant of a common ancestor."

Anyone who might reproach Darwin with having

thus deprived man of the special position which morals and religion indisputably assign to him will have to come to grips with those passages in Darwin's writings in which he presents a detailed account of how he conceives man's mental faculties to have evolved. Darwin admittedly does not, as present-day behaviour study does, speak of "moral-analogous behaviour" in animals, but he leaves us in no doubt that this is what he has in mind when he refers to the "social instincts" of animals as the forerunners of the "moral sense." Darwin is not levelling down, he is revealing genealogical relationships without overlooking the special and the new in each specific case. "The high level of development of our mental and moral faculties constitutes the main difficulty that automatically arises when we have arrived at this conclusion as to the origin of man. But everyone who accepts the principle of evolution will agree that the mental faculties of the higher animals, which are of the same quality as those of man though so different in degree, are capable of progress." Does this mean that Darwin therefore sees only gradual differences and variations between animals and people—transitions which are based on the same laws and causes? This is a question which cannot be conclusively answered. When we ask Darwin about the epistemological significance of his theory of natural selection, and indeed of any law of nature, he replies knowingly that there are also other valid ways of viewing reality: "It is indeed difficult to define accurately the meaning of the word 'nature.' By it I understand the combined action and performance of many natural laws and by 'laws' I understand the established sequence of events." And when we urge Darwin to infer from his demonstration of evolution in man's ideas about God that God does not exist, he resists and replies: "This question is of course entirely different from the higher one as to whether a Creator or World Controller exists; many of the greatest minds that have ever existed have answered this question in the affirmative."

Darwin's position in this context is not, in fact, what his overeager friends and enemies would have us believe. In an extremely guarded and typically hesitant manner he highlights the problem of man's special position, without solving it. That Darwin's importance consists not least also in this peculiarly noncommittal treatment of the question as to evolution and creation or as to the essential nature of man is something that was largely overlooked by his contemporaries, but should here be duly acknowledged and utilised. By refuting the static Platonist conceptions associated with the idea of creation as it existed in his day by his principle of evolution, Darwin appears to substitute evolutionism for creationism however conceived. Actually, however, he makes no such fundamental decision; instead, his aim is to correct particular errors in a Christian theology of creation. But at the same time Darwin, in presenting his ideas about man, clearly indicates that any evolutionism which regards itself as the only possible alternative to creationism will, with regard to man, have to preserve and re-examine the permanent and inescapable assertions of creational theology as to man's responsibility and religious beliefs. Darwin obliges his contemporaries to speak about the descent of man in such terms that the special and unique character of man remains conceivable and capable of continuation within the evolutionary framework. A philosophical legacy that has retained its validity also for present-day biologists: "Man must be excused for feeling a certain pride in having reached the topmost rung of the ladder of life, even though he has not achieved this by his own efforts. And the fact that he has risen to this height, and was not put there to start with, gives him the hope that in some distant future he will attain to an even higher destiny."

EPIGENESIS AND PREFORMATION; THE EVOLUTION THEORY IN THE CONFLICT OF IDEAS OUTSIDE THE FIELD OF BIOLOGY

Darwin's challenge was taken up. Discussion of man's origin in terms of his creation in the fullest sense of the word had led to two alternative conceptions as to how evolution proceeds: preformation and epigenesis respectively; and, associated with this distinction, there emerged two types of anthropology: an anthropology "from below" and an anthropology "from above."

While the importance of the concept of evolution lies in the fact that in general it enables us to understand how more highly organised creatures have developed from lower ones, there nevertheless remains the debatable question whether this process is associated with a continuous emergence of new quantities or qualities. Can man never be essentially anything more than the animals already were—or is a fundamentally new possibility of existence realised in him? "Supernatural" creationism had no difficulty on this score. It could postulate an external cause for the new and the underivable. Not so the evolutionist: he has to face the question about the new in man without having any convenient metaphysical possibility of side-stepping the difficulty! The dispute between the preformists and the adherents of epigenesis is indeed bound up with metaphysical relationships. In his dissertation entitled *De theoria generationis* (1759) C. F.

Wolff expressed his dissent from the then dominant theory of preformation, which asserted that within the egg of every living organism that organism must already exist in every detail, with every one of its organs present in miniature, i.e., "preformed" in the sense that its entire adult diversity of structure was formed in advance. Thus embryonic development would consist merely in the growth and manifestation of this pre-existing structure. Wolff, on the other hand, took the view that the egg in its initial stages is of very simple structure and undergoes gradual differentiation in the course of the ontogenetic process, i.e., the development of the individual. This process he called epigenesis (=postformation). The preformation theory of those days was substantially in agreement with then prevalent ideas about creationism which conceived the Creator as having packed into the first specimen of each species, at the time of its creation, all the subsequent generations, more or less on the principle of an endless series of smaller and smaller boxes nesting one inside the other. The phylogenetic consequences inherent in the two theories now also become apparent ("phylogeny" denotes the evolutionary history of the whole species). If embryonic development indeed consists merely in the enlargement and manifestation of preformed structures which were there from the start, then the formation of any really new structures or qualities in the course of phylogenetic development is not really possible at all, only a quantitative gradation of consecutive forms being conceivable. With epigenesis, on the other hand, it is possible to conceive a continuous process in which new qualities are constantly emerging.

An interesting change of position occurred in Darwin's time. A powerful group of preformists rallied to the support of his evolution theory, who were insistent upon the formation of new species in accordance with that theory, but attached an excessively mechanical interpretation to the process. The formation of species was now presupposed as self-evident, but the over-all development was conceived in mechanical terms so contrived that only that which was intended from the beginning of time would in fact be accomplished. This basic conception is formulated in many variants in Haeckel's writings: "The general theory of development, the theory of progenesis or evolution (in the widest sense), as a comprehensive philosophical world view, assumes that in nature as a whole there occurs a great uniform, uninterrupted and eternal process of development and that all natural phenomena without exception—from the motions of the heavenly bodies and the fall of the rolling stone to the growth of plants and consciousness of man—take place in accordance with one and the same great causal law and that all these things ultimately are reducible to the mechanics of atoms: mechanical or mechanistic world view, or in one word: monism" (Haeckel 1878). And more specifically with reference to man: "The evolution of man therefore takes place in accordance with the same eternal inexorable laws as the evolution of any other natural object. These laws everywhere bring us back to the same simple principles: the fundamentals of physics and chemistry." (Haeckel 1903.)

It should, incidentally, be noted that Haeckel did not, in the end, adhere rigorously to his physiomonistic conception of man and, instead, weakened it by his delving into spiritual phenomena and by his idealistic pathos. What seems to be of greater importance is to note that the blindness to the true nature of the problems, peculiar to the mechanistic outlook, has persisted down to the present time. To the superficially theoretical mind the atomistic assertion that all life, including human life, is reducible to physical laws is confirmed by the general progress achieved in biophysics and biochemistry. In this view of the genetic function of the deoxyribonucleic acid (DNA) molecule in the nucleus of the cell, the actual substance of heredity is regarded as fresh evidence of the correctness of the preformation theory. What the fertilised ovum (in this modern view) contains is not a miniature prototype of the adult individual, but the coded program for the development of the adult; the DNA molecule is the bearer of this code. With this, as the latter-day preformists see it, the central data source of all living entities has been tracked down. Discussion now focusses merely on the gains and losses of information contained in that data source during the development of the embryo and of the species as a whole. Such a position is entirely in line with Haeckel's interpretation of the "classic" evolutionary determining factors: heredity and selection. But this does not dispose of the question whether, with regard to ontogeny and phylogeny (the development of the individual and the evolution of the species respectively), other determining factors must not also be taken into account, not to mention the fundamental question as to the essential nature of "information" in connection with biological processes. The discovery of the "material of inheritance," the blueprint for organic growth and development, sheds light merely on one half of the problem presented by the higher organisms. In the central nervous system there exists a second determining system—and one which by no means always exercises merely a copying function—whose influence in connection with heredity and selection calls for careful reassessment.

The advantages and disadvantages offered by the epigenetic opposing point of view are much harder to evaluate. Insofar as epigenesis is in accord with vitalistic arguments, the drawbacks and fallacies are relatively easy to detect. Yet the epigenetic insistence upon the irreducible processual character of biological evolutionary phenomena, even including human history, contains a very compelling suggestion that the creationist and evolutionist arguments on the problem are potentially reconcilable (see below).

Committed to the view that life cannot entirely be explained in terms of physical laws, but is determined by a creative and purposive force, the vitalists have constantly endeavoured to derive proof for their hypothesis from the physiology of organic development. Hans Driesch, who utilised the results of his classic regeneration experiments to provide the basis of vitalism, writes: "Vitalism starts by establishing something negative, namely, the non-mechanical character of the events under consideration. But this negation contains a positive nucleus: what is seen to be at work here functions intelligently, like the human mind, though not consciously. We may indeed speak of a soul-like agency." Adopting a term which Aristotle has already used in a somewhat different meaning, I have called this "entelechy." The assumption of entelechy certainly does not mean that the material characteristics of the embryo and the adult have now become redundant. Matter definitely plays a part in the form of chromosomes and genes, which are of such importance in the science of genetics. But there is more to the organic phenomena than just matter: it is not the whole explanation, it is merely the material with which the most important side of the fundamental form-determining agency, the entelechy, works. (Driesch 1957.) Behind the vitalistic reservation lies the constantly expressed conviction that organic systems function with a higher degree of wholeness than inorganic systems do. Apposite though the vitalistic insistence upon the special wholeness of organic phenomena certainly is, the supernatural basis of this organic category nevertheless rules out any analysis that can bring real advance. If the dialogue between mechanism and vitalism in the last few decades had proceeded consistently, progress should have resulted in certain fields, including those relating to problems of anthropology. However, the opponents clung to their own extreme positions and thus impeded the general advancement of knowledge. Konrad Lorenz gives a striking description of this sham fight: "Whereas the vitalists turned the organised wholeness of organic phenomena into a supernatural factor, which made any attempt at causal analysis into something sacrilegious, the mechanists, for their part, quite deliberately ignored the wholeness of these phenomena and lapsed into an extreme, methodically erroneous atomism, the most detrimental effects of which have manifested themselves as the 'explanatory monisms' already referred to. The vitalists turned the expediency of animal behaviour into a miracle, declaring it to be a direct effect of a supernatural entelechial factor, while the mechanists, on the other hand, avoided taking this expediency into consideration, even when it was expediency aimed at preserving the species . . ." (Lorenz 1971.)

A similar stagnation in arguments and ideas is discernible in large areas of the discussion concerning the special position of man in nature, initiated by philosophical anthropology (Scheler, Gehlen, Plessner). Assertions of the kind which state that animals, contrary to expectation, are able to do all manner of things and that there are therefore no grounds for claiming a special position for man are just as inconclusive as those which state that man, in consequence of some cause or other, has been picked out as something uniquely special which sets him apart from the rest of the animal kingdom. The mind of man, his soul, his thought processes, his faculty of speech, his imagination, his deficient instincts, his curiosity, his social behaviour, his technical intelligence, his learning ability, his industriousness, his self-consciousness, his erect gait, even his nakedness—we may view all the celebrated arguments for and against man's "special position," but they invariably fall foul of one snag: they argue in typological isolation either "from below" or "from above" and thus miss the heart of the problem, namely, the reflection on the underivable in the derivable, on the discontinuous in the continuous, on the creative in the evolutionary. In principle, no objections can be urged against the epistemological value of such distinctions, as are indeed also made in this book. What is of decisive importance, however, is the underlying intention. What matters is the "more" on the human side, whereby man is singled out from among the animals and is yet joined with them in sharing a long evolutionary descent. "There is certainly no objection to mentioning this vast dimensional difference [between man and animals] in principle," says Otto Koehler in his article, "but man's emergence from animal precursors is something that is brought home to us once and for all by any newborn infant."

IMMANENT CREATIVE EVENTS?

Preformation or epigenesis, mechanism or vitalism, anthropology "from below" or anthropology "from above"—the inescapable epistemological commitment inherent in Darwin's theory of evolution is felt on both sides of the controversy, except that those on one side persist in making their stand at the level where life originated, i.e., in the inorganic world, while the others take refuge in the supernatural, although this way has in effect been closed at least since Darwin's day. Judged from the standpoint of epistemology the two positions illustrate the assertion contained in the title of this book, namely, that the "creatural" conception in man's intellectual reflection about himself and his place in nature is unavoidable and not to be relinquished, because it either lies concealed in the guise of a materialistic ideology or emerges overtly as an idealistic disturbing factor in biological discussions.

The problem posed by Darwin, namely, to conceive the underivably "creatural" character of man in terms of the derivability of biological developments, still awaits solution. There are, however, good reasons for supposing that the prospects of arriving at the solution are now better than ever before. The views of present-day philosophers and scientists on the subject of "creative evolution" converge to such an extent that it is worthwhile to take stock of the situation. Inspired by the progress being achieved in every field of science and freed from self-criticism arising from old and obsolete points of view, there is everywhere emerging a new understanding of immanence and transcendence, of creationism and evolutionism, which eventually also culminates in a new view of man. Marxists, theologians, philosophers and biologists have moved closer together in their endeavour to assign to man the degree of freedom and restraint that he has, and needs, to bring forth the new from within the old and to undertake responsibility for it. Ernst Bloch writes in this context:

Nihilism, one of the pestilential phenomena of the declining bourgeoisie, besides being the reflex of decline, undoubtedly also has its roots in mechanistic materialism; it has these in its cosmological aimlessness and lack of purpose. Existence as the mere cycle of matter in motion has no meaning: in this absolutising disenchantment it has arrived at apes, the dog, the atom. On the other hand, dialectic materialism (with the inscription over its gateway: "no mechanist shall enter") acknowledges a continuous series of starting points, foci of production, outside the physicochemical phenomena: the cell, active and industrious man, the closely qualitative interlocking of substructure and superstructure. He knows from within himself, as the explanation of the world, the diverse material features of a continuous process turning from quantity to quality. He knows, above all, the real problem of a humanly qualified realm of freedom: all antidotes to triviality and nihilism or activation of all that which was precisely not opium but was in fact imposed idolatry in religion. But dialectic materialism, by hearing and understanding the mighty voice of the trend in this world, and by permitting and commanding it to function according to its "whereto" and "wherefor," has wrested from dead religion that which is alive without religion, the transcendent without transcendence: the subject-object of well-founded hope. (Bloch 1972.)

The reproach that Bloch, in his aphorism-laden attack, levels against mechanistic materialism as well as against religious supernaturalism is the faulty dialectic in its discussion of matter. The materialist who has arrived at apes, the dog, the atom "absolutises"—as does also the supernatural idealist—a section of reality without taking notice of that which is underivably new in each particular organisation stage attained. In such terms as "starting point," "focus of production," "closely qualitative interlocking of substructure and superstructure," "process turning from quantity to quality," "transcendent without transcendence," Bloch attempts over and over again to indicate how we should think of matter in the ascending line from atom to man and indeed beyond man. The dialectic lies in the interlocking of continuity and discontinuity.

To the anthropological specialist the abstractness of the terms that Bloch uses may be annoying, but when we examine the details we nevertheless find confirmation of Bloch's views. Traditionally speaking, man is an intellectual being, a "mind-being," and is by virtue thereof, despite all continuous transitions, essentially different from his nearest relatives in the animal kingdom, those primates in which he shared his common ancestry with today's apes. In his article in this book Gerhard Heberer highlights this situation by drawing, with regard to the descent of man, a distinction between a subhuman and a human phase and by considering as a new telic factor peculiar to the latter stage the evolutionary activity of civilised man. Elsewhere he writes: "In this human phase of their evolution the hominids became, as already stated, evolutionary-active. They were now able to intervene as a purposive telic factor in their own evolution. To what end?" (Heberer 1968.) The evolutionary biologist Julian Huxley endorses this with the concept of "phychosocial evolution," which again seeks to emphasise man's special shaping and control of his environment and moreover calls attention to the new forms of human communication. "On this new phychosocial level the evolutionary process gives rise to new organisation types and higher degrees of organisation.

On the one hand, we have new forms of co-operation of individuals—co-operation for the practical control of matter . . . On the other, are a new system of thinking, new forms of organisation of consciousness . . ." (Huxley 1966.) The cultural anthropologist Mühlmann states the transcendence of biological by psychosocial evolution in that he disposes of the old contrast of "nature versus civilisation" by a new interlocking concept of nature as "potential" and civilisation as "manifestation" of nature. "When considered in terms of phenomenology the differences between man and animal are situated not so much in the level of achievement as in the multiplicity of achievement, the change of achievement and the increase of achievement" (Mühlmann 1966). In the philosophical anthropology of Landmann the comprehensive interpretation of man as a "singular type" and "evolutionary link" takes us far beyond the classic philosophical-anthropological isolation of man and thus makes possible the interlocking of substructure and superstructure upon which Bloch insists. "Classic evolution sees in the line of development only the continuity, whereas typology sees also revolutions and the fresh starts which occur on the basis of continuity. The two are not mutually exclusive; we must not—as was unfortunately so often done—for the sake of the fresh starts turn against and dispute continuity." (Landmann 1965.) And finally many biologists, such as, for example, the animal behaviour researchers K. Lorenz and W. H. Thorpe, find themselves in agreement with the theologist Teilhard de Chardin in that they seek to interpret the major phylogenetic stages: life, soul, mind, but also the hidden individual steps, as the realisation of respective fresh "creative events." "All these small and great acts of real creation have one thing in common: always there emerges an entity of higher order from a multiplicity of parts and members which already existed, but which do not thereby become more similar to one another but instead usually become more dissimilar. Many thinkers have observed this . . . Teilhard de Chardin has expressed this with great poetic force in a few simple words: créer c'est unir." (Lorenz 1967.) In many ways Teilhard de Chardin's writings endorse Bloch's call for the "transcendent without transcendence." In his attempt to overcome the immobilism of the mechanistic and the supernaturalistic approach, Teilhard tries to conceive the world's reality and the reality of God's thought. In doing this he is, with regard to the dynamic forces he considers, largely in sympathy with Darwin's theory of evolution and with the newer theology of creation, as described above. The problem lies in effecting a synthesis. In Teilhard's view the emergence of man marks a new phase of evolution, conceived as the culmination of the biosphere in the noosphere, but this conception as such does not go significantly beyond the views held by the anthropologists who have been cited above. What is new about it is the fact that now the theologian, too, so radically takes up Darwin's legacy of thinking about man's evolution as though we were thinking about his creation and carries it further without having recourse to traditional metaphysical suppositions.

To try to force any of the above-mentioned authors into the wake of the theologian or of the dialectic materialist would in effect belittle their intellectual achievement. There is, instead, an amazing convergence in the assessment of man's special position, and these various anthropologists, philosophers and theologians, approaching the problem from their respective world views, mark the outer and inner boundaries, as it were, of the issues at stake. In the final analysis it is a question of so recognising the difference between creationism and evolutionism, between God and man, and so taking it into account that God can gain stature in man, and man in God. The interlinking of evolutionism and creationism requires critical examination if it is not to remain bogged in a noncommittally visionary sphere of thought. It should at least be attempted to resolve the issue into its determining factors. And in connection with this the old question as to purpose, or goal, of the whole process inescapably presents itself.

SELECTION AND BEHAVIOUR—A MODIFICATION OF THE SELECTION THEORY

The starting point for any discussion of the causality of the evolution of organisms, including man, continues to be Darwin's theory of natural selection. Admittedly, the old hope of having discovered in this theory "the" mainspring of human history has not been fulfilled. Social Darwinism with its too direct application of the selection mechanism to social relationships has failed dismally, as is explained in the article by Hans-Günter Zmarzlik. But this by no means exhausts the question as to the biological factors of human history. It is instead important to give a differentiating analysis which accomplishes the interlocking of the biological with the psychosocial factors, to find as it were a fundamental category that links the prehuman to the human and thus overcomes the disparity between evolutionism and creationism.

On the basis of numerous observations of behaviour study (Wickler 1967, von Wahlert 1968 and others) the controlling function of behaviour within the context of the general process of evolution has received fresh recognition. In connection with the transforma-

tion of characteristics, which is what essentially constitutes evolution, certain modes of behaviour may
serve as "pacemakers" in that they run ahead of the
more variable elements on the way to new adaptations and pull the slower transformations of the organs
along after them. In this sense behaviour can have a
decisively important share in determining the direction of the selection process. In its dual capacity as a
product of evolution and as a controlling principle
with its share in regulating the process of evolution,
behaviour constitutes a system of feedback with regard to the evolution process as a whole: "Itself
formed in the process of evolution, it is a control
mechanism for evolution, i.e., an evolution result
which retroactively initiates and controls the overall
evolution" (von Wahlert 1968).

With the ethological modification of the selection
theory, whereby the part played by behaviour is
brought into the picture, it becomes possible to arrive at a more consistent conception of the higher development of organisms, more particularly the transition from animal to man, than has hitherto been the
case. The conception of behaviour exercising a controlling function on the feedback principle makes the
evolution of organisms, including the human species,
independent of metaphysical purpose-directed factors
and, instead, interprets this evolution as a continuous
gradation of living systems which become progressively more complex and function in a self-controlling
and self-correcting manner. And this avoids the necessity of having to force the totality of the vital phenomena into a mechanistic scheme. Here the concept
of epigenesis is applicable in its full sense. The function of modelling the variable genetic substratum is
now no longer performed by selection alone, but is to
an increasingly great extent subject also to the control

exercised by behaviour—whether the behaviour of lower organisms or the civilised behaviour of man. Thus each evolutionary step leading from lower to higher stages of organisation is fundamentally similar in character, but is, on account of the constantly increasing influence of behaviour, nevertheless unique. In this it is transcendent in relation to the evolutionary steps that have preceded it. The change from quantity to quality, the discontinuous in continuity, have been conquered and yet continue to be respected. Thus it does not constitute a levelling-down when we make a phylogenetic classification of certain modes of animal and human behaviour and seek to derive them from one another. Nor should it, by the same token, be regarded as undue overestimation to call attention to the special characteristics of man, to the multiple achievement of his civilisation, to his enhanced freedom from the bondage of instincts, to his high level of self-consciousness which allows him an entirely new degree of controlling influence. The definition of comparative behaviour study as a "turntable" of the sciences, which Otto Koenig gives in his article, applies the newly understood importance of behaviour to the system of the sciences and thus gives an important stimulus to interdisciplinary research. And so it is quite appropriate that within the context of this book, behaviour study performs a special mediatory function in the treatment of the comparison between animal and man.

GOD—THE FUTURE REVELATION OF MAN?

When a theologian adopts a concept of evolution such as Teilhard de Chardin has attempted with his definition of biosphere and noosphere, he can, to begin with, do this only by reference to the power of the

one Creator God manifesting itself in human history
(see above). In the testimony of the Bible concerning
the re-emergence of divine action in the continuum
of history the pattern of thought is essentially no different from that in evolutionism, except that in the
former case the new and discontinuous is derivable
from the loyalty of God existing outside the world
and not, as in the latter, from the continuous process
of change in nature and history. In its efforts to conceive God's reality and the world's reality as merging
together, theology can quite properly accept the epigenetic interlinkage of transcendence and immanence
within the framework of evolution as a whole. In the
conception of a change from quantity into quality the
biblical testimony of God's creative action has been
appropriately varied—and, what is more, the reality
envisaged therein has been suitably transposed. The
process of creation, as conceived in the emergence of
higher order from lower order, is unacceptable to creationism only if it is cut short by immaturely conceived definitions of man.

According to the Bible, the "creatural" nature of
man exists, on the one hand, in that the human species,
like all other forms of life, is presented as having a
beginning, but, on the other hand, also in that man
must move onward to a new and ultimate destiny. If
the purpose were to ensure for God a final place in the
time dimension, now that he is no longer to be found
in the spatial realm, the theological reservation which
has been expressed would indeed be merely a last
rearguard action in a losing battle. The real issue,
however, is the qualification of the natural and technical development that man has to control, the continuation of evolution in human history, and therefore
also the qualification of evolution as a whole. Not for
God's but for man's sake, not for heaven's but for

earth's sake, for the sake of this breathtakingly daring and frighteningly threatened civilisation of the human species, we must hope for the new and the ultimate which raises mankind's progress to a new level and safeguards it. After all, the situation is not one where man with his multiple behaviour patterns and, especially, civilised man with his multiple facilities for exercising control has the guarantee of being permitted to continue his development in health and peace. (See the articles contributed by Helmut Baitsch and Niko Tinbergen.) It is not an enterprise in straightforward and purposefully directed evolution. The experiment "mankind" is an extremely risky venture. The predictions of the experts range from downright pessimism to speculative optimism. Hans-Günter Zmarzlik calls attention to the socio-political responsibility of the scientific experts and thus indicates the wider range of vision to which man is committed in the psycho-social phase of his evolution. In his hope to achieve the accomplishment of his humanness the general direction of organic creation may indeed provide man—as Lorenz has reminded us (1967)—with a signpost and a criterion; but ultimately man has to depend on what he is not yet, but wants to be, i.e., on what is yet to come, the truly human, the uncorruptedly creatural! The divine? When Bloch speaks of "transcendent without transcendence," he envisages this presentiment of the future freedom of man, of which we can as yet only speak hopefully as an ultimate goal and which can be planned only subject to our renouncing its complete realisation. "Atheism with concrete utopianism is in one and the same fundamental act the destruction of religion and of the heretic hope of religion, placed on a human footing. Concrete utopianism is the philosophy and practice of the trend-content latently present in the world—i.e., matter qualified to the ultimate: small enough not to contain any self-alienating elements, large enough, omega enough, to give the most daring utopian scheme the remote possibility of a real meaning, a meaning which is of this world." (Bloch 1972.)

In his method of thinking the theologian can agree with the dialectic materialist. The point at issue is: that matter, in the association of utopianism and planning, be qualified to the ultimate. In this at last does the world—the long chain of qualifications, acts of creation—gain its accomplishment. It would, however, be disastrous if, in so doing, man wanted to guide the intentions of his actions only by what has been. He should enhance and absolutise whatever is as yet no more than a detail and a single step towards that which is to come. Thus man could make absolute the evolutionary step that separates him from the animal kingdom and seek to comprise in this the mystery of all transcendence. But he could also, in total incomprehension of what is coming towards him, deny the difference with regard to the most high and ultimate, the divine, and thus deprive himself of a hope which he needs in order to become truly human.

The "creatural" nature of man is preserved in the hope of that realm, since that which is comprised in the conception of God gains stature in the human (as the critic of religion in the manner of Feuerbach might put it), or since God is God and man is man (as the theologian might prefer to express it). Vercors it right. Man is "of rebellious spirit." In such "rebellion" he demands to know what separates him from the animal kingdom and what makes him equal to God. In the cipher "human creature" lies the key for a comprehensive answer: according to the wisdom of a Chinese proverb, all that is animal is present in man, but not all that is human is present in the animal; similarly, all that is human is present in God, but not all that is divine is present in man. Man's question about himself will not tolerate a quick answer; it continues to pose itself to man. Creationism and evolutionism are modes of human comprehension by means of which man inquires about the unity of his being: according as the clarity of the one increases, the other moves out of focus. The full truth about himself manifests itself only to the man who, in steadfastly traversing both roads to understanding, perseveres in posing the question about himself and, in so doing, commits himself to moving in the direction of a hope that he can never catch up with.

Glossary

ANAPHASE: Stage of nuclear division when daughter chromosomes are separating.

ANEUPLOID: Having other than an integral multiple of the haploid number of chromosomes.

ANTHROPOLOGY: Study of the human being with regard to bodily form, racial characteristics and social development.

ATELIC: Without predetermined aim or purpose.

AUTOSOME: Chromosome other than a sex chromosome.

BEHAVIOURISM: Theory of psychology which seeks to explain all human behaviour in terms of stimulus and response, to the exclusion of conscious processes.

BRACHIATION: Arboreal locomotion by using the arms for swinging from branch to branch.

CYTOPLASM: All the protoplasm of a cell excluding the nucleus.

DEMIURGE: Creator of the world.

DENTITION: Layout of the teeth.

DIALECTIC: A systematic process of deductive reasoning dealing with metaphysical contradictions and their solutions.

DIPLOID: Having the chromosomes in pairs (in the nucleus), so that twice the haploid number is present.

ECOLOGY: Study of the relations of organisms (particularly animal and plant communities) to their environment.

ENDOGENIC: Originating or developing from within.

ENTELECHY: Realisation as actual of what was potential.

EPIGENESIS: Theory that an entirely new structure originates during embryonic development.

EPISTEMOLOGY: Theory of knowledge; metaphysics concerned with the nature and validity of knowledge.

ETHNIC: Tribal; relating to racial groups.

ETHNOLOGY: Study of the culture, customs, social relationships, etc. of peoples and races.

ETHOLOGY: Behaviour study; more particularly, study of the behaviour of animals in their natural surroundings.

FOLKLORE: Study of traditional beliefs, superstitions, customs, myths, etc.

GAMETE: Germ cell; haploid reproductive cell, either male or female.

GENE: The carrier of a hereditary factor in a chromosome.

HAPLOID: Having half the usual number of chromosomes, i.e., the nucleus contains a single set of unpaired chromosomes.

HOMINID: Used as adjective and noun with reference to the Hominidae, (cf. hominoid).

HOMINOID: Used as adjective and noun with reference to the Hominoidea, a category comprising the Pongidae (anthropoid apes) and the Hominidae (fossil subhuman species and fossil or contemporary human species).

PLATE 40: *A fish (Carassius) choosing between patterns comprising four equal and four unequal squares respectively (M. Tigges 1963).*

PLATE 41: *Pablo painting with a brush.*

PLATE 42: *Julia, a young chimpanzee, painting with a brush.*

PLATE 43: *Scratchings by a male chimpanzee on a triangular piece of paper stuck to grey cardboard. These marks are similar to those which a one-and-a-half-year-old human child would produce.*

PLATE 44: *Fanwise diverging pattern produced with brown chalk by the same male chimpanzee as in Plate 43.*

PLATE 45: *Painting produced by chimpanzee Julia when she was about six years old. She was successively given the colours red, yellow and black.*

PLATE 46: *Another painting produced by Julia at the same age; here a tendency to apply rounded patterns predominates. The colours successively used were: red, yellow and blue.*

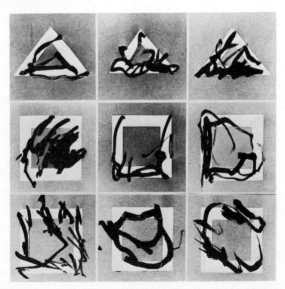

PLATE 47: *Top and middle row: brush marks applied by Lotte, a female chimpanzee, show adaptation to the shape of white paper triangles and squares stuck to grey cardboard (B. Rensch 1961).*

INTELLIGENCE QUOTIENT (IQ): Ratio of mental age to chronological age, expressed as a percentage.

KARYOTYPE: The characteristics of the set of chromosomes of a typical cell of a given species.

KINAESTHETIC: Detecting movement. Refers to sensations of movement of any part of the body arising from stimulation of sensory nerves in muscles, joints, etc.

LINKAGE: Tendency for characteristics to be linked together in hereditary transmission, due to association of two or more genes.

LOCUS: The position occupied by a particular gene in a chromosome.

MATRILINY: Descent and succession through the maternal line.

MEIOSIS: Reduction division. Cell division in which the number of chromosomes in the daughter cells is halved, i.e., becomes haploid. A normal stage in the development of gametes.

MITOSIS: The usual process of cell division (as opposed to meiosis) in which each daughter cell contains the normal (diploid) number of chromosomes.

MORPHOLOGY: Study of form and structure of organisms.

MUTATION: A variation which appears suddenly and is due to a chromosomal change, so that it is transmitted to offspring.

NON-DISJUNCTION: Abnormality in meiosis, whereby one daughter cell receives both chromosomes of a pair and the other receives neither.

NUCLEUS: A separate entity which is present in the cell and contains the chromosomes; it is the centre of life of the cell.

OCCIPUT: Region of the head at junction between skull and vertebral column.

ONTOGENY: Development of the individual organism during its life history (as opposed to phylogeny).

OVUM: Female gamete; unfertilised egg cell.

PHENOMENOLOGY: Investigation of conscious experience as experience; a method of approach to psychology.

POLYMORPHISM: Having several different forms, particularly applicable to distinct kinds of individuals belonging to one and the same species.

PREFORMATION: Theory that all the characteristics of the adult individual are present in the fertilised egg cell from the beginning.

PROTOPLASM: The living substance within the cell; differentiated into nucleus and cytoplasm.

RELEASER: Trigger mechanism; visual, audible or other signal that calls forth a specific innate response (e.g., sexual reaction, flight reaction, etc.) in other members of the species.

SPERMATOZOON: Male gamete; also referred to as "sperm," though this latter term is also used to denote the seminal fluid containing the spermatozoa.

TELIC: Purpose-directed; having a definite aim.

UXORILOCAL: Referring to marriage in which the husband lives at the wife's place of residence.

VITALISM: Biological theory which assumes a non-material agency underlying vital phenomena.

ZYGOTE: Fertilised ovum before it undergoes cleavage.

Bibliography

Chapter 1

BUETTNER-JANUSCH, J. (1966): *Origins of Man. Physical Anthropology*. Wiley, London.

CAMPBELL, D. G. (1966): *Human Evolution. An Introduction to Man's Adaptations*. Aldine, Chicago.

DART, R. A. (1957): *The Osteodontoceratic Culture of Australopithecus Prometheus*. Mem. Transvaal Mus. 10.

HEBERER, G. ed. (1967/70): *Die Evolution der Organismen. Ergebnisse und Probleme der Abstammungslehre*. 3. Auflage. Fischer, Stuttgart.

HEBERER, G. (1968): *Homo—unsere Ab- und Zukunft. Herkunft und Entwicklung des Menschen aus der Sicht der aktuellen Anthropologie*. DVA, Stuttgart.

LE GROS CLARK, W. E. (1967): *Man-Apes or Ape-Man. The Story of Discoveries in Africa*. Holt, Rinehart & Winston, New York.

REMANE, A. (1965): "Die Geschichte der Menschenaffen." In: *Menschliche Abstammungslehre, Fortschritt der "Anthropogenie" 1863–1964* (G. Heberer, ed.). Fischer, Stuttgart.

TOBIAS, P. V. (1965): "Australopithecines, Homo habilis, Tool-Making." *S. Afr. Arch. Bull.* 20, 167.

Chapter 2

COURT-BROWN, W. M. (1967): *Human Population Cytogenetics.* North-Holland Publishing Company, Amsterdam.

DOBZHANSKY, TH. (1962): *Mankind Evolving.* Yale University Press, New Haven.

DOBZHANSKY, TH. (1965): *Heredity and the Nature of Man.* Allen & Unwin Ltd., London.

EIBL-EIBESFELDT, I. (1970): *Ethology: Biology of Behaviour.* Holt, Rinehart & Winston, New York.

EICKSTEDT, E. V. (1934): *Rassenkunde und Rassengeschichte der Menschheit.* Enke, Stuttgart.

EICKSTEDT, E. V. (1937/62): *Die Forschung am Menschen.* Enke, Stuttgart.

ELSÄSSER, G. (1952): *Die Nachkommen geisteskranker Elternpaare.* Thieme, Stuttgart.

FUHRMANN, W. (1965): *Taschenbuch der allgemeinen und klinischen Humangenetik.* Wissenschaftliche Verlagsgesellschaft, Stuttgart.

GARN, ST. M. (1961): *Human Races.* Thomas, Springfield.

GEDDA, L. (1951): *Studio dei gemelli.* Orrizonte Medico, Rome.

HARRISON, G. A., WEINER, J. S., TANNER, J. M., and BARNICOT, N. A. (1964): *Human Biology.* Clarendon Press, Oxford.

JÜRGENS, H. W. (1968): *Die Wandlung der sozialanthropologischen Merkmalsbilder in Afrika südlich der Sahara.* In: *Anthropologie und Humangenetik, Festschrift für Karl Saller.* Fischer, Stuttgart.

KNUSSMANN, R. (1968): *Entwicklung, Konstitution, Geschlecht.* In: *Handbuch der Humangenetik,* Bd. I (P. E. Becker, ed.). Thieme, Stuttgart.

KOCH, H. (1966): *Twins and Twin Relations.* Chicago University Press, Chicago/London.

LENZ, W. (1959): *Ursachen des gesteigerten Wachstums der heutigen Jugend.* In: *Akzeleration und Ernährung* (J. Kühnau, ed.) Steinkopf, Darmstadt.

LINNEWEH, R., ed. (1962): *Erbliche Stoffwechselkrankheiten.* Urban und Schwarzenberg, München.

LOTZE, R. (1937): *Zwillinge. Einführung in die Zwillingsforschung.* Rau, Oehringen.

MCKUSICK, V. A. (1968): *Mendelian Inheritance in Man. Catalog of autosomal dominant, autosomal recessive and X-linked phenotypes.* Heinemann, London.

MCKUSICK, V. A. (1969): *Human Genetics.* Prentice-Hall, Englewood Cliffs, N.J.

MERGEN, A. (1968): *Der geborene Verbrecher.* Verlag Kriminalstik, Hamburg.

MOHR, H. (1967): *Wissenschaft und menschliche Existenz.* Rombach, Freiburg.

MÜHLMANN, W. E. (1968): *Geschichte der Anthropologie.* Athenäum, Frankfort/Bonn.

MÜLLER, K. V. (1956): *Heimatvertriebene Jugend.* Holzner, Würzburg.

NACHTSHEIM, H. (1966): *Kampf den Erbkrankheiten.* Decker, Schmiden b. Stuttgart.

SALLER, K. (1964): *Leitfaden der Anthropologie.* Fischer, Stuttgart.

SALLER, K., ed. (1968): *Rassengeschichte der Menschheit.* Oldenbourg, München.

SCHEINFELD, A. (1966): *Your Heredity and Environment.* Chatto & Windus, London.

SCHREIER, K., ed. (1963): *Die angeborenen Stoff-wechselanomalien.* Thieme, Stuttgart.

SCHWIDETZKY, I. (1950): *Grundzüge der Völkerbio-logie.* Enke, Stuttgart.

SCHWIDETZKY, I. (1959): *Das Menschenbild der Biologie.* Fischer, Stuttgart.

SCHWIDETZKY, I., ed. (1962): *Die neue Rassenkunde.* Fischer, Stuttgart.

SCHWIDETZKY, I. (1965): *Variations- und Typenkunde des Menschen.* In: *Handbuch der Biologie* Bd. IX, 327–436 (v. Bertalanffy, L., and Gessner, F., eds.). Athenaion, Frankfurt.

SHIELDS, J. (1962): *Monozygotic Twins. Brought Up Apart and Brought Up Together.* Oxford University Press, London/New York/Toronto.

VERSCHUER, O. V. (1954): *Wirksame Faktoren im Leben des Menschen.* Steiner, Weisbaden.

VERSCHUER, O. V. (1959): *Genetik des Menschen.* Urban and Schwarzenberg, Mündhen/Berlin.

VOGEL, F. (1961): *Lehrbuch der Allgemeinen Human-genetik.* Springer, Berlin/Göttingen/Heidelberg.

Chapter 3

DOBZHANSKY, T. (1965): *Mankind Evolving.* Yale University Press, New Haven.

KNOERINGEN, W. V., ed. (1968): *Geplante Zukunft? Aufgaben von Politik und Wissenschaft.* Hannover.

MEDAWAR, P. B. (1960): *The Future of Man.* Methuen, London.

Chapter 4

FILIP, J., ed. (1966/68): *Enzyklopädisches Handbuch zur Ur- und Frühgeschichte Europas.* 2 Bde. Kohlhammer, Stuttgart/Berlin/Köln/Mainz.

KRAFT, G. (1948): *Der Urmensch als Schöpfer. Die geistige Welt des Eiszeitmenschen.* 2. Auflage. Matthiesen, Tübingen.

MÜLLER-KARPE, H. (1966/68): *Handbuch der Vorgeschichte.* Bd. I *Altsteinzeit.* Bd. II *Jungsteinzeit.* Beck, München.

NARR, K. J. (1961): *Urgeschichte der Kultur.* Kröner, Stuttgart.

NARR, K. J., ed. (1966/70): *Handbuch der Urgeschichte,* Bd. I *Altere und Mittlere Steinzeit. Frühe Bodenbau- und Viehzuchfkulturen.* Francke, Bern/München.

SMOLLA, G. (1967): *Epochen der menschlichen Frühzeit.* Studium Universale. Alber, Freiburg/München.

Chapter 5

ADAM, L., and TRIMBORN, H. (1958): *Lehrbuch der Völkerkunde.* Enke, Stuttgart.

BEITL, R. (1955): *Wörterbuch der deutschen Volkskunde.* Kröner, Stuttgart.

BERTHOLET, A., and CAMPENHAUSEN, H. (1962): In: *Wörterbuch der Religionen* (K. Goldammer, ed.). Kröner, Stuttgart.

BOSSERT, H. TH. (1953): *Folk Art of Europe.* Praeger, New York.

BRUHN, W., and TILKE, M. (1955): *Pictorial History of Costume.* Zwemmer, London.

EIBL-EIBESFELDT, I. (1970): *Ethology: Biology of Behavior.* Holt, Rinehart & Winston, New York.

FROBENIUS, L. (1898): *Der Ursprung der afrikanischen Kulturen.*

HABERLANDT, M. (1924): *Einführung in die Volkskunde.* Zöllner, Wien.

HANSMANN, L., and KRISS-RETTENBECK, L. (1966): *Amulett und Talisman*. Callwey, München.

HEINROTH, O. (1910): "Beiträge zur Biologie, namentlich Ethologie und Psychologie der Anatiden." Verh. 5. *Int. Ornith. Kongr.* Berlin.

HIRSCHBERG, W. (1965): *Wörterbuch der Völkerkunde*. Kröner, Stuttgart.

KINERT, A., and ZDUNIC, D. (1964): *Folklore des jugoslawischen Volkes*. Graficki za rod Hravatske, Zagreb.

KISLINGER, M. (1963): *Alte bäuerliche Kunst*. Oberösterreichischer Landesverlag, Linz.

KNÖTEL, R., and SIEG, H. (1937): *Handbuch der Uniformkunde*. Schulz, Hamburg.

KOENIG, O. (1968): "Biologie der Uniform." *Naturwiss. u. Medizin* (n+m) 22, 3–19, und 23, 40–50.

KOENIG, O. (1969): *Kultur und Verhaltensforschung*. dtv, München.

KOPPERS, W. (1949): *Der Urmensch und sein Weltbild*.

KÖSTER, A. (1923): *Das antike Seewesen*. Schoetz & Parrhysius, Berlin.

KRISS-RETTENBECK, L. (1963): *Bilder und Zeichen religiösen Volksglaubens*. Callwey, München.

KULISIC, S. (1966): *Volksbräuche in Jugoslawien*. Jugoslaviga, Beograd.

LETTENMAIR, J. G. (1969): *Das gross Orient-Teppich-Buch*. Welsermühl, München/Wels.

LOMMEL, A. (1965): *Die Welt der frühen Jäger. Medizinmänner, Schamanen, Künstler*. Callwey, München.

LORENZ, K. (1969): *Man Meets Dog*. Penguin, London.

LORENZ, K. (1970/71): *Studies in Animal and Human Behaviour*. Methuen, London.

LORENZ, K., and LEYHAUSEN, P. (1968): *Antriebe tierischen und menschlichen Verhaltens,* Piper, München.

MARTIN, P. (1963): *Der bunte Rock.* Franckh, Stuttgart.

PIETSCH, P. (1963): *Die Formations- und Uniformierungs-Geschichte des preussischen Heeres 1808 bis 1914.* 2 Bde. Schulz, Hamburg.

PITTIONI, R. (1949): *Die urgeschichtlichen Grundlagen der europäischen Kultur.* Devticke, Wien.

SCHMIDT, L. (1952): *Gestaltheiligkeit im bäuerlichen Arbeitsmythos.* Wien.

SCHMIDT, W. (1937): *Handbuch der Methode der kulturhistorischen Ethnologie.*

SELIGMANN, S. (1910): *Der Büse Blick und Verwandtes.* Berlin.

SELIGMANN, S. (1927): *Die magischen Heil- und Schutzmittel aus der unbelebten Natur mit besonderer Berücksichtigung der Mittel gegen den bösen Blick.* Stuttgart.

TEUBER, O., and OTTENFELD, R. (1895): *Die Österreichische Armee von 1700 bis 1867.* Wien.

TINBERGEN, N. (1969): *Study of Instinct.* Oxford University Press, London.

TORSTEN, G., and HANIKA, J. (1963): *IRO-Volkskunde. Europäische Länder.* IRO, München.

TRANSFELDT, W., BRAND, K. H., and QUEENSTEDT, O. (1967): *Wort und Brauch im deutschen Heer.* Schulz, Hamburg.

WICKLER, W. (1968): *Mimicry in Plants and Animals.* Weidenfeld & Nicolson, Ltd., London.

WICKLER, W. (1972): *The Biology of the Ten Commandments.* Herder & Herder, New York.

WOLFRAM, R. (1951): *Die Volkstänze in Österreich und verwandte Tänze in Europa.* Müller, Salzburg.

ZIMBURG, H. (1947): *Der Perchtenlauf in der Gastein*. Braumüller, Wien.

ZUNIĆ-BAŠ, L.: *Zehn Reisen durch die jugoslawische Folklore*. Izdavacki za vod Jugoslavija, Ljubljana.

Chapter 6

This essay, Professor Tinbergen's first lecture at Oxford, was originally published in *Science* 160, 1968, pp. 1411–18. (c) 1968 American Association for the Advancement of Science.

BAGGERMAN, B. (1965): *Symp. Soc. Exp. Biol.* 20, 427.

CARSON, R. (1962): *Silent Spring*. Houghton Mifflin, Boston.

CROOK, J. H. (1965): *Symp. Zool. Soc.* 14, 181. London.

CULLEN, E. (1957): *Ibis* 99, 275.

CULLEN, E. (1961): Final Rept. Contr. AF 61 (052)–29, USAFRDC, 1–23.

HINDE, R. A. (1967): *New Society* 9, 302.

HOAR, W. K. (1962): *Animal Behaviour* 10, 247.

HOLST, E. VON, and MITTELSTAEDT, H. (1950): *Naturwissenschaften* 37, 464.

JONES, N. B. (1960): Wildfowl Trust 11th Ann. Rept. 46-52.

KNOLL, M. D. (1956): *Z. Vergleich. Physiol.* 38, 219.

KONISHI, M. (1965): *Z. Tierpsychol.* 22, 770.

KRUÜK, H. (1966): *New Scientist* 30, 849.

LORENZ, K. (1966): *Evolution and Modification of Behaviour*. Methuen, London.

MORRIS, D., ed. (1967): *Primate Ethology*. Weidenfeld & Nicholson, London.

NOTTEBOHM, F. (1967): Proc. 14th Intern. Ornithol. Congr. 265-80.

ROWELL, F. (1961): *Animal Behaviour* 9, 38.

SCHNEIRLA, T. C. (1966): *Quart. Rev. Biol.* 41, 283.

SEVENSTER, P. (1961): *Behaviour, Suppl.* 9, 1–170.

THORPE, W. H. (1961): *Bird-Song.* Cambridge University Press, New York.

TINBERGEN, N. (1959): *Z. Tierpsychol.* 16, 651.

TINBERGEN, N. (1964): *Zool. Mededelingen* 39, 209.

TINBERGEN, N. (1964): *Z. Tierpsychol.* 20, 410.

TINBERGEN, N. (1964): In: *The Pathology and Treatment of Sexual Deviation* (I. Rosen, ed.). Oxford University Press, London.

Chapter 7

EIBL-EIBESFELDT, I. (1970): *Ethology: Biology of Behavior.* Holt, Rinehart & Winston, New York.

GWINNER, E. (1964): "Untersuchungen über das Ausdrucks- und Sozialverhalten der Koldraben (Corvus Corax Corax L.)" *Z. Tierpsychol.* 21, 657–784.

HASSENSTEIN, B. (1962): "Die Spannung zwischen Individuum und Kollektiv im Tierreich." In: *Individuum und Kollektiv.* Freiburger Dies Universitatis 9.

IMMELMANN, K. (1966): "Beobachtungen an Schwalbenstaren." *J. Ornith.* 107, 37–69.

Kühme, W. (1965): "Freilandstudien zur Soziologie des Hyänhundes (Lycaon pictus lupinus Thomas 1902)." *Z. Tierpsychol.* 22, 495–541.

LAWICK-GOODALL, J. VAN (1968): "The Behaviour of Free-Living Chimpanzees in the Gombe Stream Reserve." *Animal Behaviour Monographs* (London) 1 (3), 161–311.

LORENZ, K. (1969): *Man Meets Dog.* Methuen, London; and Penguin, London.

NICOLAI, J. (1956): "Zur Biologie und Ethologie des Gimpels (Syrrhula syrrhula L.)." *Z. Tierpsychol.* 13, 93–132.

WICKLER, W. (1967): "Vergleichende Verhaltensforschung und Phylogenetik." In: *Evolution der Organismen* (G. Heberer, ed.), Fischer, Stuttgart.

WICKLER, W. (1972): *The Biology of the Ten Commandments.* Herder & Herder, New York.

Chapter 8

ADLER, M. J. (1967): *The Difference of Man and the Differences It Makes.* Holt, Rinehart & Winston, New York.

ALTNER, G. (1966): "Charles Darwin und Ernst Haeckel." *Theologische Studien,* Heft 85. EVZ, Zürich.

BAEUMER, E. (1964): *Das dumme Huhn.* Kosmos, Stuttgart.

COLLIAS, S., and JOOS, M. (1953): "The Spectrographic Analysis of Sound Signals in the Domestic Fowl." *Behaviour* 5, 175–88.

COUNT, E. W. (1968): "An Essay on Phasia, on the Phylogenesis of Man's Speech Function." *Homo* 19, 170–227.

EIBL-EIBESFELDT, I. (1961): "Über den Werkzeuggebrauch des Spechtfinken." *Z. Tierpsychol.* 18, 343–46.

EIBL-EIBESFELDT, I. (1969): *Ethology: Biology of Behaviour.* Holt, Rinehart & Winston, New York.

FRISCH, K. v. (1968): *Dance Language and Orientation of Bees.* Harvard University Press, Cambridge, Mass.

GARDNER, R. A., and W. T. (1968): "Teaching Sign Language to a Chimpanzee." *Science* 165, 664–72.

Günther, K. (1967): "Zur Geschichte der Abstammungslehre." In: Herberer, G., ed.: *Die Evolution der Organismen.* 3. Auflage, 1, 1–60.

HERRNSTEIN, R. J. (1965): "In Defence of Bird Brains." *Atlantic Monthly* 101–4.

HOCKETT, Ch. F. (1960): "The Origin of Speech." *Scientific American* 203, 3, 89–96.

HUMBOLDT, W. v. (1836): *Über die Verschiedenheit des menschlichen Sprachbaues.* Darmstadt.

KAINZ, F. (1961): *Die "Sprache" der Tiere.* Enke, Stuttgart.

KOEHLER, O. (1951): "Der Vogelgesang als Vorstufe von Musik und Sprache." *J. Orn.* 93, 1–20.

KOEHLER, O. (1952): *Vom unbenannten Denken.* Verh. D. Zool. Ges. Freiburg. Supplement Zool. Anz. 1953, 202–11.

KOEHLER, O. (1953): "Zufall, Notwendigkeit und Plan in der Welt des Lebendigen." In: *Lebendiges Wissen.* Sammlung Dieterich 99, 251–70.

KOEHLER, O. (1954): *Das Lächeln als angeborene Ausdrucksbewegung.* Z. Menschl. Vererbung und Konstitutionslehre 32, 390–98.

KOEHLER, O. (1955): "Vom Erbgut der Sprache." *Homo* 5, 97–104.

KOEHLER, O. (1955): "Vorbedingungen und Vorstufen unserer Sprache bei Tieren." *Verh. D. Ges. Zool. Tübingen,* 327–41.

KOEHLER, O. (1956): *Thinking Without Words.* Proc. 14 Internat. Congr. Zool. Copenhagen 1953, 75–88.

KOEHLER, O. (1957): "Lichtempfindlichkeit und Lichtsinn niederer Tiere." *Studium generale* 10, 75–88.

KOEHLER, O. (1960): "Darwin und wir." In: *100 Jahre Evolutionsforschung.* (Heberer und Schwanitz, ed.). Fischer, Stuttgart.

KOEHLER, O. (1960): "Le Dénombrement chez les animaux." *Journ. de psychologie normale et pathologique,* 45–58.

KOEHLER, O., *Mäuse im Hochlabyrinth*. Film B635 des Göttinger Instituts für den wissenschaftlichen Film.

KOEHLER, O. (1961): *Von der Grenze zwischen Menschen und Tieren*. Calwer Heft 45.

KOEHLER, O. (1966): "Vom Spiel bei Tieren." *Frieburger dies universitatis* 13, 79–108.

KOEHLER, O. (1967): Vogelsang. Stichwort in Riemanns Musiklexikon 3, 1049/50.

KOEHLER, O. (1968): *Die Aufgabe der Tierpsychologie*. 2. Auflage. Wissenschaftliche Buchgesellschaft, Darmstadt.

KOEHLER, O. (1968): "Der Mensch—ein besseres Tier?" In: *Was ist das, der Mensch?* Piper, München.

KOHTS, L. (1935): "Infant Ape, and Human Child." *Z. Tierpsychol.* 22, 867–70.

KONISHI, M. (1965): "Auditory Feedback in Zonotrichia." *Z. Tierpsychol.* 22, 584–94.

LAWICK-GOODALL, J. VAN (1967): "My Friends the Wild Chimpanzees." *Nat. Geogr. Mag.* 70.

LENNEBERG, E. (1967): *Biological Foundations of Language*. Wiley, New York.

LENNEBERG, E., and LEYHAUSEN, P. (1968): In: Lorenz und Leyhausen. *Gesammelte Abhandlungen*. Piper, München.

LINDAUER, M. (1956): "Über die Verständigung bei indischen Bienen." *Z. Vergleich. Physiol.* 38, 521 bis 557.

LINDAUER, M. (1962): *Communication Among Social Bees*. Harvard University Press, Cambridge, Mass.

LÖGLER, P. (1959): "Versuche zur Frage des 'Zähl' Vermögens an einem Graupapagei und Vergleichsversuche am Menschen." *Z. Tierpsychol.* 16, 179–217.

NICOLAI, J. (1964): "Der Brutparasitismus der Vidui-
nae als ethologisches Problem." Z. *Tierpsychol.*
21, 129–204.

REINERT, J. (1957): "Akustische Dressurversuche an
einem Elefanten." Z. *Tierpsychol.* 14, 100–26.

REINERT, J. (1965): "Takt- und Rhythmusunterscheidung bei Dohlen." Z. *Tierpsychol.* 22, 623–
71.

RENSCH, B., and DÜCKER, G. (1959): "Versuche über
visuelle Generalisation bei einer Schleichkatze."
Z. *Tierpsychol.* 16, 673–83.

RÉVÉSZ, G. (1953): "Der Kampf um die sogenannte
Tiersprache." *Psychologische Rundschau* 4, 81–
83.

RÉVÉSZ, G. (1956): *The Origins and Prehistory of
Language.* J. Butler (tr. from German reprint).

THORPE, W. H. (1967): *Vocal Imitation and Anti-
phonal Song and Its Implications.* Proc. XIV, Intern. Orn. Congr. Edinburgh, 245–63.

THORPE, W. H. (1969): *Der Mensch in der Evolution.
Naturwissenschaft und Religion.* Nymphenburger, München.

TRETZEL, E. (1966): "Imitation und Variation von
Schäferpfiffen durch Haubenlerchen." Z. *Tierpsychol.* 22, 784–809.

WEIZSÄCKER, C. F. v. (1949): *The History of Nature.*
University of Chicago Press.

ZEIER, H. (1966/67): "Über sequentielles Lernen bei
Tauben mit spezieller Berücksichtigung des
'Zähl'-Verhaltens." Z. *Tierpsychol.* 23, 161–89 und
24, 201–7.

Chapter 9

CRAIG, W. (1963): *The Song of the Wood Pewee
(Myochanes virens).* Mus. Bull. 334, 6–186.

DARWIN, CH. (1901): *The Descent of Man, and Selection in Relation to Sex.* Finch Press.

DARWIN, CH. (1951): *On the Origin of Species.* University of Chicago Press.

DÜCKER, G. (1963): "Spontane Bevorzugung arteigener Farben bei Vögeln." *Z. f. Tierpsychologie* 20, 43–65.

FECHNER, G. TH. (1876/97): *Vorschule der Ästhetik.* Leipzig.

KAINZ, F. (1962): *Aesthetics: The Science.* Tr. H. M. Schueller. Wayne State University Press.

KLEINEBRECHT, J. (1968): "Über die Wirkung von periodischen und nichtperiodischen Schallreizen auf das visuelle Lernen beim Haushuhn." *Zool. Beiträge* N.F. 14, 169–202.

KLÜVER, H. (1933): *Behaviour Mechanisms in Monkeys.* Chicago.

LIPPS, T. (1903/6): *Ästhetik.* 2 Bände, Hamburg.

LORENZ, K. (1966): *On Aggression.* Methuen, London.

MORRIS, D. (1966): *The Biology of Art.* Methuen, London.

REINERT, J. (1965): "Takt- und Rhythmusunterscheidung bei Dohlen." *Z. Tierpsychol.* 22, 223–71.

RENSCH, B. (1957): "Ästhetische Faktoren bei Farb und Formbevorzugungen von Affen." *Z. Tierpsychol.* 15, 447 bis 461.

RENSCH, B. (1961): "Malversuche mit Affen." *Z. Tierpsychol.* 18, 347–64.

RENSCH, B. (1965). "Über ästhelische Faktoren im Erleben Höherer Tiere." *Naturwiss. u. Medizin* (n+m) 2, 43–47.

RENSCH, B. (1968): "Manipulierfähigkeit and Komplikation von Handlungsketten bei Menschenaffen." In: *Handgebrauch und Verständigung bei*

Affen und Frühmenschen (B. Rensch, ed.), 103–30. Bern/Stuttgart.

RENSCH, B., and DÖHL, J. (1967): "Spontanes Öffnen verschiedener Kistenverschlüsse durch einen Schimpansen." *Z Tierpsychol.* 24, 476–89.

RENSCH, B., and DÖHL, J. (1968): "Wahlen zwischen zwei überschaubaren Labyrinthwegen durch einen Schimpansen." *Z. Tierpsychol.* 25, 216–31.

SCHILLER, P. H. (1951): "Figural Preferences in the Drawings of a Chimpanzee." *J. Comp. Physiol. Psychol.* 44, 101–11.

SHEPHERD, W. T. (1915): "Some Observations on the Intelligence of the Chimpanzee." *J. Anim. Beh.* 5, 391–96.

TIGGES, M. (1963): "Muster- und Farbbevorzugungen bei Fischen und Vögeln." *Z. Tierpsychol.* 20, 129–42.

TRETZEL, E. (1964/65): "Über das Spotten der Singvögel, insbesondere ihre Fähigkeit zu spontaner Nachahmung." *Verh. Dtsch. Zool. Ges. und Zool. Anz.* 28, Suppl. 556–65.

TRETZEL, E. (1967): "Imitation und Transposition menschlicher Pfiffe durch Amseln." *Z. Tierpsychol.* 24, 138–61.

ZIEHEN, T. (1923/25): *Vorlesungen über Ästhetik.* 2 Bände. Halle.

Chapter 10

For source documents and bibliography, compare with Zmarzlik's "Der Sozialdarwinismus in Deutschland als geschichtliches Problem." In: *Vierteljahreshefte für Zeitgeschichte* 11 (1963), pp. 246–73. Further literature:

ALTNER, G. (1965): *Schöpfungsglaube und Entwicklungsgedanke in der protestantischen Theologie zwischen Ernst Haeckel und Teilhard de Chardin.* EVZ, Zürich.

ALTNER, G. (1968): "Weltanschauliche Hintergründe der Rassenlehre des Dritten Reiches. Zum Problem einer umfassenden Anthropologie." *Theologische Studien,* Heft 92. EVZ, Zürich.

BOLLE, E. (1967): "Darwinismus und Zeitgeist." In: *Zeitgeist im Wandel. Das Wilhelminische Zeitalter* (H. J. Schoeps, ed.). Stuttgart.

CONRAD-MARTIUS, H. (1953): *Utopien der Menschenzüchtung. Der Sozialdarwinismus und seine Folgen.* München.

DÖRPINGHAUS, H. (1969): "Darwins Theorie und der deutsche Vulgärmaterialismus in Urteil deutscher katholischer Zeitschriften zwischen 1854 und 1914. Ein Beitrag zum Problem der Meinungsbildung und -beeinflussung im katholischen Raum." Phil. Diss. Freiburg, Ms.

ELLEGARD, A. (1958): *Darwin and the General Reader.* Adler, New York.

HOFSTADTER, R. (1959): *Social Darwinism in American Thought.* Rev. ed. Braziller, New York.

LENZ, F. (1960): "Die soziologische Bedeutung der Skelektion." In: *Hundert Jahre Evolutionsforschung. Das wissenschaftliche Vermächtnis Charles Darwins* (G. Heberer und F. Schwanitz, ed.).

MASON, ST. F. (1961): *Geschichte der Naturwissenschaft in der Entwicklung ihrer Denkweisen.* Kröner, Stuttgart.

SALLER, K. (1961): *Die Rassenlehre des Nationalsozialismus in Wissenschaft und Propaganda.*

ZMARZLIK, H.-G. (1961): "Der Sozialdarwinismus in Deutschland. Ein Betrag zur Vorgeschichte des Dritten Reiches." Freiburger Habilitationsschrift, Ms.

Chapter 12

ALTNER, G. (1966): *Charles Darwin und Ernst Haeckel. Ein Vergleich nach theologischen Aspekten.* Mit einem Geleitwort von W. E. Ankel. *Theologische Studien,* Heft 85. EVZ, Zürich.

BLOCH, E. (1972): *Atheism in Christianity.* Herder & Herder, New York.

DARWIN, CHARLES (1901): Descent of Man and Selection in Relation to Sex. Finch Press.

DARWIN, CHARLES (1962): *On the Origin of Species.* Collier-Macmillan, London.

DRIESCH, H. (1957): "Das Wunder der Regeneration." In: *Die* Natur das Wunder Gottes. Im *Lichte der modernen Forschung* (W. Dennert, ed.). Athenäum, Bonn.

FEUERBACH, L. (1967): *Lectures on the Essence of Religion.* Harper & Row, New York.

HAECKEL, E. (1878): *Freie Wissenschaft und freie Lehre. Eine Engegnung auf Fudolf Virchows Münchener Rede über Die Freiheit der Wissenschaft im modernen Staat.* Stuttgart.

HAECKEL, E. (1903): *Anthropogenie oder Entwicklungsgeschichte des Menschen. Keimes- und Stammesgeschichte.* Teil 1 und 2. Leipzig.

HEBERER, G. (1968): *Der Ursprung des Menschen. Unser gegenwärtiger Wissensstand.* Fischer, Stuttgart.

HUXLEY, J. (1966): *Essays of a Humanist.* Penguin, London.

LANDMANN, M. (1965): "Der Mensch als Evolutionsglied und Eigentypus." In: *Menschliche Abstammungslehre. Fortschritte der Anthropogenie* (G. Heberer, ed.). Fischer, Stuttgart.

LANDMANN, M. (1966): *Ursprungsbild und Schöp-*

fertat. Zum platonisch—biblischen Gespräch. Nymphenburger, München.

LORENZ, K. (1967): *Die instinktiven Grundlagen menschlicher Kultur. Die Naturwissenschaften* 15/16, 377.

LORENZ, K. (1971): *Studies in Animal and Human Behaviour.* Methuen, London.

MÜHLMANN, W. E., and MÜLLER, E. W. (1966): *Kulturanthropologie.* Kiepenheuer u. Witsch, Köln/ Berlin.

TEILHARD DE CHARDIN, P. (1959): *The Phenomenon of Man.* Fontana, London.

THORPE, W. H. (1965): *Science, Man and Morals.* Methuen, London.

VERCORS: *Zoo oder der menschenfreundliche Mörder. Eine juristische, zoologische und moralische Komödie.* Hörspielfassung von Werner Hausmann.

WAHLERT, G. v. (1968): "Latimeria und die Geschichte der Wirbeltiere. Eine evolutionsbiologische Untersuchung." In: *Fortschritte der Evolutionsforschung,* Bd. IV. Fischer, Stuttgart.

WICKLER, W. (1967): "Vergleichende Verhaltensforschung und Phylogenetik." In: *Die Evolution der Organismen,* Bd. I (G. Heberer, ed.). Fischer, Stuttgart.

INDEX